THE HISTORY OF ANCIENT ISRAEL AND JUDAH
A COMPILATION

BY

JEROME CLAYTON ROSS

DORRANCE PUBLISHING CO., INC.
PITTSBURGH, PENNSYLVANIA 15222

ISBN # 0-8059-5487-5818-5
Printed in the United States of America

First Printing

For information or to order additional books, please write:
Dorrance Publishing Co., Inc.
701 Smithfield Street
Third Floor
Pittsburgh, Pennsylvania 15222
U.S.A.
1 800 788 7654
Or visit our web site and on-line catalog at
www.dorrancepublishing.com

To Shadine with love

CONTENTS

Abbreviations and Sigla

AB	Anchor Bible Commentary Series
ANET	*Ancient Near East: Supplementary Texts and Pictures Relating to the Old Testament.* Edited by J. B. Pritchard. Princeton, 1958, 1975.
BC	Book of the Covenant (Ex. 20:22–23:33)
B.C.E.	Before the Common Era
C.E.	Common Era
CH	Chronistic History or Historian (1 and 2 Chron.)
D	Deuteronomic Code or Traditions (Deut. 12–26)
DH	Deuteronomistic History or Historian (Deut., Josh., Judg. Sam., Kgs.)
E	Elohistic Tradition or Elohist
FOTL	Forms of Old Testament Literature Series
H	Holiness Code (Lev. 17–26)
HS	Holiness School or Tradents
Int	nterpretation Commentary Series
J	Yahwistic Tradition or Yahwist
JBL	Journal of Biblical Literature
JSOT	Journal for the Study of the Old Testament Series
LXX	The Septuagint
OBT	Overtures to Biblical Theology Series
OTL	Old Testament Library Series
P	Priestly Code or Traditions
PT	Priestly Torah (same as P) or Priestly Tradents
WBC	Word Biblical Commentary Series

CHARTS

REGARDING THE HISTORY OF ANCIENT ISRAEL AND JUDAH: A COMPILATION.

To All My Colleagues in Biblical Studies:

Enclosed is the product of my lifelong effort to compile a realistic and probable reconstruction of the history of ancient Israel and Judah. The introduction of the book provides the working data that I used in exploring and compiling the information. My thesis is the history of ancient Israel and Judah is the probable reconstruction of the lives of some ancient Yahwists, who constituted a heterogeneous, culturally-diverse and politically-dominated minority that struggled to survive (pp. 1-3). In this respect I argue that the keys (my 'Rosetta Stone') for understanding the history is the seven principles for survival (pp. 1-2) that I first documented in my dissertation and subsequent works. Distinguishing and correlating theology (p. 2 n. 1) and history (p. 3 n. 3), I perceive history as the unfolding drama of what people (in this case, ancient Israel and Judah) believe that is played out in sociopolitical actions and institutions. Reading the text as a form of communication/conversation (pp. 4-5), I seek to hear the text in its manifold contexts (p. 5), that is, from the perspective of the "senders" of the text: 1. the speaker or the earliest or original proponent of the concepts within the text; and 2. the writer or the one who fixed the text in the form in which we have it or the one who put in writing the concepts that were orally transmitted (see the chart at the end of the introduction, "Helps for Reading the Text"). Here, contextual particulars (i. e., the sociopolitical locations, the addressees, the issues, the purposes, the presuppositions) are derived from the text, in order to understand it as some form of ancient communication, which reflects their developing and differing faith (pp. 1-2, especially p. 1 n. 1). The bottom-line is that I see the ancient Israelites and Judahites as a minority that struggled to survive or to maximize, even realize, freedom!

I hope that this text, meager as it is, may stimulate discussion among us and within your classes.

Jerome C. Ross

INTRODUCTION

In light of the numerous works which are required reading for understanding the history of ancient Israel and Judah, a distillation is needed which presents a basic reconstruction. This work is a revised edition of lectures which began as a *compilation* of biblical-critical scholarship that sought to explain the history of ancient Israel and Judah. It has been generated by thirty-two years of studying and twenty-one years of teaching, wherein the questions of both students and instructor have prompted numerous searches for realistic answers. It is *selective* in that the views of every available resource on ancient Israel and Judah are not directly considered, but mainly those of recent works which endeavor to present a picture of reality that is probable or reasonable according to the available data and the extant methodologies. Also, the value of this compilation, it is hoped, lies in the framework utilized for studying and presenting the history. This framework entails an integral focus—that is, a perspective for engagement which is essential to the existence of the subject. In this respect, the fundamental thread for studying the history of ancient Israel and Judah (and for that matter, any people) is *survival*.

By "survival" I mean the perpetuation and preservation of a people in some place with a purpose that makes possible community identity. It is significantly determined by the balance a people maintains between their ideals and the sociopolitical circumstances which confront and challenge them. This fundamental task has seven requirements: administrative structure—that is, some sociopolitical arrangement designed for operation (cf. Neh. 8, 10, 11; Exod. 18:13-27; Lev. 10:9-11; Num. 8); economic independence—that is, generation, acquisition, and management of the community's supplies and demands (cf. Neh. 5, 10; 13:15-22; Lev. 25); ideological standardization or intra-communal organization—that is, determination and establishment of the laws or rules for the given community (cf. Neh. 13:23-31a; Exod. 20:1-17; Deut. 5:6-21; Exod. 21:23-25; Lev. 24:10-23; Deut. 19:21); common language—that is, the spoken tongue of the group (cf. Neh. 13:23-24; Jgs. 12:1-7); selective appropriation or assimilation of the dominant culture by the dominated culture, that is, balance of extra-communal influences and intra-communal accommodation (cf. Neh. 7:6-72; 10-12; Lev. 18:1-5, 24-30; 20:22-26); people or population (cf. Neh. 7:6-72; 10-12; Gen. 12:1-4; Exod. 1:1-7; Lev. 18:21-23; 20:3-5, 13, 15-16; Deut. 25:5-10); and land or place (cf.

Neh. 5; Gen. 12:1-4; 23, 50:22-26; Exod. 13:19; Lev. 25; Josh.). Fulfillment of these requirements is normative for every people; these items must be addressed and supplied if a people are to exist meaningfully.

The fulfillment of these requirements for survival by the ancient Yahwists was complicated by several factors. Their society was heterogeneous. This mixed social situation prevented Yahwism from ever being monolithic, and thereby spawned the various theologies[1] in the Hebrew Bible, which are the expressions of the ancient Yahwists, as they struggled to survive. Their theological concerns, then, entailed religious matters which were intertwined with sociopolitical ones, which contributed to divisions among them. So, ancient Yahwistic faith must be regarded as their ideologies for living, which are manifested socially in customs, institutions, practices, symbols, and conceptually in statements or theories. The latter of these, the conceptual expressions of their faith, is their theologies, which constitute the belief-statements or the doctrines that they fostered for meaningful and purposeful existence. These are the ideological arguments they articulated and developed within their assorted historical contexts, which of necessity included and endorsed social (i.e., economic, political, cultural) action. In other words, the faith of the Hebrew Bible comprises the *sociopolitical propaganda* of the ancient Yahwists!

Furthermore, the situation of ancient Israel and Judah was compounded by the fact they were never fully free, except during the time of David. They were continually dominated by the stronger nations and were forced to accommodate these cultures. This made fulfillment of the requirements for survival difficult, because their existence depended upon marginal compliance, at least, with the policies of their overlords in deference to their own standards. The task of balancing external demands and internal standards befell the Yahwistic leaders, especially the kings. In this respect, the statements of the Bible were written by persons in different cultural contexts relevant to issues and persons within those respective contexts for the fundamental purpose of survival, particularly in light of Israel and Judah being an oppressed or dominated people for most of their existence during biblical times.[2] The powerful commissioned the writings—that is, the texts are political propaganda or designed to endorse action favorable to the state administration and their overlords. Thus, the primary concern of their history[3] is the *survival of a minority*, that is, *the quest for preservation and perpetuation of community identity or meaningful existence by a people who are not fully self-determinant.* In modern terms, ancient Israel and Judah were a two-thirds world country or a lesser nation among the superpowers of the ancient world. This quest for survival pervades the Hebrew Bible, even the Greek Testament. Therefore this motif and the corresponding requirements are the agenda items which must be employed for examining the text and reconstructing their history.

This compilation is guided by several premises. First, reality[4] is constant—that is, the natural or physiological world of the ancients is the same as that of today. Here, the ancients and the moderns share a common world! Second, reality is complex, lending itself to innumerable explanations. Sharing a common world, the ancients and the moderns differ in their explanations of that world. Yet every interpretation is a reduction or simplification; all concepts and texts are reductive, being perceptions or refractions of something that has occurred and thereby fictional. Third, concepts[5] and texts[6] are subjective or biased;[7] they are respectively collected, written, and redacted as a result of verification/confirmation of their claims, and thereby they reflect the biases of their conceivers or writers. Fourth, concepts are contextual; they originate within some cultural contexts[8] as expressions of some prevalent understanding of reality. Here, theology is contextual—that is, one's understanding of YHWH and what He requires is always connected to and practical in some specific situation.[9] Fifth, texts are contextually functional; they are used for specific purposes within specific situations for specific reasons by specific people. A text, then, is a medium of communication. Sixth, texts, contexts, and pretexts are interrelated—that is, contexts produce pretexts. The basic norm for reading is one's experience of reality.[10] The basic rules for reading are: (a) texts are read within the contexts of the readers; (b) texts are interpreted based upon the pretexts of the readers.[11] So, for the practicing theologian or believer, theological integrity is determined by biblical consistency and existential expediency—that is, a quality faith stance or faith posture requires, demands, and/or reflects affirmation of one's faith standards (traditionalism) and commitment to the reality in which one lives (realism, relevancy, or realisticness).

These premises suggest a fundamental rule for reading the text: the text must be explained as some conversation/communication between some parties that occurred some where, that pertains to some thing(s) for some purpose(s). Focusing upon the text, the content of its communication and how it was used in its respective historical context(s) must correlate the theology and the pertinent history. Here, the astute reader sees that the communicator (i.e., the speaker and/or the writer) determines/selects the form of the text (clues: structures, formulae, patterns, etc.), selects the content in the text (clues: historical references, e.g., names of peoples, places, or nations, and motifs, concepts, subjects, topics, etc.), and conveys his message through the form(s) of the text and the content in the text (clues: issues/problems which are addressed, functions/purposes the communication serves, presuppositions which are employed). The content of the text is suggestive of the context of the communicator, while the message of the text conveys endorsement of some action which addresses the issues/problems in the context(s) of the communicator and the addressees. The content in the text cannot be assumed to be accurate without investigation or research which corroborates evidence within and outside of the text. Furthermore, talking about the content in the text is distinct from talking about the form of the text or the text as a form of communication. Thus, an operative formula for reading emerges:

FORM + CONTENT = MESSAGE[Issues, Presuppositions, & Purposes]

Employing the results and methods of biblical criticism and the sensitivities discussed above, this compilation seeks to present the probable (i.e., reconstructed) contexts[12], in which the statements of the Hebrew Bible emerged, were written, and were used. Since what is communicated informs the choice of the literary form[13] that is used and what is conveyed through a work and how it is conveyed are dependent upon the quantity and the quality of the available information, the goal is to "hear the text in context"[14] — that is, to understand the Hebrew Bible as the oral or written conversations of the ancient Yahwists, as they might have occurred in their various, original sociopolitical situations. The primary objective is to read the text[15]—to hear it—from *their postures, not ours!*

Helps for Reading the Texts

A. Possible Alignments for Determining the Speaker(s) or the Writer(s) and the Addressees:[16]
  1. The Political Construct:
     a. Tribalist
     b. Monarchalist/Royalist
  2. The Tone:
     a. Conservative/Orthodox
     b. Assimilationist/Moderate/Progressive
     c. Liberal
  3. The Nationality:
     a. Northerner, i. e., Israelite
     b. Southerner, i. e., Judean or Judahite
  4. The Stance:
     a. Advocate, i. e., Pro-
     b. Opponent, i. e., Con-
     c. Sympathizer
  5. The Class:
     a. The Rich/Wealthy including the landowners, the aristocracy, etc.
     b. The Poor/Defenseless/Vulnerable including the resident aliens, the marginal, the populace, etc.

B. Data for Determining the Main Happenings or the Pertinent Descriptions/Circumstances of the Context:
  1. The Causes
  2. The Developments
  3. The Effects

C. Agenda Items for Determining the Issue(s) and the Purpose(s): "The Requirements for Survival"
  1. Administrative Structure
  2. Economic Independence
  3. Ideological Standardization or Intra-communal Organization
  4. Common Language
  5. Selective Appropriation or Assimilation of the dominant culture by the dominated culture, that is, Balance of Extra-communal Influences and Intra-communal Accommodation
  6. People or Population
  7. Land or Place

D. Possible Sources for Identifying & Determining the Presupposition(s):
  1. "The Three Criteria for Yahwism"
     a. the prioritization of YHWH

Endnotes

1. Theology is essentially interpretation of some historical phenomenon from the perspective of some beliefs, which is directed toward some concern in the life of its composer, seeking to engender, influence, or inform sociopolitical behavior. It is the concepts, statements, or theories that constitute the verbal expressions of some faith. Yahwistic theology consists of: (a) YHWH as a subject or an actor within history or human affairs; (b) the presence of the extraordinary as an indicator of the Presence of YHWH; and (c) allusions to historical entities or things in subservience to YHWH, or the dominance of YHWH. It presupposes: (a) some specific historical context(s); (b) some particular audience(s) and author(s)/writer(s); (c) some specific concern(s) or problem(s) that warranted its statements; and (d) some criteria or standards that are acceptable to its addressees and its author(s)/writer(s). It is obvious, then, that theology has the following ingredients: (a) some "interpretive" concept(s); (b) endorsement(s) of some specific socio-politico-religious posture(s); and (c) some pattern(s) of action, or policy(-ies) relevant to the specific and original historical context(s), and possibly subsequent context(s). Thus, faith is an ideology for living that is manifested in customs, institutions, practices, symbols, and concepts, statements or theories (i. e., doctrines or dogmas, which entail principles, norms, criteria, or standards). The latter expressions of faith constitute theology, which entails the belief-statements or the doctrines that are fostered for the meaningful and the purposeful existence of its proponents.

2. cf. Robert B. Coote and Mary P. Coote, *Power, Politics, and the Making of the Bible: An Introduction* (Minneapolis: Fortress, 1990), ix, x, 8, 11, 18, 28, 34f, 36f, 39, 41, 61, 70-73, 75, 78-80, 87, 92f, 101, 108f, 112, 123, 128, 135f, 139, 149-151, 159-161, 162, 164. Coote and Coote correctly contend the Bible originated as temple scriptures, was the product and the tool of power struggles between the rich or affluent, and was used to legitimate the political or power status/policies promulgated by these rich and powerful. Cf. also Morton Smith, *Palestinian Parties and Politics that Shaped the Old Testament* (London: SCM, 1987); Norman K. Gottwald, *The Hebrew Bible: A Socio-literary Introduction* (Philadelphia: Fortress, 1985), especially 596-609; and Richard Elliott Friedman, *Who Wrote the Bible?* (New York: Harper & Row, 1987).

3. History is essentially interpretation or explanation of some subject (e.g., events, people, places, etc.), which reflects the interpretive tools, methodology, and philosophy of a given author. It consists of: (a) interrelations of humans and events via causal connections; (b) normal sociopolitical circumstances; (c) inclusion of theology among other perspectives of reality that has some accreditation of its speaker(s) as a 'believer(s)', e.g., "they believed that YHWH..." History is: (a) purposeful, i.e., it is written for

some specific reason or use; (b) selective, i.e., it indicates use of a limit-ed number of sources; no history is exhaustive; (c) fictional, i.e., it is lit-erary reconstruction informed by the use of a limited number of sources. Being fictional, history is an art-form or literary art; (d) factual, i.e., it is an attempt to convey some truth about the world through the selected literary form, though the selected form may be unacceptable to a given reader's criteria or standards for understanding reality. In this respect it is obvious that history is post eventu, i.e., written after the event or fact; (e) in the Bible, pseudonymous, i.e., it is usually written by an unknown author and attributed to a renown figure as its subject or spokesperson; (f) biased, i.e., it is written from some perspective or point of view and thus reflects the given assumptions, presuppositions, or beliefs of its author. In this respect, history in the Bible is theocentric, i.e., having YHWH as the main subject or actor. Also, history in the Bible is pre-modernistic, i.e., it reflects utilization of standards or criteria peculiar to or characteristic of the ancients and their worldview.

4. Carlos Mesters, "The Use of the Bible in Christian Communities of the Common People," in *The Bible and Liberation: Political and Social Hermeneutics.* Revised Edition of A Radical Religion Reader, ed., Norman K. Gottwald (Maryknoll, NY: Orbis Books, 1983) cf. 122, 123, 132f. Reality is the grounding for relevant reading and use of the Bible, in which the text (i.e., the Bible), the context (i.e., the community), and the pretext (i.e., reality) are interrelated (122f). Interrelation of these three factors balances interpretation, checking subjectivity and undue misappropriation (132f).

5. Concepts are ideas, thoughts, or insights that originate within some con-texts by means of some personal interaction or happening, historical or natural, and thereby are interpretive.

6. Texts are written documents for purposes of recording, teaching, or propaganda.

7. David Lochhead, "The Liberation of the Bible," in *The Bible and Liberation: Political and Social Hermeneutics.* Revised Edition of A Radical Religion Reader (ed. Norman K. Gottwald; Maryknoll, NY: Orbis Books, 1983), 77-80, 81, 82, 83, 86. Contextuality is indispensa-ble (cf. 75, 83), while prejudice or bias is inevitable (cf. 77-80). Reading the text requires attentiveness to how one hears—that is, the perspec-tive(s) that one takes and the blindspots that are related to one's per-spective(s) (cf. 78, 80). In this respect, a theology of the oppressed who are simultaneously the oppressor is needed (77). See Sergio Rostagno, "The Bible: Is an Interclass Reading Legitimate?" in *The Bible and Liberation: Political and Social Hermeneutics.* Revised Edition of A Radical Religion Reader (ed. Norman K. Gottwald; Maryknoll, NY: Orbis Books, 1983), 62, 70, 71-73. Rostagno observes that the church suffers from the illusion of interclass reading of the Bible, when in fact

the church is mainly bourgeoisie, failing to realize the God of the Bible sides with the oppressed or the poor. Also, Bruce J. Malina, "The Social Sciences and Biblical Interpretation," in *The Bible and Liberation: Political and Social Hermeneutics*. Revised Edition of A Radical Religion Reader (ed. Norman K. Gottwald; Maryknoll, NY: Orbis Books, 1983), 16, 17, 18, 19, 20, 22. Malina stipulates "no model...is useful for every conceivable purpose," and that "the appropriate model depends on the type of information one seeks to generate and comprehend." Further, he states "...the social sciences along with sociolinguistics in some form are useful and necessary" (19), and notes the social science models require the interpreter to articulate and account for her/his own social location (20).

8. Contexts are the given social settings or situations in which people live, that have sociopolitical, economic, and cultural dimensions.

9. Matching of the situation in/of the text and the situation of the interpreter is informative for comprehension and consistency in practice.

10. Renita J. Weems, "Reading Her Way through the Struggle: African American Women and the Bible," in *Stony the Road We Trod: African American Biblical Interpretation* (ed. Cain Hope Felder; Minneapolis: Fortress, 1991), 62.

11. Weems, "Reading *Her Way*; cf. William H. Myers, "The Hermeneutical Dilemma of the African American Biblical Student," in *Stony the Road We Trod: African American Biblical Interpretation* (ed. Cain Hope Felder; Minneapolis: Fortress, 1991), 52-55. Myers includes as sources for pretexts "near-canonical" traditions of a given community. Pretexts, then, are the specific attitudinal or mental lenses by and through which a given community understands reality; context is the social situation (i.e., political affiliation, economic status, education level, ethnic group, believing community, etc.) that predisposes one toward reality or the world. Contexts produce pretexts!

12. These contexts constitute the most significant events in the life of the ancient Yahwists. They are considered significant because of (a) what happened, i.e., the particular acts or occurrences; and/or (b) what began, was furthered, or ceased, i.e., developments, trends, customs, concepts, etc. Here, events are interrelated by means of developments within the life of a given people. Such developments are borne through customs or concepts that are interpretive in nature and may be manifested in institutions.

13. It is a consensus that every genre has a linguistic form or structure, a specific function or purpose, a definite *Sitz im Leben*, characteristics or features indicative of its form and elements of which it is composed. In order to define a given genre, one must analyze the grammatical forms (e.g., types of sentences, tenses and persons of verbs, parts of speech, etc.), determine the structure by means of formulae, limits of thoughts or themes, topics, etc., observe and note the logic or flow of thought (i.e., how the content of the passage is presented by the grammatical

forms), determine the function(s) of the grammatical forms and the passage (i.e., how these structures are used to convey the thought and the impact of the passage for its literary setting), and seek to select that genre—kind/type of speech or writing—most characteristic of the information that is compiled.

14. The key questions for listening to the text are: (a) Who spoke it? (b) Who wrote it? (c) To whom was it spoken? (d) To whom was it written? (e) For whom was it spoken? (f) For whom was it written? (g) When was it spoken? (h) When was it written? (i) Where was it spoken? (j) Where was it written? (k) What is it addressing? (l) How is it presented? (m) Why is it presented?

15. Exegesis is reading, which consists of: (a) perception of the grammatical or linguistic forms utilized; (b) articulation of the content or sense borne by/within the forms; (c) comprehension of the reality beyond the forms/text to which it points; and (d) functional acceptance of the writer's assumptions, whereby the reader becomes acquainted with the writer's perspective and attempts to see through the writer's eyes, but not uncritically. Here, mastery of language is required—that is, conceptualization and communication skills. The reader inevitably, in most instances, takes a stance regarding the validity of the work, the writer's claims, or the factuality of what is reported. This is required and to be expected. The reader in comprehending a work judges its credibility by means of the reader's standards or criteria for interpretation.

16. See the chart "Biblical Contextuality."

CHAPTER ONE:
THE LAND OF THE ANCIENT YAHWISTS

The general location of the land of the ancient Yahwists, which is properly called Canaan or Palestine, during the biblical period is the ancient Near East. Specifically it is located along the Fertile Crescent, which stretches from the mouth of the Tigris-Euphrates river on the Persian Gulf northward along the course of the rivers, curves west to the Mediterranean Sea, and then southward through Syria and Palestine as far as the Nile Delta of Egypt.[1] The Fertile Crescent has the largest concentrations of population, the most fertile agricultural areas, the most frequently traveled routes, the territories most fought over by armies, and the great majority of powerful states in the ancient Near East.[2]

Palestine consists of four longitudinal zones: the coastal plains; the western mountains or highlands called Cisjordan; the rift valley or the Jordan River valley which included the Dead Sea; and the eastern mountains or highlands and plateau called Transjordan. These zones do not continue unbroken and are tilted from north-northeast to south-southwest, having numerous different subregions. Because the reliable farming areas are less than half of the total land area, constant struggle ensued over the choice lands.[3] Its location between the continents of Africa and Asia made it a necessary and strategic area for political stability, military control, and economic enterprise.[4] The climate of this area is rainfall deficient. The higher elevations received the heaviest precipitation, and the mountain slopes facing the cloud-bearing rains tended to be far wetter than the slopes to the leeward, making it necessary to capture and control the seasonal runoffs of the rivers.[5] Also, the climate is subtropical, except for the Jordan Valley which is almost tropical and has two seasons. The summer is hot and dry, extending from June to September, and the winter is rainy, extending from mid-October to mid-April.[6]

The geography of the land is significant for the history of the ancient Yahwists in several respects. First, the geography of the land prevented any uniform occupation of it and severely hindered unification of the peoples. Second, the climate and the location combined to precipitate migrations of people for sustenance and security, particularly in times of famine or blight. Third, the most fertile agricultural areas were the ones most heavily populated and over which most battles occurred. Fourth, the militarily stronger

1

entities usually occupied the most fertile agricultural areas. Fifth, the militarily stronger entities usually were most culturally advanced and technologically superior (cf. Judg. 1:19; 4:3; 1 Sam. 13:19-23; Isa. 2:4; Mic. 4:3). Dominance of the land, then, depended upon political stability and military might. In this respect, Israel and Judah remained an oppressed people for most of its existence during the biblical period. The period of David-Solomon is the only exception, which was possible because of the vacuum of political powers internationally. Thus, the biblical presentation of Israel and Judah reflects their struggle to survive.

The Customs of the Ancient Near East

Political structures were sacralized—that is, monarchies were given ideological justification by the cult as the administrative arms of the gods. It was believed a hierarchy of gods[7] ruled through the states, appointing and empowering kings. Since the king was the head of the state and the state religion, he directed religious affairs, regulating festivals and sacrifices. He lived adjacent to the deity—that is, the temple was next to the palace and separated from the rest of the population. He could, and would, build[8] altars and sanctuaries,[9] conduct war,[10] make deity images/statues,[11] appoint cultic officials, establish cultic procedures, make sacrifices, and authorize the cultic rituals and laws.[12] In this respect, the cultic personnel provided the *apologia*, ideological justification and authorization, for a given monarchy. Such justification included royal enthronement rituals[13] and royal ideologies, which usually perpetuated the dynastic principle and proclaimed the dynasties were eternal. At the heart of these was the view the god(s) had put the king on the throne, even through a calling, in which the king is presented as a humble man and as the vice regent of his god(s). In this regard, the institution of monarchy was viewed as sacred, or the king was regarded as divine.[14] The king's concern, then, was administration and representation of the divine order, of which the given state believed it was part. It is noteworthy, here, that writing was usually authorized by the king, utilizing common literary patterns (e.g., right and wrong, order and chaos, good and evil).[15] Thus, it was common for a monarchy to have a temple-cult, and the two institutions were regarded as counterparts. The basic presupposition was that political action was premised upon revelation of the divine will.[16]

On the other hand, cultic structures were politicized. The cult served two functions. It represented the realm of the gods, particularly the gods of the state. Also, the cult represented the state, being an administrative arm of the government. In this capacity the temple personnel, including priests and prophets, were state officials, administering laws, acquiring land, and participating in the military operations. The cult, then, is a religio-political institution which governs the lives of its proponents, endorsers, or adherents, providing a constitution (i.e., rules, standards, ideology), a mechanism of regulation (i.e., calendar of feasts), enforcers (i.e., cultic officials in conjunction with community leaders), and expressions or practices (i.e., offerings, symbols). The cult presupposes a view that certain persons are "sacred" or authorized by deity to direct the lives of the given, fostering community, which justifies or legitimates the requests and contributions of offerings. These are the cultic personnel, the priests and the prophets. Such people were employed, endorsed, or supported by some established groups (e.g., strong communal factions, tribal associations, monarchies), and in turn tended to justify the existence of their support base. They had political clout and could enforce their views, usually, including the aims and wishes of the powerful and/or the king. This means the laws of the powerful or the king were promulgated as the will/laws of the gods. The cult, then, is the place or institution which establishes the ideological basis or constitution for the lives of its proponents and adherents and the mechanism for management or administration of the economic resources of its fostering community. It is the ideological determiner or ideological interpreter of its community, whether of the local village or of the state in the case of a monarchy.[17]

However, the aims of the administration which endorses a specific cult are always central, reflecting the peculiar goals of those in control or power. First, politically speaking, the cultic calendar is the mechanism of institutional regulation of daily life, which, naturally, reflects the posture and perspective of its proponents and endorsers. It provides the occasions for collection of the offerings. Second, being located within the cult and thus understandable only on the premise that the cult directs or governs significantly daily life/routines, the offerings are the expressions of the social circumstances of the offerers—that is, their economic, sociopolitical, and existential conditions and their allegiance to the state administration and gods. The offerings, then, ritualize or symbolize the status of intra-communal relations in relation to deity, which in the case of the kingdoms of Israel and Judah was a pantheon of gods, including YHWH up until the post-exilic period.[18] So the quality of a given cult is determined by assessment or examination of the lives (or relations) of its practitioners in comparison to its ideology, not the views, perspectives, or postures of a given proponent or group.

Daily Life in Biblical Times

A. Factors:
1. 95% illiteracy of the population
2. No medicine
3. No guaranteed government amenities (i. e., social security, welfare aid, police, etc.)
4. Poor or unbalanced diets due to geography
   a. rainfall-deficient climate
   b. less than a third of the land was agricultural
5. Shortage of males due to killings in times of suppression and war, and castration/neutering
6. Polygamy due to existential circumstances
7. Dominance by hierarchies
8. Male dominance or chauvinism
9. Superstitions within religions
10. Sacralization of political structures and politicization of cultic structures

B. Characteristics:
1. Difficult
2. Short
3. 'Brutal'
4. Communally-oriented
5. 'Valued'

C. Rules:
1. If one worked on the land, that one's share was small; if one did not work, one's share was often large.[19]
2. The debilitations of poverty made life short and hard for the working people.[20]
3. Work was a given that was necessary, natural, and virtuous, having the deepest religious significance to villagers.[21]
4. The cult reflected its sponsors or proponents.[22]
5. The more land a household controlled, the less its members worked and the more they ate.[23]
6. Might made right.[24]
7. Everything was biased, cultically and politically.

Endnotes

1. Norman K. Gottwald, *The Hebrew Bible: A Socio-literary Introduction* (Philadelphia: Fortress, 1985), 39; Gösta Ahlström, *The History of Ancient Palestine from the Palaeolithic Period to Alexander's Conquest* (ed. Diana Edelman; JSOT Sup. 146; England: Sheffield, 1993), 61-66; J. Alberto Soggin, *An Introduction to the History of Israel and Judah* (trans. John Bowden; Valley Forge, PA: Trinity International, 1993), 8-10.

2. Gottwald, *The Hebrew Bible*, 39; Ahlström, *History*, 67-69; Soggin, *History*, 16-20.

3. Gottwald, *The Hebrew Bible*, 41-42; Ahlström, *History*, 62-66, 67-69.

4. Gottwald, *The Hebrew Bible*, 39; Ahlström, *History*, 67-69; Soggin, *History*, 16-20.

5. Gottwald, *The Hebrew Bible*, 37f. and Ahlström (*History*, 67) note the rainfall generally decreases from west to east and from north to south.

6. Ahlström, *History*, 66f.

7. Lowell K. Handy, "The Appearance of Pantheon in Judah," in *The Triumph of Elohim: From Yahwisms to Judaisms* (ed. Diana Vikander Edelman; Grand Rapids, MI: Eerdmans, 1995), 27-43. Handy argues that Judah followed a four-tiered pantheon of gods, characteristic of Ugaritic traditions (32-43). See Pss. 8:6; 29:1; 82; 86:8; 89:7; 95:3; 97:7; 135:5; 138:1; 148.

8. Ahlström, *History*, 427, 473, 507. Kings conducted extensive building projects, expressing their power as authorized by the gods and their positions as shepherds. Consonant with this view is the belief the gods were the owners of the land (328). So, in taking over a land, the gods of the land were worshiped as they were or by means of identification of them with one's own gods for the purpose of gaining blessings, i. e., crops, birth, etc. (146, 328). Walled cities were usually built for purposes of protection, serving as fortresses (357); thus, walling of cities by subject peoples was regarded as an act of preparation for rebellion (828, 863). Such protective measures were necessary, for villagers, as a rule, were conservative (538) and probably provided sources of tension and strife to the city-states, while opposing states were obvious threats. Lastly, kings sought to expand their kingdoms through conquests or treaties (385). Such expansion and building was necessary because the god's power was extended by such. This even included naming of cities.

9. Ahlström, *History*, 471. In this light, threshing floors served as temporary cult places during harvest seasons where the rites of harvest were performed, since they were also used for official gatherings and decision making.

10. Ahlström, *History*, 631. Similarly, "ripping open all the pregnant women" was an established method of warfare, guaranteeing that no new

opponents or soldiers would be born. See also Gottwald, *The Hebrew Bible*, 39; Ahlström, *History*, 67-69; Soggin, *History*, 16-20. For the consideration of war as an interpreted expression of YHWH's legal judgment, see Robert M. Good, "The Just War in Ancient Israel," *Journal of Biblical Literature* 104 (1985): 385-400.

11. Ahlström, *History*, 524, 533. The lion was a symbol of divinity and royalty. Pillars symbolized the entrances to the heavens.

12. Ahlström, *History*, 179f, 374, 383, 388f, 426f, 430f, 438 n. 4, 453, 475f, 491, 507, 523f, 529-531, 582, 588, 603, 611, 773.

13. Ahlström, *History*, 431. Designation by a prophet was part of the ritual.

14. Ahlström, *History*, 588.

15. Ahlström, *History*, 375.

16. Ahlström, *History*, 116-118, 199, 251, 264, 300, 328, 453, 475f, 499 n. 3, 523f, 598, 603, 610 n. 6, 638, 773.

17. See Niels Peter Lemche, *Ancient Israel: A New History of Israelite Society* (England: Sheffield, 1995), 34 n. 1, 56, 119-124, 164f, 169.

18. Handy, "The Appearance of Pantheon" 32-43; Herbert Niehr, "The Rise of YHWH in Judahite and Israelite Religion: Methodological and Religio-Historical Aspects," in *The Triumph of Elohim: From Yahwisms to Judaisms* (ed. Diana Vikander Edelman; Grand Rapids, MI: Eerdmans, 1995), 45-72, especially 52, 59, 65f.

19. Robert B. Coote, *Early Israel: A New Horizon* (Minneapolis: Fortress, 1990), 10.

20. Coote, *Early Israel*, 17.

21. Coote, *Early Israel*, 26.

22. Coote, *Early Israel*, 27.

23. Coote, *Early Israel*, 28.

24. Coote, *Early Israel*, 31.

CHAPTER TWO:
THE RISE TO DOMINANCE OF THE YAHWISTS

The present scholarly consensus relates that there was no conquest of high-land Palestine by outside invaders (e.g., the Bible), no infiltration of disparate nomads into the Palestinian hills to merge gradually in a tribal league (e.g., Alt[1] and Noth[2]), and no peasant revolution (e.g., Mendenhall and Gottwald[3]).[4] This consensus is based upon the absence of archeological data, including extra-biblical references which corroborate the biblical presentations and the general trend toward late dating of the composition of the Hebrew Bible.[5] Two archaeological givens provide the basis for reconstructing the pre-monarchic history of Israel: the reference of Merneptah (ca. thirteenth century B.C.E.); and the spread of villages on the settlement frontiers of Palestine (ca. twelfth-eleventh centuries B.C.E.).[6] Since the Hebrew Scriptures were not written in early Israel, and its writers knew little or nothing about the origin of Israel, there can be no narrative history of early Israel.[7]

Regarding the early (i.e., premonarchic) history of Israel, the following represents the present, scholarly consensus. First, the Israelites were indigenous to Palestine, and their lives were dominated by the struggle of hierarchical factions linked to outside powers, such as Egypt, Assyria, Babylonia, etc.[8] This signifies that the Israelites were Canaanites.[9] Their primary concern was survival—securing their basic needs and satisfying the demands of their overlords. This concern required an egalitarian emphasis as women participated alongside men until circumstances led to changes.[10] As a rule, workers received smaller shares than those who did not work but owned the land;[11] the debilitation of poverty made life short and hard for the working people;[12] and the more land a household controlled, the less its members worked, and the more they ate.[13] Work, then, was the central or integrating focus of existence, having the deepest religious significance. Thus, the cult or religion served economic and political purposes.[14]

Second, Egyptian imperial power dominated Palestine from the late sixteenth century B.C.E., and peaked in the thirteenth and early twelfth centuries B.C.E.[15] Egypt, Assyria, and Babylonia constituted the major nations or superpowers during the history of Israel, and thus were standard setters for the other smaller states and villages. The first nation to dominate Israel was Egypt. The Egyptian "New Kingdom" domination began about 1550 B.C.E., and its time of greatest administrative intensity in Palestine was 1300-1150

B.C.E.[16] They maintained their dominance by means of conquest and control of the lowland of Palestine, with extension into the hills, and implementation of a policy of "divide and rule"—varied degrees of control. This rule was marked by Egyptian expansion into Palestine, which secured trade and tribute and provided a buffer against attack.[17] So, before the end of the Egyptian "New Kingdom" domination and the late Bronze Age, Israel existed, but not with the later structure that emerged during the monarchy and that is reflected in the biblical texts. The "New Kingdom" domination collapsed about 1150 B.C.E. during the reign of Ramesses VI (ca. 1141-1133 B.C.E.).[18]

Third, during the first three centuries of Egyptian power in Palestine economic and political exploitation disrupted social relations and aggravated intraregional hostilities, resulting in retreat of settlements from the frontier zones and population decline.[19] Specifically, during the period of the Egyptian "New Kingdom" domination in Palestine, Israel developed and settled the highlands under Egyptian endorsement, later becoming an established kingdom.[20] They settled the sparsely inhabited highlands during the twelfth and eleventh centuries B.C.E., surviving through diversified subsistence production—pastoralism and extensive land use. This was prompted by the economic and political insecurity of the urban centers, which discouraged agriculture and encouraged pastoralism.[21] Settlements occurred along the coast and the main trade ways, which contrasted and conflicted with settlements at harbors on the coast to the north and Egyptian strongholds in the southern plains. The shift toward pastoralism and the restriction and reduction of settlement, agriculture, and population growth then resulted from the Egyptian defense policy, which destroyed the walls of cities, leaving large and strategic sites unfortified.[22] As a result of these changes, settlements were occupied and areas were farmed that had never been previously occupied, which provided the agricultural heartland for the monarchy of Israel that formed shortly thereafter.[23]

Also, as late as 1207 B.C.E. Israel, an ally of Egypt,[24] was a strong tribal confederacy developed by Egypt and Palestinian chiefs for the purpose of overseeing tribal interests and the border zone between the Egyptians and the Hittites.[25] However, during the latter half of the thirteenth century B.C.E., European and Anatolian invaders overran lowland Palestine, with their strongest families taking over many areas and replacing the Egyptians and the Palestinians as a ruling class.[26] These invaders included a significant aristocratic component, which probably prompted employment of them as mercenaries by Egypt. In this respect, the Sherden (or Shardana) and the Shekelesh were supporters of Egypt, while the Lukka (or Lycians) and the Tjekers were opponents to Egypt.[27] It is probable the Philistines were initially opponents of Egypt, but became allies of Egypt, mastering the lowlands of Palestine with a pentapolis (i.e., Gaza, Ashkelon, Ashdod, Gath, and Ekron).[28] Still, Israel remained affiliated with Egypt through the time of Saul.

With the collapse of the Hittite and the Egyptian empires and the rise of the European and Anatolian strongmen, expansion of settlement and population in the tribal frontier zones in Palestine occurred, particularly those areas controlled by Israel. This enlarged the tribes and the territories of Israel, whose chiefs were probably regarded by the western Palestinians as the legitimate alternative to European and Anatolian rule.[29] Also, the Philistines replaced Egypt as the dominant power in Palestine and became the opponents to Israel. Though Israel may have been initially sponsored by Egypt against the Philistines,[30] Israel increasingly gained independence from Egypt[31] and decisively ended its vassalship with Egypt during the time of David, after having inhabited recently founded villages in the highland and becoming a mostly highland group, thereby establishing a monarchy.[32] So the establishment of a monarchy was necessary for protection, in light of the change in the political climate, the spread of Israel's settlements, and the increase of Israel's agriculture, all of which required order and security.[33]

Finally, the Israelite tribal society came under the monarchy of Saul (ca. 1000 B.C.E.) and was usurped by the Davidic regime,[34] during whose administration the Hebrew Scriptures began to be formed in the court, containing significant hints of conditions and developments before 1000 B.C.E. but no historical account of Israel's origin and early history. Hence there was no golden age of Israel, since early Israel constituted a typical, complex tribal conglomerate in a Palestinian context which was ruled by a tribal elite.[35]

Chapter Synopsis:
The Key Dates

1550-1150 B.C.E.	Egyptian "New Kingdom" Domination
1290-1223 B.C.E.	Reign of Rameses II
1200-1100 B.C.E.	End of the Occupation of the Land: Beginning of the Overthrow or Rejection of Egyptian Domination by the YHWH-worshippers

Causes:

1. decline of the XVIII-XX Egyptian dynasties or collapse of the Egyptian "New Kingdom"
2. influx or migration of European and Anatolian rovers [e.g., Philistines, Lukka, Tjeker] and conquest of coast and lowlands
3. efficient organization of YHWH-worshippers for protection initiated under Egyptian domination and furthered by circumstances of Egyptian decline, including occupation of the highlands and diversified subsistence production [e.g., pastoralism and extensive land use]
4. desire for freedom or self-determination
5. securing of technology or technological advancement of tribal confederation

Developments:

1. integration and association of YHWH-worshippers and Palestinian chiefs [i.e., pre-Israelite elements] to form "Israel"
2. compilation, assimilation, and sequencing of the various traditions of the Israelites

Effects:

1. birth of conception of YHWH as socio-political deliverer or warrior
2. birth of "Israel" as a formidable political coalition and contender for the land of Palestine, conducting defensive and offensive wars
3. formulation of patriarchal traditions [Gen. 12 - Deut., Jos.]

Interpretations:

1. explanation of the overthrow of Egyptian domination as 'exodus from Egypt' or 'deliverance by YHWH' [Exod. 1-15]
2. beginning of relationship with YHWH described as 'covenant' as the socio-political rubric of organization of Israel [Exod. 19-34; also Gen. 12, 15, 17; Exod. 6]
3. land as gift from YHWH [Jos.]
4. Israel as sons of Jacob [Gen. 29:31-30:24; 49:1-27; Num. 26:4-51]

5. disobedience as hindrance/prevention of complete occupation/dominance of the land [Jgs. 1-2]

The Selected Interpretations

#1: Explanation of the Overthrow of Egyptian Domination as 'Exodus from Egypt' or 'Deliverance by YHWH' [Exod. 1-15]

A. Perspectives:
  1. Speaker: early Yahwists
  2. Writer: J (earliest) or David's court

B. Addressees:
  1. of the Speaker:
    a. the Yahwistic tribes
    b. the unaligned tribal components
  2. of the Writer:
    a. the kingdom of David-Solomon
    b. the marginal people or the bedouins on the southwestern border

C. Contexts:
  1. of the Speaker:
    a. the aftermath of the demise of the Egyptian dynasties
    b. the struggles between the Sea Peoples and the Yahwistic tribes
  2. of the Writer: the formation of the Davidic state

D. Issues: "security"
  1. of the Speaker:
    a. the low morale due to early defeats
    b. the potential threat of unaligned tribal components siding with Israel's enemies
  2. of the Writer:
    a. the soured relations that ensued due to David's methods of conquest and accrual of his state
    b. the potential threat of unaligned marginal components siding with Egypt

E. Purposes:
  1. of the Speaker:
    a. encouragement of the war effort
    b. recruitment or solicitation of non-participants

11

2. of the Writer: "propaganda or public relations"
    a. appeasement of opponents to, and suppression of rumors about, David, i.e., to improve David's image, particularly among the Northern Yahwists or the Israelite tribes
    b. recruitment or solicitation of northern factions that David had soured

F. Presuppositions:
    1. of the Speaker:
        a. the historicity of YHWH's activity
        b. YHWH as Warrior
        c. YHWH as God of Israel, i.e., Israel as chosen people by YHWH
        d. the oneness of YHWH, i.e., the political solidarity of Yahwistic tribalism
    2. of the Writer:
        a. the historicity of YHWH's activity
        b. YHWH as Warrior
        c. YHWH as God of Israel, i.e., Israel as chosen people by YHWH
        d. David as being Mosaic, i.e., a liberator/deliverer
        e. the oneness of YHWH, i.e., the political solidarity of Yahwistic monarchalism
        f. YHWH as being with David [1 Sam. 16:1, 12f, 18; 17:37, 45-48; 18:12, 14, 28-29; 23:14; 30:6; 2 Sam. 3:1; 5:10; 8:6, 14]

#2: Beginning of Relationship with YHWH described as Covenant as the Socio-Political Rubric of Organization of Israel [Exod. 19-34; cf. Gen. 12, 15, 17]

A. Perspectives:
    1. Speaker: early Yahwists
    2. Writer: J (earliest) or David's court

B. Addressees:
    1. of the Speaker:
        a. the Yahwistic tribes
        b. the pre-Israelite components or potential Israelites who are being recruited
    2. of the Writer:
        a. the pre-Israelite components

b. the Northern Yahwists or Israelites

C. Contexts:
1. of the Speaker:
    a. the early struggles for control of Palestine
    b. the intra-tribal rivalry for control of the group
2. of the Writer: the kingdom of David-Solomon

D. Issues:
1. of the Speaker:
    a. the competing views/models of organization
    b. the competing ideologies with their respective gods/cults
2. of the Writer:
    a. the competing views/models of organization
    b. the competing ideologies with their respective gods/cults
    c. contesting of the South's (re-)organization of the State

E. Purposes:
1. of the Speaker:
    a. administrative structure
    b. ideological standardization
2. of the Writer: "propaganda or public relations"
    a. establishment of the ideological basis for the State
    b. appeal to the original Yahwistic faction(s) for support of the Davidic state

F. Presuppositions:
1. of the Speaker:
    a. YHWH as God of Israel, i.e., Israel as chosen people by YHWH
    b. the oneness of YHWH, i.e., the political solidarity of Yahwistic tribalism
    c. the historicity of YHWH's activity
2. of the Writer:
    a. YHWH as God of Israel, i.e., Israel as chosen people by YHWH
    b. David as being Mosaic, i.e., a liberator/deliverer
    c. YHWH as being with David [1 Sam. 16:1, 12f, 18; 17:37, 45-48; 18:12, 14, 28-29; 23:14; 30:6; 2 Sam. 3:1; 5:10; 8:6, 14]
    d. the oneness of YHWH, i.e., the political solidarity of Yahwistic monarchalism
    e. the historicity of YHWH's activity

#3: Land as Gift from YHWH [Jos.]

A. Perspectives:
    1. Speaker: early Yahwists
    2. Writer: J (earliest) or David's court

B. Addressees:
    1. of the Speaker:
        a. the Yahwistic tribes
        b. the rivals for control of the land
        c. those among the Yahwistic group with competing claims
    2. of the Writer:
        a. the Davidic state
        b. the peoples in the land who were conquered by David or under his domination

C. Contexts:
    1. of the Speaker:
        a. the early struggles for control of Palestine
        b. the intra-tribal rivalry for control of the group, reflected in competing ideological claims
    2. of the Writer:
        a. the competing ideological claims
        b. the assertion of land-claims by the Northern Yahwists or Israelites

D. Issues: land-rights or land-claims

E. Purposes:
    1. of the Speaker: assertion and establishment of ownership
    2. of the Writer: justification of the acquisition of the national land-base

F. Presuppositions:
    1. of the Speaker:
        a. YHWH as God (i.e., the Owner and Giver) of the land
        b. YHWH as God of Israel, i.e., Israel as chosen people by YHWH
        c. the oneness of YHWH, i.e., the political solidarity of Yahwistic tribalism
        d. the historicity of YHWH's activity
    2. of the Writer:
        a. YHWH as God (i.e., the Owner and Giver) of the land

    b.   YHWH as God of Israel, i.e., Israel as chosen people by YHWH

    c.   YHWH as being with David [1 Sam. 16:1, 12f, 18; 17:37, 45-48; 18:12, 14, 28-29; 23:14; 30:6; 2 Sam. 3:1; 5:10; 8:6, 14]

    d.   the oneness of YHWH, i.e., the political solidarity of Yahwistic monarchalism

    e.   the historicity of YHWH's activity

#4: Israel as Sons of Jacob [Gen. 29:31-30:24; 49:1-27; Num. 26:4-51]

A. Perspectives:
1. Speaker: the Central-Northern Israelites
2. Writer: J (earliest) or David's court

B. Addressees:
1. of the Speaker: the rivals or competing factions within the tribal association
2. of the Writer:
    a.   the Northern Yahwists or Israelites
    b.   the Southern Yahwists or the newly-assimilated Israelites

C. Contexts:
1. of the Speaker: the early intra-tribal struggles for control of the group
2. of the Writer: the rivalry between the Northern Yahwists and the Southern Yahwists, in which the latter dominated the former

D. Issues:
1. of the Speaker: identification of the group, i.e., its origins and constituency
2. of the Writer: redefinition of Israel according to the Davidic administration

E. Purposes:
1. of the Speaker:
    a.   administrative structure
    b.   ideological standardization
2. of the Writer:
    a.   incorporation of the newly-assimilated Israelites or peoples
    b.   accommodation/acceptance of the Southern arrangement

F. Presuppositions:
  1. of the Speaker:
     a. YHWH as God of Israel, i.e., Israel as chosen people by YHWH
     b. the oneness of YHWH, i.e., the political solidarity of Yahwistic tribalism
     c. the historicity of YHWH's activity
  2. of the Writer:
     a. YHWH as God of Israel, i.e., Israel as chosen people by YHWH
     b. YHWH as being with David [1 Sam. 16:1, 12f, 18; 17:37, 45-48; 18:12, 14, 28-29; 23:14; 30:6; 2 Sam. 3:1; 5:10; 8:6, 14]
     c. the oneness of YHWH, i.e., the political solidarity of Yahwistic monarchalism
     d. he historicity of YHWH's activity

#5: Disobedience as Hindrance/Prevention of Complete Occupation/ Dominance of the Land [Jgs. 1-2]

A. Perspectives:
  1. Speaker: the early Yahwists
  2. Writer: J (earliest) or David's court

B. Addressees: those who had suffered defeats/setbacks in their struggles for control of the land

C. Contexts:
  1. of the Speaker: the struggles for control of the land
  2. of the Writer:
     a. the struggles for control of the land
     b. the aftermath of David's conquest of Palestine

D. Issues:
  1. of the Speaker:
     a. the efforts toward acquisition of land
     b. the inability to dominate the land and to accumulate land-base
  2. of the Writer: motivation for maintenance of land-rights

E. Purposes:
  1. of the Speaker:
     a. explanation of defeats in efforts to control the land
     b. incentive for compliance with the tribal arrangement/alliance

16

2. of the Writer: incentive for compliance with the Davidic state

F. Presuppositions:
    1. of the Speaker:
        a. YHWH as God (i.e., the Owner and Giver) of the land
        b. YHWH as God of Israel, i.e., Israel as chosen people by YHWH
        c. the oneness of YHWH, i.e., the political solidarity of Yahwistic tribalism
        d. the historicity of YHWH's activity
    2. of the Writer:
        a. YHWH as God (i.e., the Owner and Giver) of the land
        b. YHWH as God of Israel, i.e., Israel as chosen people by YHWH
        c. YHWH as being with David [1 Sam. 16:1, 12f, 18; 17:37, 45-48; 18:12, 14, 28-29; 23:14; 30:6; 2 Sam. 3:1; 5:10; 8:6, 14]
        d. the oneness of YHWH, i.e., the political solidarity of Yahwistic monarchalism
        e. the historicity of YHWH's activity

Endnotes

1. Albrecht Alt, "The Settlement of the Israelites in Palestine," in *Essays on Old Testament History and Religion* (Garden City, N. Y.: Doubleday, 1968), 173-221.

2. Martin Noth, *The History of Israel* (3d ed.; trans. Peter R. Ackroyd; New York: Harper and Row, 1958).

3. Norman K. Gottwald, *The Tribes of Yahweh: A Sociology of the Religion of Liberated Israel*, 1250-1050 B.C.E. (Maryknoll, N. Y.: Orbis Books, 1979); also *The Hebrew Bible: A Socio-literary Introduction* (Philadelphia: Fortress, 1985), 272-275, 284-286. In the latter work, he argues "Israel burst into history as an ethnically and socioeconomically mixed coalition composed of a majority of tribally organized peasants along with a lesser number of pastoral nomads, mercenaries and freebooters, assorted craftsmen, and renegade priests...(that) joined in a combined sociopolitical and religious revolution against the imperial and hierarchic tribute-imposing structures of Egyptian-dominated Canaan" (284). For a critique, see Jacob Milgrom, "Religious Conversion and the Revolt Model for the Formation of Israel," *Journal of Biblical Literature 101* (1982): 169-176, especially 169, 173, 175.

4. Robert B. Coote, *Early Israel: A New Horizon* (Minneapolis: Fortress, 1990), 2; J. Alberto Soggin, *An Introduction to the History of Israel and Judah* (trans. John Bowden; Valley Forge, PA: Trinity International, 1993), 33, 157f, 162f; Gösta Ahlström, *The History of Ancient Palestine from the Palaeolithic Period to Alexander's Conquest* (ed. Diana Edelman; JSOT Sup. 146; England: Sheffield, 1993), 241, 344f, 347f, 418. Gottwald ["Sociological Method in the Study of Ancient Israel," *The Bible and Liberation: Political and Social Hermeneutics*. Revised Edition of a Radical Religion Reader (ed. Norman K. Gottwald; Maryknoll, NY: Orbis Books, 1983), 26-37] concedes it is erroneous to assume early Israel arose along only one trajectory (32).

5. Cf. Philip R. Davies, *In Search of 'Ancient Israel'* (JSOT Sup. 148; England: Sheffield, 1992).

6. Coote, *Early Israel* 4; cf. "Israel Stela," translated by John A. Wilson(*ANET*, 231); cf. "A Campaign of Seti I in Northern Palestine," translated by John A. Wilson (*ANET*, 182f); "The Report of a Frontier Official," translated by John A. Wilson (*ANET*, 183f).

7. Coote, *Early Israel*, 2f; Davies, *In Search*; J. Alberto Soggin, *An Introduction to the History of Israel and Judah* (trans. John Bowden; Valley Forge, PA: Trinity International, 1993), 3, 26, 28, 67, 95, 114, 136, 138, 148, 175f; Ahlström, *History*, 43, 45-52, 413, 490 n. 3, 491 n. 4, 540 n. 5, 557 n. 4, 561, 597f, 621 n. 2, 623, 650 n. 1, 677 (n. 3), 702 (n. 1), 706 (n. 2), 720 n. 3, 770f, 775 n. 1, 777, 804, 822, 838, 844-847, 859 n. 3, 876, 883, 885-887; Niels Peter Lemche, *Ancient Israel: A New History of Israelite Society* (Sheffield, England: Sheffield, 1995), 29-73, 119-124.

8. Coote, *Early Israel*, 4; Soggin, *History*, 20, 27, 158, 163; Ahlström, *History*, 234-236, 277, 285f, 349, 355, 404.

9. The biblical writers present the view of Israel as being the sons of Jacob, and thereby "blood-related" (Gen. 16-18; 25:1-6, 19-26; 29:1-30:24; 35:16-21; 49:1b-27; Num. 26:4b-51). This is merely an ideological or polemical argument, designed to promote political unity, as traditions from the various tribal units were compiled and sequenced to express a common origin and destiny. This does not discount the fact there was association through propagation and marriage. The point is association was necessary and occurred for the purposes of protection and provision, obviously having political, economic, and religious dimensions. See Coote, Early Israel, 75-77, 79, 81, 86f; Gottwald, *The Hebrew Bible*, 272-275, 284-286; see later "Assimilation and Syncretism in Israelite History."

10. Phyllis A. Bird, "Images of Women in the Old Testament," *The Bible and Liberation: Political and Social Hermeneutics*. Revised Edition of A Radical Religion Reader (ed. Norman K. Gottwald; Maryknoll, NY: Orbis Books, 1983), 252-288; Carol L. Meyers, "The Roots of Restriction: Women in Early Israel," *The Bible and Liberation: Political and Social Hermeneutics*. Revised Edition of A Radical Religion Reader (ed. Norman K. Gottwald; Maryknoll, NY: Orbis Books, 1983), 289-306. Bird argues that though in the social arena women were generally subordinated to men, the ancient Israelite literature shows their status and role in ancient Israel varied at different periods and in different social circles, and these varied stances were self-critical and counter-critical (cf. 260f, 262, 263, 264, 267, 268, 269, 270, 271, 274, 276, 278). Moreover, Meyers explains that due to severe depopulation in the late Bronze Age, there was a dire need for child-bearing women rather than female participation in the egalitarian peasant movement, resulting in a circumstantial restriction of the roles of women that was continually perpetuated in subsequent generations (cf. 292, 294, 295, 296, 297-300, 302f).

11. Coote, *Early Israel*, 10.

12. Coote, *Early Israel*, 17.

13. Coote, *Early Israel*, 28.

14. Coote, *Early Israel*, 25-27, 29f.

15. Coote, *Early Israel*, 4; Ahlström, *History*, 218f, 287; see also Soggin, *History*, 20, 27, 158, 163; "Amarna Letters," translated by H. L. Ginsberg (ANET, 262-277).

16. Coote, *Early Israel*, 34, 50, 52; Ahlström, *History*, 218f.

17. Coote, *Early Israel*, 33-35, 46f; Ahlström, *History*, 287.

18. Coote, *Early Israel*, 56f.

19. Coote, *Early Israel*, 5.

20. Coote, *Early Israel*, 59f, 62, 64, 66, 68-70; Ahlström, *History*, 285-286.

21. Coote, *Early Israel*, 59f, 60f, 62.
22. Coote, *Early Israel*, 64, 66, 68f.
23. Coote, *Early Israel*, 70.
24. Coote, *Early Israel*, 92. The pact between Egypt and Israel lasted until the time of David.
25. Coote, *Early Israel*, 5, 88-90; Ahlström, *History*, 286f, 418; see Niels Peter Lemche, "Kings and Clients: On Loyalty between the Ruler and the Ruled in Ancient "Israel," *Semeia* 66 (1994): 119-132 .
26. Coote, *Early Israel*, 5; "The War Against the Peoples of the Sea," translated by John A. Wilson (ANET, 185f).
27. Coote, *Early Israel*, 96, 99, 100, 101, 102, 108; Ahlström, *History*, 282-333.
28. Coote. *Early Israel*, 92, 102, 108; Ahlström, *History*, 241, 248, 288-291. Coote sees the Philistines as the opponents to Egypt, who replaced the Egyptian counterparts and renewed the threat to Egypt, when the Egyptian "New Kingdom" collapsed (ca. 1150 B.C.E.). On the other hand, Ahlström regarded the Philistines as agents of Egypt. Nevertheless, the Philistines filled the void left by Egypt's decline.
29. Coote, *Early Israel*, 5, 113-117, 130f, 133f 135, 136-138; Ahlström, *History*, 334f, 346, 348-350, 360, 369, 487; Soggin, *History*, 167, 169. These new settlements occurred during the twelfth-eleventh centuries B.C.E., and were mostly villages in the highland territories of Israel, northern Galilee, the Negeb, and parts of the Transjordan. These settlements, which came under Israelite control, established the agricultural base for the later, Israelite monarchy. Israel explained their acquisition of these territories as land-grants from YHWH, asserting their ownership or land-rights (Jos.) and later critiquing their multi-culturality by regarding their inability to control, or their loss of, certain areas as due to disobedience to YHWH (cf. Judg. 1-2; also Judg. 1:19; 4:3; 1 Sam. 13:19-23; Isa. 2:4; Mic. 4:3).
30. Coote, *Early Israel*, 116f. Once the Europeans had removed Hatti from the stage, Ramesses III countered by bolstering the tribes of Israel. However, when Egypt was forced out altogether by the Europeans, the Palestinian lowland came under the control of the newcomers, and the Palestinian elite clients of the Egyptian occupation were removed.
31. This acquisition of freedom and emergence of Israel as a self-determining political entity was explained as the result of deliverance by the high god of the tribal association, YHWH (Exod. 1-15). The biblical tradition is a cult legend, reflecting numerous pentateuchal tradents, who share in common the view that YHWH is a warrior-god, who has claimed Israel as His vassal, thereby establishing their identity through an exclusive covenant existence with them (cf. Exod. 19-34; cf. Gen. 12, 15, 17; Exod. 6).

32. Coote, *Early Israel*, 72, 88-90, 92f; Ahlström, *History*, 285-288; Soggin, *History*, 169. According to Coote the nature of the political change was "from a tribal confederation located mainly in northern lowland and frontier Palestine, supported by village agriculture and military subsidies, and tied to Egypt to a tribal confederation located mainly in the central highlands, still supported by village agriculture, and at first in its fortunes more tied to Egypt, but with the fall of the New Kingdom much less so" (119).

33. Coote, *Early Israel*, 116; Douglas A. Knight, "Political Rights and Powers in Monarchic Israel," *Semeia* 66 (1994): 93-117; Lemche, "Kings and Clients," 119-132.

34. It must be noted that the factuality of David and his reign has been questioned by some scholars. See Herbert Niehr, "The Rise of YHWH in Judahite and Israelite Religion: Methodological and Religio-Historical Aspects," in *The Triumph of Elohim: From Yahwisms to Judaisms* (ed. Diana Vikander Edelman; Grand Rapids, MI: Eerdmans, 1995), 53; Bernard Goldstein (private discussions); Philip R. Davies, *In Search of "Ancient Israel"* (JSOT Sup. 148; Sheffield: JSOT Press, 1992), 16-48.

35. Coote, *Early Israel*, 5f; Soggin, *History*, 51, 53f. See Robert B. Coote and David Robert Ord, *The Bible's First History: From Eden to the court of David with the Yahwist* (Philadelphia: Fortress, 1989); also Harold Bloom, *The Book of J* (trans. David Rosenberg; New York: Vintage Books, 1990).

Principles for Survival in Israel*

The Mirror:	The Reflections:	The Truths:
Exodus-Numbers	Ezra-Nehemiah	Requirements for Survival
Exod. 18:13-27 Lev. 10:9-11; Num. 8	Neh. 8, 10, 11	Administrative Structure
Lev. 25	Neh. 5; 10; 13:15-22	Economic Independence
Exod. 20:1-17; Deut. 5:6-21 (Exod. 21:23-25; Lev. 24:10-23; Deut. 19:21)	Neh. 13:23-31a	Intra-Communal Organization or Ideological Standardization
Jgs. 12:1-7	Neh. 13:23-24	Common Language
Lev. 18:1-5, 24-30; 20:22-26	Neh. 7:6-72; 10-12	Balance of Extra-Communal Influences & Intra-Communal Accommodation, i.e., Selective Appropriation or Assimilation of the dominant culture by the dominated culture
Gen. 12:1-4; Exod. 1:1-7; Deut. 25:5-10	Neh. 7:6-72; 10-12	Population or People
Gen. 12:1-4; 23; 50:22-26 Exod. 13:19; Josh.	Neh. 5	Land or Place

EXCURSUS ONE:
SOCIALIZATION—ASSIMILATION AND SYNCRETISM IN ISRAELITE HISTORY

The history of ancient Israel—and for that matter, any people—can be appropriately described as a process of assimilation. Assimilation is the naturalization or adjustment process that any people undergo, when occupying or settling a new locale, undergoing a new experience, or encountering a foreign culture, which consists of adoption and adaptation. Adoption is the acquisition or taking over of some thing, for example, customs, places, names, concepts. Adaptation is the modification, adjustment, or changing of some thing that has been adopted according to some standards or criteria that are normative to the ones implementing the process. Ancient Israel conceived of itself, including its god, in terms of a covenant, that is, the 'suzerainty-vassal' treaty.[1] In the case of Israel it is possible that the most significant or indispensable covenant-standards[2] were: *prioritization* of YHWH;[3] *selective imaging* of YHWH;[4] and historicity of YHWH's activity,[5] which distinctly emerged in the form of Yahwistic monotheism in the post-exilic period.[6] Assimilation began when the proto-Israelite, tribal elements started to form or emerge. Here, their circumstances in the land, including their achieving control of it, led to their association and consolidation into a tribal coalition, which shared language,[7] historical experience, location, and religio-political traditions.[8] Changes in their lifestyle were reflected in the institutions that they established and developed, particularly the political constructs and the cultic systems. Since the end-products usually were not the same as the original conceptions, as long as a given institution marginally complied with the normative standards for the Israelite community, it was generally tolerated and perceived as divine in its origin (cf. 1 Sam. 9:1-10:16 regarding the monarchy). If a given institution failed to comply or proved to be destructive to the community, it was usually perceived as a violation of the divine will, warranting and reflecting divine punishment (cf. 1 Sam. 7:2-8:22; 10:17-27a; 12:1-25; 1 Sam. 13:1-2 Sam. 2:7 regarding the monarchy). When an institution was felt to be in violation of the orthodox standards, syncretism predominated. Here, syncretism signifies adoption without adequate adaptation. It is non-selective acquisition or appropriation of some cultural feature that is incompatible with the orthodox standards of the group appropriating such. However, note that such assessments were relative, that is, based upon the stance of those who were in power. Once tribalism had established the

23

norms for Israel, subsequent developments were perceived as syncretistic in some respect.

The interplay of assimilation and syncretism as trends within the life of ancient Israel led to the grouping of the people in assorted socio-politico-religious postures.[9] Generally, the people could be grouped as: the orthodox or conservative Yahwists; the moderate Yahwists or assimilationists; and the liberal or left-wing Yahwists. These postures are based upon the degree of consistency with, or deviation from, the normative standards of Yahwism as established and fostered by the prevalent leaders. Included within these postures were corresponding political constructs and economic status. Here, three general groups[10] emerged in the early history of Israel: clans and tribes, whose family leaders were the *paterfamilias* and the firstborn sons, whose political construct was tribalism, whose political representatives were the elders and the Yahwistic prophets, whose cultic institutions were the local altars and sanctuaries, and whose cultic leaders were the Levitical priesthood; royal dynasties and households, whose family leaders were the kings and their successors, whose political construct was monarchalism, whose political leaders were the kings and the royal courts (i. e., elders, scribes, sages, and prophets), whose cultic institutions were temples, and whose cultic personnel were royally-appointed or royally-approved priests and cultic prophets; and post-exilic, Judean families, whose leaders were the *paterfamilias*, whose political arrangement was colonialism, whose political leaders were appointees or governors, selected and installed by the respective overlords, whose cultic institutions were temples and/or synagogues, whose cultic leaders were Aaronite priests, headed by a high priest and ruling over the Levites. According to this scheme the earliest institutions became normative for Israel and subsequently were established as orthodox. Benevolent forms of the monarchy, if they were ever existent, were obviously accepted, though not by all (see the "people of the land"—and the Rechabites—2 Kgs. 10:15; Jer. 35).

Furthermore, the varying forms of organization, including their respective cults, competed, often conflicting. In this respect, there were popular forms of Yahwism that circulated in the areas surrounding the cities and that countered the monarchical forms that were fostered by a given administration.[11] Though these early institutions were normative, it is to be noted that with all probability an extremely small sector of Yahwists were strictly monotheistic, and this was due to the composite nature of the formulative traditions and the polytheistic and the pluralistic backgrounds of the members that eventually formed Israel. In essence, only the Yahwism as practiced by the orthodoxy was possibly strictly monotheistic; the other forms were syncretistic. However, the theoretical arguments for both that were eventually transcribed and transmitted maintained a monotheistic overtone.

It may be concluded that the economic, the social, the political, and the religious posture of an Israelite were mutually-influential and mutually-determinative! Internal struggles between the tribal culture and the monarchic culture continued throughout the period of the monarchy into the post-monarchic periods, spawning numerous, ideological arguments which eventually were recorded as the Hebrew Scriptures.[12]

JEROME C. ROSS

BIBLICAL CONTEXTUALITY

Institutions:

Family   Political Constructs   Cult

Clans & Tribes   Tribalism Local Altars & Sanctuaries

Leaders: Paterfamilias   Leaders: Elders   Leaders: Levitical Priesthood

& Firstborn Sons   Representatives: Yahwistic Prophets

Royal Dynasties &   Monarchalism   Temples

Households   Leaders: Kings & Royal CourtsLeaders: Royal Priesthood

Leaders: Kings &   [=Elders, Scribes, Sages, & Prophets]   & Cult Prophets

Successors

Judean Families   Colonialism   Temple & Synagogues

Leaders: Paterfamilias   Leaders: Appointees or Governors   Leaders:

Aaronite/Zadokite

Priesthood with High

Priest & Levites

Constitutional Data: Ideology

A. Criteria: 1. Prioritization of YHWH

2. Selective Imaging of YHWH

3. Historicity of YHWH's Activity

B. Principles: 1. Righteousness

2. Compassion

3. Justice

C. Concepts: 1. Covenant

2. Law

The Significance of the Cult in Israel

1. A cult is a religio-political institution that governs the lives of its proponents, endorsers, or adherents, providing a constitution (i. e., rules, standards, ideology), a mechanism of regulation (i. e., calendar of feasts), enforcers (i. e., cultic officials in conjunction with community leaders), and expressions or practices (i. e., offerings, symbols).

2. The cult pre-supposes a view that certain persons are 'sacred' or authorized by deity to direct the lives of the given, fostering community, which justifies or legitimates the requests and contributions of offerings. Such persons, for Israel, were endorsed or supported by some established groups (e. g., strong communal factions, tribal associations, monarchies), and in turn justified the existence of its support-base.

3. The cult functions religio-politically, i. e., it is the place or institution that establishes the ideological basis or constitution for the lives of its proponents and adherents and the mechanism for management or administration of the economic resources of its fostering community. This ideology is reflected in the numerous law-collections: the Book of the Covenant (called BC: Exod. 20:22-23:33); the Deuteronomic Code (called D: Deut. 12-26); the Priestly Collection (called P: Exod. 19 - Num. 10:10 minus BC + H); the Holiness Code (called H: Lev. 17-26).

4. The quality of the cult is determined by assessment or examination of the lives or relations of its practitioners in comparison to its ideology, not the views, perspectives, or postures of a given proponent or group.

5. The cultic calendar or feasts is the mechanism of institutional regulation of daily life, which, naturally, reflects the posture and perspective of its proponents and endorsers. There are several calendars: Exod. 23:10-19 (the Northern calendar); Exod. 34:18-26 (the Southern calendar); Deut. 16:1-17 (a northern version); Num. 28-29 (the P version); Ezek. 45:18-25 (a southern variant); and Lev. 23 (the H version).

6. The offerings are located within the cult and thus are understandable only on the premise that the cult directs or governs significantly daily life/routines.

7. The offerings are the expressions of the social circumstances of the offerers, i. e., their economic, socio-political, and existential conditions.

8. The offerings ritualize or symbolize the status of intra-communal relations in relation to deity, here YHWH.

9. "Faith" is 'that ideology by which a people live that is manifested in customs, institutions, practices, symbols, and concepts, statements, or theories (i. e., doctrines or dogmas, which entail their criteria, norms, principles, or standards). The basis of faith is belief or unquestioning/uncritical assumption or pre-supposition of the existence and activity of some god, not necessarily doctrines or dogmas. In essence the basis of faith is 'living trust'.

Endnotes

1. Norman K. Gottwald, *The Hebrew Bible: A Socio-literary Introduction* (Philadelphia: Fortress, 1985), 202, 204-206. "Covenant" (בְּרִית bᵉrît) is a political term, denoting "treaty", which could be a 'parity treaty' or a 'suzerainty-vassal treaty'. Israel used the latter type as a model for its self-organization (204f). For Israel YHWH was the suzerain, and they were His vassal. According to Israelite usage "covenant" signified: 1. an ordered relationship between God and people that is two-sided, though not necessarily evenhanded in the involvements and obligations of both parties (202); 2. Israel's way of symbolizing the ground and origin of the proper ordering of its communal life, i. e., a sociopolitical reality; 3. Israel's formulation of its self-definition as a people and its basic social institutions; and 4. a way of binding together the tribes so that they could effectively subordinate their separate interests to the common project of winning their collective freedom and security from Canaanite city-states that tried to subject them to state domination (204). The structural elements of the suzerainty treaty form are: 1. preamble or title of the author/superior party to the treaty (Exod. 20:2a; Deut. 5:6a; Josh. 24:2a); 2. historical prologue or antecedent history of relations between the treaty partners (Exod. 20:2b; Deut. 1-3; 5:6b; Josh. 24:2b-13); 3. stipulations stating the obligations imposed upon the vassal or inferior party to the treaty (Exod. 20:3-17; Deut. 5:7-21; 12-26; Josh. 24:14); 4. provision for deposit of the treaty text in a temple and periodic public reading (Exod. 25:21; 40:20; Deut. 10:5; 27:2-3; 31:10-11); 5. lists of gods (or elements of nature/people) as witnesses to the treaty (Josh. 24:22, 27; Isa. 1:2; Mic. 6:1-2); 6. curses and blessings invoked for dis-obedience/obedience to the treaty stipulations (Deut. 27-28; cf. Lev. 26:3-45); 7. oath by which the vassal pledges obedience to the treaty (Exod. 24:3; Josh. 24:24); 8. solemn ceremony for formalizing the treaty (Exod. 24:3-8); and 9. procedure for initiating sanctions against a rebel vassal (Hos. 4:1-10; Isa. 3:13-15) (206). Though the concept of covenant influenced Israelite thinking, the strict monotheistic tendency could have emerged late and would have been read back into the earlier tradi-tions. See Diana Vikander Edelman, ed., *The Triumph of Elohim: From Yahwisms to Judaisms* (Grand Rapids, MI: Eerdmans, 1995); also Niels Peter Lemche, *Ancient Israel: A New History of Israelite Society* (England: Sheffield, 1995), 163-170.

2. Norman K. Gottwald, "The Theological Task after *The Tribes of Yahweh*," *The Bible and Liberation: Political and Social Hermeneutics*. Revised Edition of A Radical Religion Reader (ed. Norman K. Gottwald; Maryknoll, NY: Orbis Books, 1983), 190-200. Gottwald notes that the egalitarian intertribal movement created its own culture,

spawning numerous exceptional new developments (191): 1. the sole high god usurps the entire sacred domain, calling for the exclusive recognition of one deity in the life of the people; 2. the sole high god is alone active in the world; 3. the sole high god is conceived by egalitarian sociopolitical analogies, that is, the representations of YHWH are chiefly those of a warrior-leader who brings the distinctive intertribal community into existence and defends it; 4. the sole high god is coherently manifested or experienced as powerful, just, and merciful; 5. the sole high god is in bond with an egalitarian people, an intertribal formation (193); and 6. the sole high god is interpreted by egalitarian functionaries (194).

3. See Lowell K. Handy, "The Appearance of Pantheon in Judah," in *The Triumph of Elohim: From Yahwisms to Judaisms* (ed. Diana Vikander Edelman; Grand Rapids, MI: Eerdmans, 1995), 27-43; Herbert Niehr, "The Rise of YHWH in Judahite and Israelite Religion: Methodological and Religio-Historical Aspects," in *The Triumph of Elohim: From Yahwisms to Judaisms* (ed. Diana Vikander Edelman; Grand Rapids, MI: Eerdmans, 1995), 45-72.

4. Brian B. Schmidt, "The Aniconic Tradition: On Reading Images and Viewing Texts," in *The Triumph of Elohim: From Yahwisms to Judaisms* (ed. Diana Vikander Edelman; Grand Rapids, MI: Eerdmans, 1995), 75-105. Schmidt argues that the second commandment (Deut. 5:8-10 = Exod. 20:4-6) assumes the existence of other gods beside YHWH that were worshiped, even along with Him, and that there could have been legitimate images of YHWH, though it does not say (80, 83, 86, 88, 91, 102). This commandment, then, addresses the propensity of the Yahwists to worship other gods above YHWH, and condemns their tendency to make illegitimate images of Him (84, 85), disregarding the appropriate symbolisms ([Deut. 4:15-20]; 85f). In this respect, the images that are forbidden are certain groups of theriomorphic forms, that is, those faunal forms that inhabit the sky, earth, and sea (81, 82). On the other hand, YHWH astral imagery was an indigenous Israelite tradition ([Deut. 17:3]; 88). The only biblical evidence that suggests the existence of such images is the ritual animation (Exod. 24:15-18; 33:9; 40:34-38) that is connected with the cloud (ענן 'anan) and the incense (קטרת qetôret), which accompany Moses's use of the mask ([Exod. 34:29-35; 40:35]; 92-96). He concludes that the appropriate YHWH image is a *Mischwesen*, that is, a composite form that consists of human and animal elements (102-105). Also, see Walter Brueggemann, *Old Testament Theology: Essays on Structure, Theme, and Text* (ed. Patrick D. Miller; Minneapolis: Fortress, 1992). Brueggemann perceives, then, the main tendencies of Yahwistic faith to the polarity of tension between "aniconic religion/egalitarian social practice (the combination of which is called "pain-embracing")"

and "iconic religion/monopolistic social practice (the combination of which is called "structure legitimation")" [137; see 118-149].

5. See Werner H. Schmidt, *The Faith of the Old Testament: A History* (trans. John Sturdy; Philadelphia: Westminster, 1983) 1-2, 57, 59, 60, 70, 72, 74, 77, 81, 83-84, 86, 87, 93-95, 143, 178-181. Schmidt has argued that the basic commandments fostered the oneness, and the imagelessness, of YHWH, and the historicity of His activity. However, Brian Schmidt refines or qualifies the aniconic understanding of YHWH ["The Aniconic Tradition," 75-105].

6. See Niehr, "The Rise of YHWH;" Brian B. Schmidt, "The Aniconic Tradition," 75-105, especially 81f, 86, 88, 102-105; Thomas L. Thompson, "The Intellectual Matrix of Early Biblical Narrative: Inclusive Monotheism in Persian Period Palestine," in *The Triumph of Elohim: From Yahwisms to Judaisms* (ed. Diana Vikander Edelman; Grand Rapids, MI: Eerdmans, 1995), 107-124; Thomas M. Bolin, "The Temple of why at Elephantine and Persian Religious Policy," in *The Triumph of Elohim: From Yahwisms to Judaisms* (ed. Diana Vikander Edelman; Grand Rapids, MI: Eerdmans, 1995), 127-142. Thompson argues that Yahwism developed from *inclusive monotheism* under the Persian administration to *exclusive monotheism* under the Hellenistic rule (112-124), while Bolin specifically locates the emergence of *inclusive monotheism* during the reign of Xerxes (128, 137, 139f, 141).

7. See Daniel I. Block, "The Role of Language in Ancient Israelite Perceptions of National Identity," *Journal of Biblical Literature* 103 (1984): 321-340. Block argues that language is a function of nationality rather than geography, and should not be overemphasized as an indicator of kinship, but considered as the most important dialect within a nation (338f).

8. See Martin Noth, *The History of Israel* (3d ed.; trans. Peter R. Ackroyd; New York: Harper & Row, 1958), 3-4, 53, 71f, 87, 106f; W. Schmidt, *The Faith of the Old Testament*, 10-27; Robert B. Coote, *Early Israel: A New Horizon* (Minneapolis: Fortress, 1990), 113-139; Gottwald, *The Hebrew Bible*, 272-275, 284-286. Noth argues that Israel became Israel through association, consolidation, and minor wars, up to the time of David, in the process of occupation of the land. Gottwald refines Noth, arguing for a multi-faceted and multi-fronted social revolution involving a mixed coalition. Coote argues from a different base, that is, that Israel was a tribal ally or vassal of Egypt, which broke away during shifts in power due to the migrations and settlements of European and Anatolian settlers, particularly the Philistines.

9. See Morton Smith, *Palestinian Parties and Politics that Shaped the Old Testament* (London: SCM Press Ltd., 1987); Robert B. Coote & Mary P. Coote, *Power, Politics, and the Making of the Bible: An Introduction*

(Minneapolis: Fortress, 1990); Douglas A. Knight, "Political Rights and Powers in Monarchic Israel," *Semeia* 66 (1994): 93-117; Niels Peter Lemche, "Kings and Clients: On Loyalty between the Ruler and the Ruled in Ancient "Israel"", Semeia 66 (1994): 119-132 .

10. See the diagram and notes on "Biblical Contextuality".

11. See Jerome C. Ross, *The Composition of the Holiness Code* (Lev. 17-26) (Dissertation: University of Pittsburgh, 1997), 157 n. 40. From study of the Holiness Code [Lev. 17-26], I have observed the following characteristics of "popular religion" : 1. involvement of the elders, or invoking of the clan leaders, as representatives of the populace [Alan Cooper and Bernard Goldstein, "At the Entrance to the Tent: More Cultic Resonances in Biblical Narrative, *Journal of Biblical Literature* 114 (1997), 206f; Jer. 26:11, 16f]; 2. the prevalence of the veneration of the clan deities [Alan Cooper and Bernard Goldstein, "Exodus and Massot in History and Tradition, *MAARAV* 8 (1992), 29f; idem, "The Cult of the Dead and the Theme of Entry into the Land, *Biblical Interpretation* 1 (1993), 294f; cf. Schmidt, "The Aniconic Tradition"]; 3. the promulgation of the "all-Israelite" view [Israel Knohl, *The Sanctuary of Silence: The Priestly Torah and the Holiness School* (Minneapolis: Fortress, 1995), 65, 190f]; 4. the elevation of Shabbat to an equal status with the Tabernacle [Knohl, *The Sanctuary of Silence*, 16-19]; 5. the inclusion of the gêr [Knohl, *The Sanctuary of Silence*, 21, 18]; 6. the anthropomorphizing, and personalizing, of "God" [Knohl, *The Sanctuary of Silence*, 170-172]; and 7. the view of the covenant between YHWH and Israel as being reciprocal [Knohl, *The Sanctuary of Silence*, 173f]. The latter five characteristics are features of H, that show evidence of influence by popular forms of Yahwism. Being 'priestly-popular', I perceive that H: 1. assumes that the elders are leaders, but not over the priests; 2. advocates the holiness of all Israelites, even the land, but in grades (94 n. 27; also 144f); 3. elevates *Shabbat* to an equal status with the Temple (151f); 4. denounces the clan deities (cf. Lev. 17:7; 19:4, 31; 26:1); 5. includes the gêr as equal on conditions of compliance (140-146); 6. adopts anthropomorphisms in describing YHWH; and 7. personalizes the covenant between YHWH and the people of Israel (see my discussion of the divine self-introduction formulae—the short form and the long form—and the holiness formula: 47-51, 81-87, 175f). In this respect, I define "Israelite popular religion" as 'an unofficial form of Yahwism that was headed by local leaders, who were not backed by the political overlords or the authorities in power.'

12. Brueggemann, *Old Testament Theology: Essays*, 137; see 118-149. The tension between Yahwistic tribalism and Yahwistic monarchalism or foreign monarchalism that sponsored the Yahwistic temple-cultus in the post-exilic period is reflected in Brueggemann's polarity "aniconic

religion/egalitarian social practice (the combination of which is called "pain-embracing")" versus "iconic religion/monopolistic social practice (the combination of which is called "structure legitimation")," which the text presents as an accommodation of the popular trends by the official tradents, in which the latter maintains an upper hand. See, for example, the understanding of H in Ross, *The Holiness Code*, 131-146, 147-161.

CHAPTER THREE:
THE EARLY YAHWISTIC MONARCHIES

Since the final form of the biblical texts that pertain to the early Yahwistic monarchies is late, even post-exilic[1] caution must be taken in assuming that their history occurred according to the presentations in these texts. In light of the texts being political propaganda,[2] they must be read contextually, giving attention to the specific problems and issues that are addressed, the understandings that are fostered, and the purposes that these texts serve. Note that several views of the monarchy are rendered. First, the monarchy is regarded as an institution that is in conflict with Yahwistic tribalism. Here, the word *melek* (מלך) is used for "king", and the theological assessment is that the institution constitutes a rejection of YHWH as king or sovereign (1 Sam. 7:2-8:22; 10:17-27a; 12). The view of monarchy reflected in these passages is that of an advanced or developed stage, in which the king exercises executive privileges over his subjects. Second, the monarchy is regarded as compatible with Yahwistic tribalism. Here, the word *nagîd* (נגיד) is used for "king", and the theological assessment is that the institution marks the intervention of YHWH as deliverer through the Spirit-endowed, military leader (1 Sam. 9:1-10:16). Third, the monarchy of David is specifically endorsed and given priority over Yahwistic tribalism. In this instance, a dynasty is established under the auspices of an eternal promise from YHWH to David (2 Sam. 7). Theologically, this promise to David, which has the connotations of an eternal covenant, supersedes the Mosaic covenant of Yahwistic tribalism, in which YHWH purportedly delivered Israel from the domination of a sociopolitical hierarchy (Exod. 1-15, 19, 24, 32-34). In this arrangement the Davidic dynasty and its southern constituency gained dominance over and exploited the central and northern, Palestinian tribes, until the rebellion of the North under Jeroboam. Following this split, tension persisted between the two nations for most of their duration, with the Northern Kingdom maintaining enough political advantage to preserve its independence from the Southern Kingdom. That the Northern Kingdom was destroyed before the South, or the Southern Kingdom was the last to be destroyed, privileged the South with the last word. The traditions covering the period of the kings (i. e., DH, CH)[3] reflect a blatant bias in favor of the Davidic dynasty in the South and in degradation of the Northern kings.[4] From such a critical posture only a general sketch of Israelite history is possible.

The formation of the monarchy was not the result of a democratic process. Its development in Israel was spawned by two general factors. First, when Egypt's sponsorship of Israel as a tribal ally was impeded by European and Anatolian invaders, Israel was left with minimal Egyptian support, and thus was forced by circumstance to organize more efficiently. The emerging threat of the Philistines provided the external impetus for Israel to develop a monarchy. In other words, the monarchy in Israel was developed out of necessity, in order to provide defense against the Philistines, in light of the inefficiency of the tribal arrangement.[5] In its inception and operation, a monarchy is designed to supply the needs or requirements for survival: a fixed administrative structure (e. g., a king with a royal family and heirs, a court, temple(s), and personnel); a stable economy that undergirds the life of the state; set laws, including a calendar for regulation and synchronization; control, even check, of foreign cultural influences; a national language; increased population; and stable, preferably increasing, territory. In no uncertain terms, a monarchy is designed primarily for the self-perpetuation and self-preservation of the king and his family, and secondarily for the people. Second, the collapse of the Hittite and the Egyptian empires coincided with a period of international dormancy in the Mesopotamian area. Without major rivals contesting for Palestine, the smaller entities within Palestine were able to develop and expand extensively, particularly during the Davidic regime.[6] Thus, the development of a monarchy in Israel was normative for their situation.

Saul was the first king, and probably state-builder, of Israel, in spite of the bias of the biblical texts (1 Sam. 9-31).[7] He was initially endorsed by Samuel, but asserted himself in opposition to Samuel and eventually seized control of the tribal association from him[8] (see 1 Sam. 9; also 10:8; 11:15; 13:9, 11b-12; cf. 2 Sam. 6:17; 24:25; 1 Kgs. 9:25). His base of operations probably was his hometown, Gibeon, from which he waged guerrilla warfare, maintaining control over the highlands and keeping the Philistines in check, but not having sufficient weaponry to counter them on the plains.[9] His main victory was over the Amalekites (1 Sam. 15), whose king he spared. The description of this event in the biblical text is the theological presentation that provides the purported grounds for removing Saul from office. However, during his reign (ca. 1020-1000 B.C.E.) the institution of monarchy probably remained compatible with Yahwistic tribalism, that is, the two institutions were interwoven or complemented each other.[10] No doubt, conflicts between the two institutions ensued and were spearheaded by their respective representatives: for tribalism, the Yahwistic prophets, of which Samuel is pictured as a prototype; for the monarchy, the king. Here, Yahwistic prophetism was Yahwistic tribalism's check on the monarchy.[11] Though the conflicts between Saul and Samuel may be understood as apological, that is, explanations for the demise of Saul and the rise of

David (1 Sam. 16:14 - 2 Sam. 5:25) who purportedly replaced him,[12] these conflicts must also be seen as an indication of actual or strained relations between Saul and Samuel, due to efforts on the part of Saul to seize control.

In light of the overt bias of the biblical texts in favor of David and generally the styles of ancient texts, extreme caution must be taken in understanding the reign of David (ca. 1000-961 B.C.E.). In fact, the *David* of the biblical texts (1 Sam. 16-1 Kgs. 2:11) does not correspond with the *David* of history, that is, what can be reasonably reconstructed. First of all, David may be considered an indigenous Canaanite from the hills of Judah,[13] who served in Saul's army and sought to seize the throne from Saul (1 Sam. 16-17; Ruth 4:18-22; 1 Chron. 2:50-51). David's exploits in Saul's army probably drew attention to him and prompted him to go over to the Philistines. While in service for them, David conquered Ziklag and used it as his base of operations, from which he conducted numerous military raids south of Judah and toward Egypt (1 Sam. 27). He was made king at Hebron (2 Sam. 2:1-4), and reigned over Judah, no doubt, ethnically integrating the two areas. The Hebronite-Judean kingdom of David confronted Israel in battle at Gibeon (2 Sam. 2:12-32), and through the services of Abner, who went over to David, Saul's daughter, Michal, was obtained by David. Also, numerous figures (i. e., Abner, formerly one of Saul's generals; Jonathan; Eshbaal, the last, remaining son of Saul), all in Saul's family, were murdered or eliminated, paving the way for David's acquisition of the throne of Israel.[14] The biblical accounts of these episodes merely camouflage the ruthless maneuvers, whereby David's machinery gained control, and they seek to counter the obvious negatives of David. Upon gaining control over Israel, David's kingdom more than doubled in size, including most of Palestine with the exception of the coastal plains and Jerusalem.[15] Shortly thereafter, David captured Jerusalem, a non-Yahwistic city, and made it his capital (2 Sam. 5:6-8). Later, he conducted several battles against the Philistines and was victorious (2 Sam. 5:17-25; 8:1; 21:15-22; 2 Chron. 20:4-8).[16] It is noteworthy to remember that the conquest of these territories did not include exportation of the native peoples or their cults, but integration of these cultures into that of David's. This cultural diversity, coupled with the ruthlessness with which David conquered some of the territories (i. e., the Moabites, the Ammonites, the Edomites),[17] posed a major challenge to David in regard to organization.

Second, David made significant political adjustments in order to solidify his kingdom. Modeling his kingdom after the Egyptian governmental system,[18] he made all of his subjects officially "Israelites", that is, YHWH became the main god for all of his domain. This entailed stationing of priests and other government officials in newly incorporated cities and in their sanctuaries, in order to teach the law of the kingdom. In this respect, Yahwism was further blended with the religions of the recently subjugated peoples.[19] It became the ideology of the kingdom of David and was represented by the

Zionistic pantheon in which YHWH and his female cohort were claimed as the head.[20] The main concern of this ideology was provision of political policy and justification of David as king, particularly in light of the later claims of Judaism to be the sole heir of Yahwism. The preponderance of legendary material in DH, which elevates David over Saul, in all probability, is mainly apologetic and fictional, that is, the David material reflects the Southern Kingdom's, even Judaism's, redaction of the pre-exilic Northern traditions, that aims at establishing its sovereignty over the Northern Kingdom, at least traditionally, since the North dominated the South during most of the existence of the two kingdoms. This bias is shown in the valuation of David as "good," that is, the establishment of David as the measure or canonical figure for the Yahwistic monarchy, since he achieves what no other Yahwistic king does (i. e., freedom). Also, that the South outlasted the North enabled the elevation and the prioritization of the Southern traditions.[21] Moreover, two, major themes that are found in DH (which is post-exilic in its final form) are: the presentation of YHWH as being with David, which serves to explain his success as the result of being divinely endorsed (1 Sam. 16:1, 12f, 18; 17:37, 45-48; 18:12, 14, 28-29; 23:14; 30:6; 2 Sam. 3:1; 5:10; 8:6, 14); and the Davidic king as being the "adopted son" of YHWH, which serves to validate and establish a Davidic dynasty (2 Sam. 7), in contradistinction to the import of the covenant traditions of Moses. This elevation and prominence of "Zionistic" Yahwism was, then, symbolized in the moving of the ark of YHWH to Jerusalem (2 Sam. 6) and the promotion of YHWH and his cohort as the heads of a Judean pantheon of gods.[22] Also, Jerusalem was made his capital. This choice was strategic, for Jerusalem was neutral turf and owned by David. Its administrative personnel were probably continued, but under a new regime, that is, David's. Because of the cultural diversity of his kingdom, he appointed officials that were representative of the respective cults, that is, Abiathar and Zadok as cultic personnel, Joab as head of the tribal militia, Benaiah as head of the Cerethites and Pelethites (the royal guards), and his sons as priests (2 Sam. 8:15-18 || 1 Chron. 18:14-17; 20:23-26; 1 Kgs. 4:1-6).[23] Third, David organized a census, probably for the purpose of raising revenue from the non-Yahwistic elements in Hermon and Galilee (2 Sam. 24:2-9). This triggered unrest and dissatisfaction among the different groups of people, which later became a backdrop for the revolts of Abshalom and Sheba (2 Sam. 15-20). Since David's acts were necessary and especially favorable to Judah and the most productive lands were located in the central and north Palestinian area, the discontent of the North is understandable.[24] This discontent would continue to simmer and eventually erupt in the rebellion of Jeroboam and the secession of the North. Thus, David was responsible for assembling and establishing the largest Israelite state.

The reign of David ended with struggles over the throne. Since he held jurisdiction over numerous regions, beginning at different times, and had many sons,[25] the heir to his throne was not so apparent. The biblical text that presents the scenario of the occupation of David's throne is the so-called *Succession Story*[26] (2 Sam. 9-20; 1 Kgs. 1-2). Its purpose is to explain how Solomon became the successor of David, when he was not a legitimate heir, and thereby to justify his reign. Briefly stated, according to DH, Solomon became the coregent of David, as a result of a promise David made to Bathsheba, his favorite wife, which, for all intentional purposes, was a maneuver orchestrated by Bathsheba and Nathan the prophet (1 Kgs. 1-2). Thus, Solomon began his reign with intrigue and, after David's death, a *coup d'e`tat*, as he secured his throne.[27]

The reign of Solomon (ca. 961-926 B.C.E.) may best be characterized as a period of extensive urbanization (1 Kgs. 1-11). After eliminating all contenders to the throne, the Jerusalemite-Jebusite party gained control and fostered the Jerusalemite ideology, which hailed YHWH of Zion and his cohort as the undisputed heads of the gods. Commensurate with this development, Zadok became the undisputed leader of the official national Yahwistic cult, while Benaiah became the commander-in-chief of the army. The Zion ideology became more accentuated and overshadowed the Sinaitic ideology.[28] Solomon followed the Canaanite model, which significantly reflected Egyptian influence,[29] in building a temple and other structures (e. g., a palace, stables). Such building projects, which were perceived to express and extend the domain of the god(s) of the state, required administrative reorganization. These were primarily carried out in Israelite regions and Jerusalem,[30] probably to enforce Solomon's policy and to secure his homebase. Thus, Solomon reorganized twelve political units that David had formed (cf. the royal district list in 1 Kgs. 4:7-19), which coincided with the geographical areas. This served the purpose of levying taxes, providing provisions for the king and royal court and coordinating forced labor (1 Kgs. 5:27-32 [English: 5:13-18]), and was consonant with provisions of centers for commerce for the population of the countryside and with protection for the village population.[31]

Solomon's extensive building projects proved extremely costly. He became indebted to Hiram of Tyre (1 Kgs. 5:24 [English: 5:10]; 7:13-14; 9:10-14, 26-27) and gave him 20 cities, which were located in western Galilee and part of the Phoenician territories that were conquered by David, as payment.[32] As a result of Solomon's building projects and the administrative activities that generated economic support, deficit spending ensued and oppression and exploitation of the North occurred.[33] This constituted the main grounds for discontent among the North, which, following Solomon, led to the secession of the North. Thus the syncretism and its social consequences that were fostered by the state were regarded as the major cause for Israel's defection from YHWH, which was manifested as sociopolitical crises.[34]

Solomon's reign effected several, enduring structural features. First, political centralization[35] was efficiently developed. Power was concentrated in the hands of the king and his court and secured by means of militia, fortresses, and districts. Included in this development is the construction and operation of the temple. It is to be noted that the royal temple served the purposes of the administration, in this case, Solomon's. This focus of power in the hands of the few enabled and precipitated other developments. Second, social stratification[36] began, as the economic fortunes segregated the populace into different groups. The power of taxation, conscription, and draft was mainly targeted at the 'subject' population, who incurred deficits, depending upon the national fortunes in domestic and foreign relations. For example, persons could be taxed out of their land, and thus would become tenants on property that was formerly theirs. On the other hand, absentee landlords arose, as property was taken in lieu of debts. Third, and obvious, is shifts in land tenure.[37] Though the land may have been regarded as tribal property, economic fortunes that were precipitated by international deficits or military losses forced changes in ownership. Also, the kings could exercise the *power of imminent domain*, depending upon the prevalent ideologies that were in vogue. Fourth is domestic repercussions of foreign trade, diplomacy, and war.[38] The geographical situation of Palestine[39] provided the basis for its historical fortunes. Being a connecting link between the major political centers (i. e., Anatolia-Mesopotamia in the north, and Egypt in the south), the political status of the Palestinian states and peoples was always dependent upon the dominant nation(s) at the time. Thus, the Yahwistic nations, with the exception of the period during the beginning of the Davidic regime, were always vassals[40] to some 'superpower' nation. In sum, these features persisted until the end of both monarchies.

The Division of the Kingdom of David-Solomon[41]

The unfavorable circumstances that began during the reign of David and that escalated during the reign of Solomon prompted a confrontation between Solomon's heir, Rehoboam, and the leaders of the North. The proposed policy of Rehoboam, which was to be a continuation of his father's administration,[42] was rejected by the elders, who asserted their independence from the Davidic regime (1 Kgs. 12:1-19; a series of prophetic legends - 11:29-40; 12:21-24; 14:1-18; extracts from annals - 12:25-31; 14:21-31). The key representative from the North was Jeroboam, who had returned from Egypt. It is surmised that Jeroboam had the backing of Egypt, which soon began excursions into Palestine, in order to reclaim it.[43] The secession of the North was a major loss to the South, which had exploited the former's resources. Also, it is obvious that the North was stronger than the South, for the latter was not able to quench the rebellion or to retake the North.[44]

After the severance of their political ties, both nations became vulnerable to stronger nations that were larger or of comparable size. This was evidenced by the assertion of independence on the part of nations that were subjugated under David's regime: Ammon severed ties; Moab continued to pay tribute to Judah; and Edom remained in alliance with Judah.[45] Also, as previously mentioned, Egypt began to resurge under Pharaoh Shoshenq (Shishak) I.[46] The Philistines in the southwest, the Arameans of Damascus and east of the Jordan, and eventually the Assyrians began to rival the two kingdoms.[47] In light of the growing national threats, both kingdoms had to reorganize politically. This was somewhat simpler for the South, for the dynastic principle of kingship was operative. However, with the North it was necessary to construct a whole administration, for it lacked such mechanisms and, consisting of the best lands in Palestine, was most attractive to prospective conquerors. This Jeroboam did by establishing a royal city, that is, Shechem, Penuel, the land west of the Jordan, the city of Tirzah, and finally Samaria (1 Kgs. 16), and establishing royal sanctuaries at Dan and Bethel, in order to service his subjects and to prevent defecting to Jerusalem in the south (1 Kgs. 12:25-33).[48] A key part of the administrative reorganization in the North was establishment of some policy of rule. In asserting independence for the North Jeroboam no doubt resorted to the Mosaic or Sinaitic covenant traditions[49] and probably developed a form of monarchy that resembled the charismatic form developed during the reign of Saul. However, necessity dictated that this form would be changed, particularly in light of the international climate. So, dynasties were attempted in the North, specifically to stabilize the nation.[50]

Also, Jeroboam established new festivals in the eighth month of the Israelite calendar, in contrast to the principal festivals that were observed in the seventh month in Judah (1 Kgs. 12:32-33), and introduced a civil calendar that began in the spring, in contrast to the one used in Judah wherein the year began in the autumn.[51] These changes were made, based upon the ideological traditions utilized in the North, and sought to prevent the loss of offerings to the cult in the South. Here, regulation of the life of the community was at stake, as the court of Jeroboam propagated a new ideology.

In sum the two kingdoms of Israel that emerged after the reign of Solomon were merely joined by the reign of David. There was never a homogeneous, Yahwistic nation, that is, a united monarchy in Israel under David is a misnomer. Instead, two Yahwistic entities were marginally joined and separated due to sociopolitical differences.

Chapter Synopsis:
The Key Dates

1020-1000 B.C.E. Reign of Saul

Causes: 'Need'
1. threat of the Philistines
2. incompleteness of the tribal association

Developments:
1. assimilation
2. existence of Israel as a dual socio-political entity

Effects:
1. development of a "limited monarchy"
2. conflict of monarchy with tribal system
3. rise of Yahwistic prophetism as proponents of the tribal system and check of the kings

Interpretations:
1. king as rejection of YHWH [1 Sam. 7:2-8:22; 10:17-27a; 12]
2. king as instrument of YHWH [1 Sam. 9:1-10:16]

1000-961 B.C.E. Reign of David

Causes:
1. military strategies of David, including elimination of Saul's heirs/contenders for throne
2. lack of international rivals
3. conquest of the Philistines
4. faithfulness to the tribal system

Development: tribal acceptance of the "limited monarchy"

Effects:
1. development of the "limited monarchy"
2. incorporation of extensive land and subject peoples

Interpretations:
1. YHWH as being with David [1 Sam. 16:1, 12f, 18; 17:37, 45-48; 18:12, 14, 28-29; 23:14; 30:6; 2 Sam. 3:1; 5:10; 8:6, 14]
2. justification of the monarchy, i. e., king as "adopted son" of YHWH [e. g., 2 Sam. 7; also the Yahwistic Tradition]

961-926 B.C.E. Reign of Solomon

Causes:
1. inheritance from David his father
2. trickery by Bathsheba his mother & Nathan the prophet

Development: urbanization of the kingdom of Israel

Effects:
1. elimination of rivals/opponents
2. internal/administrative development
3. expensive and extensive building projects [e. g., temple, palace, etc.]
4. corvee labor & taxation
5. enduring structural effects:
   a. political centralization
   b. social stratification
   c. shifts in land tenure
   d. domestic repercussions of foreign trade, diplomacy, & war
6. deficit spending

Interpretations:
1. justification of the monarchy, i. e., legitimation of Solomon as David's successor [2 Sam. 9-20; 1 Kgs. 1-2]
2. monarchy as major cause for Israel's defection from YHWH [cf. DH; e. g., 1 Kgs. 4]

926-922 B.C.E. Division of the Kingdom of David-Solomon

Causes:
1. oppressive economic & political policies that continued with Rehoboam, Solomon's son
2. disfavor of northern tribes with dominance of the southern tribes in the monarchical arrangement

Developments:
1. revolution of the northern tribes led by Jeroboam I
2. formation of two socio-political entities under Yahwism
3. conflicts of interest due to contrast of tribalism and monarchalism

Effects:
1. internal:
   a. establishment of two principles of kingship

      b. frontier disputes between the two kingdoms
      c. establishment of a new administrative order by the northern tribes [1 Kgs. 12:25-33; 16]
      d. negative assessment of the monarchy by E, D, & D-Hist.
      e. co-regencies from the time of Asa
  2. external:
      a. vulnerability to larger/stronger & comparable nations
      b. struggles with neighboring states
      c. eventual subjection to stronger nations, i. e., vassal status

Interpretations:
  1. monarchy as the fundamental cause of Israel's defection from YHWH [DH; e. g., 1 Kgs. 4]
  2. monarchy or state syncretism as cause of religious/ideological syncretism [1 Kgs. 9-11], particularly the monarchy of David-Solomon
  3. division as caused by YHWH [1 Kgs. 12:1-24]

The Selected Interpretations
#1: King as Instrument of YHWH [1 Sam. 9:1-10:16]

A. Perspectives:
  1. Speaker: the progressive Yahwists who endorsed assimilation and formation of a Yahwistic monarchy
  2. Writer: Deuteronomistic Historian [DH]

B. Addressees:
  1. of the Speaker:
      a. those Yahwistic tribalists who rejected a monarchy as an option for administrative structure
      b. those Yahwistic tribalists who were tentative or undecided about organization of a Yahwistic monarchy
  2. of the Writer: the exilic Judeans

C. Contexts:
  1. of the Speaker: the struggle between the Philistines and the Israelites
  2. of the Writer: the exile and the demise of the Judean (and last Yahwistic) monarchy

D. Issues:
  1. of the Speaker: determination of the most appropriate means of protection and survival, i. e., how and whether to assimilate

2. of the Writer: sanity, i. e., comprehension of the national crisis/catastrophe

E. Purposes:
  1. of the Speaker:
     a. endorsement of a moderate form of monarchy, that was compatible with Yahwistic tribalism, as the administrative structure
     b. maintenance of and preference for the early Yahwistic tribal traditions as the standard ideology
     c. ideological endorsement or justification of Saul's monarchy/state
  2. of the Writer:
     a. explanation of the national crisis as due to departure from the early Yahwistic orthodoxy
     b. engendering of hope through endorsement of the continuation of the Davidic lineage

F. Presuppositions:
  1. of the Speaker:
     a. YHWH as King/Sovereign of Israel
     b. YHWH as Warrior and Deliverer
     c. YHWH as Just and Merciful
     d. the oneness of YHWH, i. e., the political solidarity of Yahwistic tribalism
     e. the historicity of YHWH's activity
  2. of the Writer:
     a. YHWH as Universal Sovereign
     b. YHWH as Warrior, Deliverer, and Judge
     c. YHWH as Just and Merciful
     d. the oneness of YHWH, i. e., the political solidarity of Yahwistic monarchalism
     e. the historicity of YHWH's activity
     f. Jerusalem (or Mount Zion) as the City of YHWH and the Sole Yahwistic Cult Center

#2: King as Rejection of YHWH [1 Sam. 7:2-8:22; 10:17-27a; 12]

A. Perspectives:
  1. Speaker: the conservative Yahwists who preferred tribalism
  2. Writer: Deuteronomistic Historian [DH]

B. Addressees:
1. of the Speaker: the tribal culture that first endorsed the Yahwistic monarchy
2. of the Writer: the exilic Judeans

C. Contexts:
1. of the Speaker: the struggle between the Philistines and the Israelites
2. of the Writer: the exile and the demise of the Judean (and last Yahwistic) monarchy

D. Issues:
1. of the Speaker: determination of the most appropriate means of protection and survival, i. e., how and whether to assimilate
2. of the Writer: sanity, i. e., comprehension of the national crisis/catastrophe

E. Purposes:
1. of the Speaker:
   a. implicit endorsement of a more flexible administrative structure
   b. adherence to the early Yahwistic tribal traditions as the standard ideology
   c. opposition to Saul's formation of a monarchy/state
2. of the Writer:
   a. explanation of the national crisis as punishment for departure from the early Yahwistic orthodoxy, and the subsequent future possibilities
   b. engendering of hope through endorsement of Davidic-Zionistic Yahwism

F. Presuppositions:
1. of the Speaker:
   a. YHWH as King/Sovereign of Israel
   b. the oneness of YHWH, i. e., the political solidarity of Yahwistic tribalism
   c. the historicity of YHWH's activity
2. of the Writer:
   a. YHWH as King/Sovereign of Israel
   b. Universalism of YHWH's Sovereignty
   c. YHWH as Just and Merciful
   d. the historicity of YHWH's activity

#3: YHWH as being with David [1 Sam. 16:1, 12f, 18; 17:37, 45-48; 18:12, 14, 28-29; 23:14; 30:6; 2 Sam. 3:1; 5:10; 8:6, 14]

A. Perspectives:
1. Speaker: J or David's court
2. Writers:
    a. J or David's court
    b. Deuteronomistic Historian [DH]

B. Addressees:
1. of the Speaker:
    a. the Northern Yahwists or the Israelites who backed Saul and witnessed David's usurpation of Saul's monarchy
    b. the marginal people or the bedouins on the southwestern border
2. of the Writers:
    a. early:
        i. the Northern Yahwists or the Israelites who backed Saul and witnessed David's usurpation of Saul's monarchy
        ii. the marginal people or the bedouins on the southwestern border
    b. late:
        i. the exilic Judeans
        ii. he Northern Yahwists or the Samaritans

C. Contexts:
1. of the Speaker:
    a. the conquest of Palestine by David
    b. the struggles between the Philistines and the Israelites
    c. the usurpation of Saul's regime by David
2. of the Writers:
    a. early:
        i. the conquest of Palestine by David
        ii. the struggles between the Philistines and the Israelites
        iii. the usurpation of Saul's regime by David
    b. late: the exile and the demise of the Judean (and last Yahwistic) monarchy

D. Issues:
1. of the Speaker: determination of the legitimate Yahwistic monarchy, including the successor to Saul
2. of the Writers:
    a. early: determination of the legitimate Yahwistic monarchy, including the successor to Saul

    b.   late: sanity, i. e., comprehension of the national crisis/catastrophe

E. Purposes:

    1.   of the Speaker:

    a.   endorsement of the Davidic state, including his usurpation of Saul's regime

    b.   reconciliation of David's usurpation of Saul's regime and the Yahwistic traditions

    c.   justification of David's monarchy/state

    d.   explanation of David's success

    e.   presentation and promotion of David as innocent

    2.   of the Writers:

       a.   early:

          i.   endorsement of the Davidic state, including his usurpation of Saul's regime

          ii.   reconciliation of David's usurpation of Saul's regime and the Yahwistic traditions

          iii. justification of David's monarchy/state

          iv.   presentation and promotion of David as innocent

       b.   late:

          i.   explanation and endorsement of the continuation of the Davidic lineage and right to administrative privilege

          ii.   presentation and promotion of David as innocent

          iii.   solicitation for resettlement and reconstruction of Judah

F. Presuppositions:

    1. of the Speaker:

       a.   YHWH as Warrior and Deliverer

       b.   YHWH as King/Sovereign of Israel and Judah

       c.   YHWH as Just and Merciful

       d.   the oneness of YHWH, i. e., the political solidarity of Yahwistic monarchalism

       e.   the historicity of YHWH's activity

       f.   Jerusalem (or Mount Zion) as the City of YHWH and the National Yahwistic Cult Center

    2.   of the Writers:

       a.   YHWH as Warrior, Deliverer, and Judge

       b.   YHWH as Universal Sovereign

       c.   YHWH as Just and Merciful

       d.   the oneness of YHWH, i. e., the political solidarity of Yahwistic colonialism

       e.   the historicity of YHWH's activity

    f.   Jerusalem (or Mount Zion) as the City of YHWH and the Sole Yahwistic Cult Center

#4: King as Adopted Son of YHWH [2 Sam. 7]

A. Perspectives:
1. Speaker: J or David's court
2. Writers:
   a. J or David's court
   b. Deuteronomistic Historian [DH]

B. Addressees:
1. of the Speaker:
   a. the Northern Yahwists or the Israelites who backed Saul and witnessed David's usurpation of Saul's monarchy
   b. the marginal people or the bedouins on the southwestern border
2. of the Writers:
   a. early:
      i. the Northern Yahwists or the Israelites who backed Saul and witnessed David's usurpation of Saul's monarchy
      ii. the marginal people or the bedouins on the southwestern border
   b. late:
      i. the exilic Judeans
      ii. the Northern Yahwists or the Samaritans

C. Contexts:
1. of the Speaker:
   a. the conquest of Palestine by David
   b. the usurpation of Saul's regime by David
2. of the Writers:
   a. early:
      i. the conquest of Palestine by David
      ii. the usurpation of Saul's regime by David
   b. late: the exile and the demise of the Judean (and last Yahwistic) monarchy

D. Issues: explanation of the legitimacy of David's state and rule

E. Purposes:
1. of the Speaker:
   a. justification of David's dynasty

    b.   attempted reconciliation of the early Yahwistic (Mosaic-Sinaitic) traditions and the newly-formulated (Davidic-Zionistic) traditions

    c.   explanation of the templeless cult of David and justification of the temple cult of Solomon, David's son

2. of the Writers:

    a.   early:

       i.   justification of David's dynasty

      ii.   attempted reconciliation of the early Yahwistic (Mosaic-Sinaitic) traditions and the newly-formulated (Davidic-Zionistic) traditions

     iii.   explanation of the templeless cult of David and justification of the temple cult of Solomon, David's son

  b. late:

       i.   explanation, and endorsement, of the continuation of the Davidic lineage and right to administrative privilege

      ii.   promotion of reconstruction of the temple cult in Jerusalem

     iii.   solicitation for resettlement and reconstruction of Judah

F. Presuppositions:

1. of the Speaker:

    a.   YHWH as Warrior and Deliverer

    b.   YHWH as being with David [1 Sam. 16:1, 12f, 18; 17:37, 45-48; 18:12, 14, 28-29; 23:14; 30:6; 2 Sam. 3:1; 5:10; 8:6, 14]

    c.   YHWH as King/Sovereign of Israel and Judah

    d.   YHWH as Just and Merciful

    e.   the oneness of YHWH, i. e., the political solidarity of Yahwistic monarchalism

    f.   the historicity of YHWH's activity

    g.   Jerusalem (or Mount Zion) as the City of YHWH and the National Yahwistic Cult Center

2. of the Writers:

    a.   YHWH as Warrior, Deliverer, and Judge

    b.   YHWH as Universal Sovereign

    c.   YHWH as Just and Merciful

    d.   the oneness of YHWH, i. e., the political solidarity of Yahwistic colonialism

    e.   the historicity of YHWH's activity

    f.   Jerusalem (or Mount Zion) as the City of YHWH and the Sole Yahwistic Cult Center

#5: Legitimation of Solomon as David's Successor [2 Sam. 9-20; 1 Kgs. 1-2]

A. Perspectives:
    1.   Speaker: J or David's (and Solomon's) court
    2.   Writers:
        a.   J or David's (and Solomon's) court
        b.   Deuteronomistic Historian [DH]

B. Addressees:
    1.   of the Speaker:
        a.   the Northern Yahwists or the Israelites who backed Solomon's brothers
        b.   the potential rebels or the disgruntled factions in the kingdom
        c.   the marginal people or the bedouins on the southwestern border
    2.   of the Writers:
        a.   early:
            i.   the Northern Yahwists or the Israelites who backed Solomon's brothers
            ii.   the potential rebels or the disgruntled factions in the kingdom
        b.   late:
            i.   the exilic Judeans
            ii.   the Northern Yahwists or the Samaritans

C. Contexts:
    1.   of the Speaker:
        a.   the coup d'état of Solomon
        b.   the trickery by Bathsheba and Nathan
    2.   of the Writers:
        a.   early:
            i.   the coup d'état of Solomon
            ii.   the trickery by Bathsheba and Nathan
        b.   late: the exile and the demise of the Judean (and last Yahwistic) monarchy

D. Issues:
    1.   of the Speaker:
        a.   the security of Solomon's kingdom
        b.   the legitimacy of Solomon as heir to David
    2.   of the Writers:
        a.   early:
            i.   the security of Solomon's kingdom

        ii.   the legitimacy of Solomon as heir to David
    b.   late: the legitimacy of Solomon as heir to David

E. Purposes:
    1.   of the Speaker:
        a.   justification of Solomon's acts
        b.   explanation of the legitimacy of Solomon as heir to David
        c.   presentation and promotion of Solomon as a wise administrator
    2.   of the Writers:
        a.   early:
            i.   justification of Solomon's acts
            ii.   explanation of the legitimacy of Solomon as heir to David
            iii.   presentation and promotion of Solomon as a wise administrator
        b.   late:
            i.   justification of Solomon's acts
            ii.   explanation of the legitimacy of Solomon as heir to David
            iii.   presentation and promotion of Solomon as a wise administrator
            iv.   explanation and endorsement of the continuation of the Davidic lineage and right to administrative privilege

F. Presuppositions:
    1.   of the Speaker:
        a.   YHWH as being with David [1 Sam. 16:1, 12f, 18; 17:37, 45-48; 18:12, 14, 28-29; 23:14; 30:6; 2 Sam. 3:1; 5:10; 8:6, 14]
        b.   King as Adopted Son of YHWH [2 Sam. 7]
        c.   YHWH as King/Sovereign of Israel and Judah
        d. the oneness of YHWH, i. e., the political solidarity of Yahwistic monarchalism
        f.   the historicity of YHWH's activity
        g.   Jerusalem (or Mount Zion) as the City of YHWH and the National Yahwistic Cult Center
    2.   of the Writers:
        a.   YHWH as Warrior, Deliverer, and Judge
        b.   YHWH as Universal Sovereign
        c.   YHWH as Just and Merciful
        d.   the oneness of YHWH, i. e., the political solidarity of Yahwistic colonialism
        e.   the historicity of YHWH's activity
        f.   Jerusalem (or Mount Zion) as the City of YHWH and the Sole Yahwistic Cult Center

#6: The Monarchy as Major Cause for Defection from YHWH [cf. DH, e. g. 1 Kgs. 4]

A. Perspectives:
   1. Speaker: Solomon's court
   2. Writer: Deuteronomistic Historian [DH]

B. Addressees:
   1. of the Speaker:
      a. the Northern Yahwists or the Israelites who backed Solomon's brothers
      b. the potential rebels or the disgruntled factions in the kingdom
      c. the marginal people or the bedouins on the southwestern border
   2. of the Writer:
      a. the exilic Judeans
      b. the Northern Yahwists or the Samaritans

C. Contexts:
   1. of the Speaker:
      a. the oppressive economic policies of Solomon
      b. the deficit spending that ensues from Solomon's enterprizes
   2. of the Writer: the exile and the demise of the Judean (and last Yahwistic) monarchy

D. Issues:
   1. of the Speaker:
      a. the security of Solomon's kingdom
      b. the relations between the Northern Yahwists and the Southern Yahwists
   2. of the Writer: sanity, i. e., comprehension of the national crisis/catastrophe

E. Purposes:
   1. of the Speaker:
      a. justification of Solomon's acts
      b. explanation of the legitimacy of Solomon as heir to David
      c. presentation and promotion of Solomon as a wise administrator
   2. of the Writer:
      a. explanation of the national crisis as punishment for departure from the early Yahwistic orthodoxy, and the subsequent future possibilities

    b.   engendering of hope through endorsement of Davidic-Zionistic Yahwism

    c.   explanation and endorsement of the continuation of the Davidic lineage and right to administrative privilege through qualified criticism

F. Presuppositions:
1. of the Speaker:
   a. YHWH as being with David [1 Sam. 16:1, 12f, 18; 17:37, 45-48; 18:12, 14, 28-29; 23:14; 30:6; 2 Sam. 3:1; 5:10; 8:6, 14]
   b. King as Adopted Son of YHWH and the Eternality of the Davidic Dynasty [2 Sam. 7]
   c. YHWH as King/Sovereign of Israel and Judah
   d. the oneness of YHWH, i. e., the political solidarity of Yahwistic monarchalism
   f. the historicity of YHWH's activity
   g. Jerusalem (or Mount Zion) as the City of YHWH and the National Yahwistic Cult Center
2. of the Writer:
   a. YHWH as Warrior, Deliverer, and Judge
   b. YHWH as Universal Sovereign
   c. YHWH as Just and Merciful
   d. the oneness of YHWH, i. e., the political solidarity of Yahwistic colonialism
   e. the historicity of YHWH's activity
   f. Jerusalem (or Mount Zion) as the City of YHWH and the Sole Yahwistic Cult Center

#7: The Monarchy or State Syncretism as the Cause of Religious/Ideological Syncretism [1 Kgs. 9-11]

A. Perspectives:
1. Speaker: the conservative Yahwists who worked in Solomon's court or were sympathizers with the early (Mosaic-Sinaitic) Yahwists
2. Writer: Deuteronomistic Historian [DH]

B. Addressees:
1. of the Speaker: the sympathizers with the Northern (Mosaic-Sinaitic) Yahwists or the proponents of the Davidic-Solomonic regime
2. of the Writer:
   a. the exilic Judeans including the Judean sympathizers with the early (Mosaic-Sinaitic) Yahwists
   b. the Northern Yahwists or the Samaritans

C. Contexts:
1. of the Speaker:
   a. the official or the popular assessment of the administration's policy
   b. the conflicts of interest due to the secession of the Northern Yahwists
2. of the Writer: the exile and the demise of the Judean (and last Yahwistic) monarchy

D. Issues:
1. of the Speaker:
   a. national security
   b. ideological contamination, i. e., violation of the constitution and Yahwistic diversity
2. of the Writer:
   a. sanity, i. e., comprehension of the national crisis/catastrophe
   b. management of cultural diversity

E. Purposes:
1. of the Speaker:
   a. mild solicitation of the Northern Yahwists who defected to rejoin the South
   b. reconciliation of the internal differences regarding national policy
2. of the Writer:
   a. explanation of the national crisis as punishment for departure from the early Yahwistic orthodoxy, and the subsequent future possibilities
   b. engendering of hope through endorsement of Davidic-Zionistic Yahwism
   c. explanation and endorsement of the continuation of the Davidic lineage and right to administrative privilege through qualified criticism
   d. reconciliation of Yahwistic diversity

F. Presuppositions:
1. of the Speaker:
   a. YHWH as being with David [1 Sam. 16:1, 12f, 18; 17:37, 45-48; 18:12, 14, 28-29; 23:14; 30:6; 2 Sam. 3:1; 5:10; 8:6, 14]
   b. YHWH as King/Sovereign of Israel and Judah
   c. King as Adopted Son of YHWH and the Eternality of the Davidic Dynasty [2 Sam. 7]
   d. the oneness of YHWH, i. e., the political solidarity of Yahwistic monarchalism

      e.   the historicity of YHWH's activity

2. of the Writer:
      a.   YHWH as being with David [1 Sam. 16:1, 12f, 18; 17:37, 45-48; 18:12, 14, 28-29; 23:14; 30:6; 2 Sam. 3:1; 5:10; 8:6, 14]
      b.   YHWH as Universal Sovereign
      c.   King as Adopted Son of YHWH and the Eternality of the Davidic Dynasty [2 Sam. 7]
      d.   the oneness of YHWH, i. e., exclusive Yahwistic monotheism and the political solidarity of Yahwistic colonialism
      e.   Zionistic Yahwism as the Legitimate (Sole) Heir of early Yahwism
      f.   the historicity of YHWH's activity
      g.   Jerusalem (or Mount Zion) as the City of YHWH and the Sole Yahwistic Cult Center

#8: The Division as Caused by YHWH [1 Kgs. 12:1-24]

A. Perspectives:
1. Speaker: the conservative Yahwists who worked in Solomon's court or were sympathizers with the early (Mosaic-Sinaitic) Yahwists
2. Writer: Deuteronomistic Historian [DH]

B. Addressees:
1. of the Speaker: the sympathizers with the Northern (Mosaic-Sinaitic) Yahwists or the proponents of the Davidic-Solomonic regime
2. of the Writer:
      a.   the exilic Judeans including the Judean sympathizers with the early (Mosaic-Sinaitic) Yahwists
      b.   the Northern Yahwists or the Samaritans

C. Contexts:
1. of the Speaker:
      a.   the official, or the popular, assessment of the administration's policy
      b.   the conflicts of interest due to the secession of the Northern Yahwists
      c.   the decrease of the territory and the jurisdiction of the Davidic-Solomonic state
2. of the Writer: the exile and the demise of the Judean (and last Yahwistic) monarchy

D. Issues:
1. of the Speaker:

      a. national security, i. e., "public relations"
      b. ideological contamination, i. e., violation of the constitution and handling of Yahwistic diversity

  2. of the Writer:
      a. sanity, i.e., comprehension of the national crisis/catastrophe
      b. management of cultural diversity

E. Purposes:
  1. of the Speaker:
      a. mild solicitation of the Northern Yahwists who defected to rejoin the South
      b. reconciliation of the internal differences regarding national policy
      c. explanation of the Southern administration's ineffectiveness in stopping the secession of the Northern Yahwists
      d. explanation of the partisan postures within the Southern administration

  2. of the Writer:
      a. explanation of the national crisis as punishment for departure from the early Yahwistic orthodoxy, and the subsequent future possibilities
      b. engendering of hope through endorsement of Davidic-Zionistic Yahwism
      c. explanation and endorsement of the continuation of the Davidic lineage and right to administrative privilege through qualified criticism
      d. reconciliation of Yahwistic diversity

F. Presuppositions:
  1. of the Speaker:
      a. YHWH as being with David [1 Sam. 16:1, 12f, 18; 17:37, 45-48; 18:12, 14, 28-29; 23:14; 30:6; 2 Sam. 3:1; 5:10; 8:6, 14]
      b. YHWH as King/Sovereign of Israel and Judah
      c. King as Adopted Son of YHWH and the Eternality of the Davidic Dynasty [2 Sam. 7]
      d. the oneness of YHWH, i. e., the political solidarity of Yahwistic monarchalism
      e. the historicity of YHWH's activity

  2. of the Writer:
      a. YHWH as being with David [1 Sam. 16:1, 12f, 18; 17:37, 45-48; 18:12, 14, 28-29; 23:14; 30:6; 2 Sam. 3:1; 5:10; 8:6, 14]
      b. YHWH as Universal Sovereign
      c. King as Adopted Son of YHWH and the Eternality of the

Davidic Dynasty [2 Sam. 7]

d. the oneness of YHWH, i. e., exclusive Yahwistic monotheism and the political solidarity of Yahwistic colonialism

e. Zionistic Yahwism as the Legitimate (Sole) Heir of early Yahwism

f. the historicity of YHWH's activity

g. Jerusalem (or Mount Zion) as the City of YHWH and the Sole Yahwistic Cult Center

Endnotes

1. Robert B. Coote, *Early Israel: A New Horizon* (Minneapolis: Fortress, 1990), 2f; Philip R. Davies, *In Search of 'Ancient Israel'* (JSOT Sup. 148; England: Sheffield, 1992); J. Alberto Soggin, *An Introduction to the History of Israel and Judah* (trans. John Bowden; Valley Forge, PA: Trinity International, 1993), 3, 26, 28, 67, 95, 114, 136, 138, 148, 175f; Gösta Ahlström, *The History of Ancient Palestine from the Palaeolithic Period to Alexander's Conquest* (ed. Diana Edelman; JSOT Sup. 146; England: Sheffield, 1993), 43, 45-52, 413, 490 n. 3, 491 n. 4, 540 n. 5, 557 n. 4, 561, 597f, 621 n. 2, 623, 650 n. 1, 677 (n. 3), 702 (n. 1), 706 (n. 2), 720 n. 3, 770f, 775 n. 1, 777, 804, 822, 838, 844-847, 859 n. 3, 876, 883, 885-887; see especially Davies, *In Search*.

2. Robert B. Coote & Mary P. Coote, *Power, Politics, and the Making of the Bible: An Introduction* (Minneapolis: Fortress, 1990); Soggin, *History*, 29.

3. DH is the siglum for the Deuteronomistic History, which consists of Deut., Josh., Jgs. Sam., and Kgs. CH is the siglum for the Chronistic History, which is a post-exilic redaction of DH.

4. Norman K. Gottwald, *The Hebrew Bible: A Socio-literary Introduction* (Philadelphia: Fortress, 1985), 348-351; Martin Noth, *The History of Israel* (3d ed.; trans. Peter R. Ackroyd; New York: Harper & Row, 1958), 232-234; Robert B. Coote & David Robert Ord, *The Bible's First History: From Eden to the court of David with the Yahwist* (Philadelphia: Fortress, 1989). Jerusalem is assumed by DH and CH to be the only authorized sanctuary, and every king—northern and southern—is judged according to their attitude toward the exclusive legitimacy of the Temple in Jerusalem. Also, the monarchy is presented as the fundamental cause for Israel's defection from and unfaithfulness to YHWH. See Niels Peter Lemche, *Ancient Israel: A New History of Israelite Society* (England: Sheffield, 1995), 119-124, 161-172.

5. Coote, *Early Israel*, 5, 72, 88-90, 92f, 113-117, 130f, 133-138; André Lemaire, "The United Monarchy," in *Ancient Israel: A Short History from Abraham to the Roman Destruction of the Temple* (ed. Hershel Shanks; Washington, D. C.: Biblical Archaeology Society/Englewood Cliffs, NJ: Prentice-Hall, 1988), 86f; Ahlström, *History*, 432-439; Soggin, *History*, 169f; Gottwald, *The Hebrew Bible*, 319; Lemche, Ancient Israel, 100-104.

6. Coote, *Early Israel*, 5, 72, 88-90, 92f, 113-117, 130f, 133-138; Soggin, *History*, 47; Gottwald, *The Hebrew Bible*, 321; Ahlström, *History*, 454, 487.

7. Ahlström, *History*, 448-454; Soggin, *History*, 49-53; Coote, *Early Israel*, 92; cf. 88-90. Lemaire ["The United Monarchy," 90f] perceives Saul's kingship as essentially a "family matter". However, the persistent effort of DH to overshadow Saul with David suggests that historically Saul was

more significant than the biblical texts show. See also Lemche, *Ancient Israel*, 130-137.

8. Ahlström, *History*, 434-440.
9. Lemaire, "The United Monarchy," 88; Ahlström, *History*, 435-439.
10. Lemche, *Ancient Israel*, 138.
11. Gerhard von Rad [*The Message of the Prophets* (New York: Harper & Row,1962, 1965)] has argued that Yahwistic prophetism as evidenced by the classical prophets is a conservative counter-movement to the syncretistic degeneracy of orthodox Yahwism precipitated by the formation and development of the Israelite state. These prophets interpreted the crises to the nations of Israel as YHWH's judgment upon Israel. The emergence of this movement is connected with: 1. the degeneracy of Yahwism due to syncretism; 2. political autonomy or systematic emancipation from YHWH and his offer of protection brought about by the formation of the state (9); 3. oppressive and exploitative economic and social developments; and 4. the rise of the Assyrians (10). Their messages reflected several common factors: 1. rootedness in the basic sacral traditions of the early period, i. e., Yahwistic tribalism; 2. an intensive view into the future (11-12); 3. proclamations of judgment coupled with the beginnings of a new movement toward salvation (12); and 4. spiritual independence and religious immediacy, i. e., involvement in the traditions and general religious ideas of their environment (13). See Lemche, *Ancient Israel*, 155-156. Caution must be taken here, for the classical Yahwistic prophets also operated within a pantheistic view, in which YHWH was the supreme god (cf. Lowell K. Handy, "The Appearance of Pantheon in Judah," in *The Triumph of Elohim: From Yahwisms to Judaisms* (ed. Diana Vikander Edelman; Grand Rapids, MI: Eerdmans., 1995), 27-43; Herbert Niehr, "The Rise of YHWH in Judahite and Israelite Religion: Methodological and Religio-Historical Aspects," in The Triumph of Elohim: From Yahwisms to Judaisms (ed. Diana Vikander Edelman; Grand Rapids, MI: Eerdmans, 1995), 45-72; Isa. 2:18-20; Jer. 1:4-6; 7:9-19, 30-31; 9:20; Ezek. 8:10-16; Hos. 2:15; 11:2; 13:1-4, 14). However, this aspect of the prophets' activity may reflect a change in emphasis of their roles from cultic to sociopolitical affairs [cf. Samuel E. Balentine, "The Prophet as Intercessor: A Reassessment," *Journal of Biblical Literature* 103 (1984): 161-173].
12. Ahlström, *History*, 448-454, 455 n. 1; Soggin, *History*, 49-53; Coote, *Early Israel*, 92; cf. 88-90.
13. Ahlström, *History*, 455-458.
14 Ahlström, *History*, 456-462; Lemaire, "The United Monarchy," 92f;
15. Ahlström, *History*, Map. 14. At its farthest expanse David's kingdom included: 1. Judah; 2. Israel; 3. Jerusalem; 4. Ziklag; 5. Ammon; 6. Edom; and 7. Tyre. His vassals were: 1. Aram/Damascus; and 2. Moab. See

Soggin, *History*, 56-63. It is noteworthy that the kingdoms of Judah and Israel were and remained distinct entities, merely sharing a single ruler. Their distinctiveness must be attributed to ideological and geographical differences. Also, it must be considered that these presentations of the Davidic kingdom are in DH, which is exilic, and may be apologetic, that is, fostering the elevation of the South over the North.

16. Ahlström, *History*, 463-469; Soggin, *History*, 58.
17. Ahlström, *History*, 481, 484 n. 6, 485, 489f; Soggin, *History*, 65.
18. Ahlström, *History*, 474; Soggin, *History*, 64f; Coote, *Early Israel*, 154f; Lemche, *Ancient Israel*, 139f.
19. Ahlström, *History*, 469f, 476-479; Lemaire, "The United Monarchy," 93f; Soggin, *History*, 67-69; Coote, *Early Israel*, 154f.
20. Coote and Ord [*The Bible's First History*] argue that J was a social product of urban Israel composed to validate the establishment of the royal house of David, which replaced the less centralized political arrangement of inter-tribalism in the highlands of Palestine (3, 6, 7, 29f, 201), and thus is nationalistic, state propaganda (246) with YHWH as the god of the nation of Israel (250). See Richard Elliott Friedman, *Who Wrote the Bible?* (New York: Harper & Row, 1987), 50-88; Harold Bloom, *The Book of J*, trans. David Rosenberg (New York: Vintage Books, 1990), 9-48. Friedman argues that J was written after the reign of Solomon (848-7?? B.C.E.) (87); Bloom argues that J is post-Solomonic and written by a *Gevurah* ("great lady") of Davidic blood, who is essentially a comic author (10, 19, 26). See Niehr, "The Rise of YHWH," 59, 63-67; Handy, "The Appearance of Pantheon in Judah," 36-41. See 1 Sam. 4:4; 2 Sam. 6:2 = 1 Chr. 13:6; 2 Kgs. 19:15 = Isa. 37:16; Ps. 80:2; 99:1; Isa. 6; 1 Kgs. 22:19-22; Pss. 46:2-12; 48:5-9; 76:3-10; 82.
21. See Niehr, "The Rise of YHWH," 52-59, 63-67.
22. Ahlström, *History*, 471-473, 503; Lemaire, "The United Monarchy," 96, 98f; Soggin, *History*, 67-69, 75f. Though he did not build a temple, close reading of 2 Sam. 7 suggests that he planned such. See Carol Meyers, "David as Temple Builder," in *Ancient Israelite Religion* (eds. Patrick D. Miller, Jr., Paul D. Hanson, and S. Dean McBride; Philadelphia: Fortress, 1987), 357-376; Lemche, Ancient Israel, 164f, 170-172. See Saul Olyan, "Zadok's Origins and the Tribal Politics of David," *Journal of Biblical Literature* 101 (1982): 177-193, especially 185, 189-193; Niehr, "The Rise of YHWH;" Thomas L. Thompson, "The Intellectual Matrix of Early Biblical Narrative: Inclusive Monotheism in Persian Period Palestine," in *The Triumph of Elohim: From Yahwisms to Judaisms* (ed. Diana Vikander Edelman; Grand Rapids, MI: Eerdmans, 1995), 107-124. Though he regards such creation theology as exilic (65), Niehr presents the following as evidence of the use of mythological elements in Yahwism: 1. "The stability of the earth, which is effected by YHWH's

creation, is an indicator of YHWH's faithfulness (cf. Pss. 90:2; 102:26-27);" 2. "By virtue of his creation, YHWH proves to be higher than the gods (cf. Isa. 40:18-26; Jer. 10:1-16; Pss. 89:7-13; 96:4-5; 135:5-7; 136:2-9), almighty (cf. Job 26:5-14; Ps. 135:6-7) and incomparable (cf. Isa. 40:25-26; Job 38-39);" 3. "YHWH is the owner of the creation (cf. Isa. 43:1; Pss. 8:4; 29:1-2; 74:16; 89:12; 95:5-7; 100:3; 115:15-16) and full power over the natural forces belongs to him (cf. Jer. 10:12-13 = 51:15-16; Pss. 29; 104; 135:6-7);" and 4. "As creator of heaven and earth YHWH is also the lord of history (cf. Isa. 42:5-8; 44:24-28; 45:1-8, 9-13; 51:9-16; Jer. 18:1-12; 27:4-8; Zech. 12:1-2; Ps. 135:6-12) (66). See also 1 Sam. 4:4; 2 Sam. 6:2 = 1 Chr. 13:6; 2 Kgs. 19:15 = Isa. 37:16; Ps. 80:2; 99:1; Isa. 6; 1 Kgs. 22:19-22; Pss. 46:2-12; 48:5-9; 76:3-10; 82. The Jerusalem pantheon of gods probably was appropriated from the cults of the dead, which were prevalent in the North and the South; thus the death cult legislation (e. g., Lev. 19:26, 31; 20:6, 27; Deut. 18:10-11; 26:14) was aimed at diverting allegiance and funds from the local cultic operations to that of the Jerusalem Temple cult. See Elizabeth Bloch-Smith, "The Cult of the Dead in Judah: Interpreting the Material Remains," *Journal of Biblical Literature* 111 (1992): 213-224, especially 219-224. Note the use of elôhîm אלהים for the deified dead [Bloch-Smith, "The Cult of the Dead in Judah," 220]. See, also, Alan Cooper and Bernard Goldstein, "The Cult of the Dead and the Theme of Entry into the Land," *Biblical Interpretation* 1 (1993): 285-303.

23. Ahlström, *History*, 474f; Coote, *Early Israel*, 154; Soggin, *History*, 64f.

24. Ahlström, *History*, 488-490, 495-501; Lemaire, "The United Monarchy," 96; Soggin, *History*, 65f; Lemche, *Ancient Israel*, 143-145.

25. David had sons born at several locations: at Hebron (2 Sam. 3:2-5) and at Jerusalem (2 Sam. 5:14-16). His firstborn sons, according to 2 Sam. 3:2-5, are: 1. Amnon, whose mother was Ahinoam from Jezreel in Judah (1 Sam. 25:43; 2 Sam. 13-14); 2. Chileab, whose mother was Abigail from Nabal in Carmel; 3. Abshalom, whose mother was Maacah, daughter of the king of Geshur (2 Sam. 13:39; 14:1; 15-19); 4. Adonijah, whose mother was Haggith (1 Kgs. 1:5, 7-8);5. Shephatiah, whose mother was Abital; 6. Ithream, whose mother was Eglah; and 7. Solomon, whose mother was Bathsheba (2 Sam. 11:2-12:25; 5:14; 1 Kgs. 1:11-40, especially 28-40). Now, the first four constituted legitimate candidates to throne. The first six were born to David in Hebron. Note that Solomon was not a firstborn or legitimate heir! Consider, also, that David deprived Michal, Saul's daughter, of children (1 Sam. 18:27; 2 Sam. 6).

26. L. Rost, *Die Uberlieferung von der Thronnachfolge Davids*.

27. Ahlström, *History*, 497-501; Soggin, *History*, 66f; Lemaire, "The United Monarchy," 98; Zafrira Ben-Barak, "The Status and Right of the *Gebîrâ*," *Journal of Biblical Literature* 110 (1991): 23-34; Susan Ackerman,

"The Queen Mother and the Cult in Ancient Israel," *Journal of Biblical Literature* 112 (1993): 385-401. Ben-Barak attributes the presence of the queen mothers to the deuteronomic redactor, who develops the text to show uninterrupted dynastic continuity with the house of David (24). However, this phenomenon is not conventional, and the isolated instances reveal in common the accession of a younger son who was not by right in line for the throne and who acquires the throne by means of the maneuvers of his mother on his behalf (34). For queen mothers, see Bathsheba, the daughter of Eliam (2 Sam. 11:3), Maacah, the daughter of Abishalom (1 Kgs. 15:2), Hamutal, the daughter of Jeremiah of Libnah (2 Kgs. 23:31), Nehushta, the daughter of Elnathan (2 Kgs. 24:8), Jezebel, the daughter of Ethbaal, king of the Sidonians, and wife of King Ahab (1 Kgs. 16:31), and Athaliah, the daughter of Ahab (2 Kgs. 8:18) or the daughter of Omri (2 Kgs. 8:26). Further, Ackerman argues that the queen mother had an official responsibility in Israelite religion (i. e., to devote herself to the cult of the mother goddess Asherah within the king's court), which was primary among her other obligations, and that the queen mother had sociopolitical responsibilities within ancient Israel, particularly with regard to succession upon the old king's death, which cannot be divorced from her cultic role as "surrogate mother" within the royal ideology (388, 394f, 400f).

28. Ahlström, *History*, 503; Soggin, *History*, 68f, 75f; Lemaire, "The United Monarchy," 98f.

29. Ahlström, *History*, 509, 531-539; Soggin, *History*, 74. Soggin sees Solomon as building a Canaanite temple, while Ahlström noted that Solomon followed the Egyptian model of organization.

30. Ahlström, *History*, 520-524. It is possible that Solomon's temple was also a fortress.

31. Ahlström, *History*, 507-515.

32. Ahlström, *History*, 515-517.

33. Soggin, *History*, 200-205; Gottwald, *The Hebrew Bible*, 322f, 342; Noth, *History*, 226f; Lemche, *Ancient Israel*, 137-146. See the discussions of Solomon as the foil for Josiah [Marvin A. Sweeney, "The Critique of Solomon in the Josianic Edition of the Deuteronomistic History," *Journal of Biblical Literature* 114 (1995): 607-622, especially 609-611, 613-615, 619, 621, 622], and the response [David A. Glatt-Gilad, "The Deuteronomistic Critique of Solomon: A Response to Marvin A. Sweeney," *Journal of Biblical Literature* 116 (1997): 700-703], and the present issues pertaining to the "United Monarchy" [Gary N. Knoppers, "The Vanishing Solomon: The Disappearance of the United Monarchy from Recent Histories of Ancient Israel," *Journal of Biblical Literature* 116 (1997): 19-44, especially 19, 21, 25, 27].

34. Gottwald, *The Hebrew Bible*, 348-351; Noth, *History*, 232-234; Coote & Ord, *The Bible's First History*; see von Rad, *The Message of the Prophets*.
35. Gottwald, *The Hebrew Bible*, 323; Lemaire, "The United Monarchy," 96. This trend began during the reign of David.
36. Gottwald, *The Hebrew Bible*, 323f.
37. Gottwald, *The Hebrew Bible*, 324.
38. Gottwald, *The Hebrew Bible*, 324f.
39. See earlier "The Land of Israel;" Ahlström, *History*, 487; Lemche, *Ancient Israel*, 24-27.
40. Vassal status typically consisted of: 1. forced acceptance of the administrative arrangement of the suzerain, i. e., a suzerainty-vassal treaty; 2. required payment of tribute; 3. forced acceptance of the religion of the suzerain; and 4. required, unconditional loyalty, i. e., no foreign alliances. Violation of any of the stipulations constituted treason or insurrection and was severely penalized. See Gottwald, *The Hebrew Bible*, 202-206; Soggin, *History*, 235f.
41. 1 Kings 11:1-40.
42. Soggin, *History*, 200-202; Ahlström, *History*, 543-548.
43. Ahlström, *History*, 545; Soggin, *History*, 207f; Siegfried H. Horn, "The Divided Monarchy," in *Ancient Israel: A Short History from Abraham to the Roman Destruction of the Temple* (ed. Hershel Shanks; Washington, D. C.: Biblical Archaeology Society/Englewood Cliffs, NJ: Prentice-Hall, 1988), 111f; Lemaire, "The United Monarchy," 104.
44. Lemche, *Ancient Israel*, 125-128.
45. Noth, *History*, 227f; Soggin, *History*, 206f.
46. "The Campaign of Sheshonk I," translated by John A. Wilson (ANET, 187).
47. Noth, *History*, 238-240, 244-245; see Ahlström, *History*, 545, 557-560; Soggin, *History*, 207-208; Horn, "The Divided Monarchy," 111-112; Lemaire, "The United Monarchy," 104.
48. Noth, *History*, 230-232; Soggin, *History*, 205-206; Ahlström, *History*, 548-552, 556-557. The biblical view (1 Kgs. 12:27-31) that Jeroboam set up golden calves to be worshiped reflects the polemical attack and bias of the South, which had its own cult objects (1 Kgs. 7:15-47). This bias is felt to have been inserted into the early traditions, when or after J and E were combined (Exod. 32).
49. Robert B. Coote, *In Defense of Revolution: The Elohist History* (Minneapolis: Fortress Press, 1991); Alan W. Jenks, *The Elohist and North Israelite Traditions* (Missoula, Montana: Scholars Press, 1977). Coote's thesis is that E originated as a written supplement to J in the court of Jeroboam to justify his revolution against and secession from the Davidic kingdom (2, 13, 17, 19, 61, 63, 67, 69, 75, 90, 92, 94, 95, 96, 98, 101, 103, 107, 112, 114, 119, 120, 121, 139f). Jenks's thesis is that the E traditions

comprise the fragments of an originally continuous and independent epic tradition, which was formulated ca. 922 B.C.E. from the northern Israelite traditions located among the Mushite (Gershonite) or Levitical priesthood, i. e., "prophetic-levitical" group, at Shiloh, after the death of Solomon, when the kingdom divided and an independent state in the north was being established, and was designed for cult or covenant renewal and teaching (1 Kgs. 11:16-12:33) (cf. 102, 104, 105, 120). See also Friedman [*Who Wrote the Bible?*], who dates E ca. 922-722 B.C.E. (86f).

50. Noth, *History*, 228-229; Gottwald, *The Hebrew Bible*, 346f; Ahlström, *History*, 548-550, 561-562. Coregencies are reported from the time of Asa in the South, while Omri was the first to establish a dynasty in the North, which lasted 44 years. See Horn, "The Divided Monarchy," 120-123.

51. Horn, "The Divided Monarchy," 112.

CHAPTER FOUR:
THE TWO YAHWISTIC KINGDOMS

Following the secession of the North from the South, struggles occurred between the two kingdoms for about forty years. Due to its economic and productive potential, the North was more successful than the South. War continued throughout the reigns of Rehoboam (ca. 922-915 B.C.E.), Abijah (ca. 915-913 B.C.E.), and Asa (ca. 913-873 B.C.E.) of Judah, and Jeroboam I (ca. 922-901 B.C.E.), Nadab (ca. 901-900 B.C.E.), and Baasha (ca. 900-877 B.C.E.) of Israel.[1] DH, which presents an abbreviated overview of the monarchy, is extremely sketchy, providing *regnal resumés*.[2] Coupled with the fact that DH is of Southern origins, the information provided therein is brief and biased. Therefore, the general trends that persisted will be discussed, giving attention to outstanding developments.

First, during the reign of Asa the Southern Kingdom gained an advantage over the North. This was facilitated by a treaty Asa made with Aram-Damascus, which in turn broke up the alliance between Baasha of Israel and Aram-Damascus (1 Kgs. 15:18-20). It is possible that this new alliance was spurred by Egyptian backing of Judah (2 Chron. 14:8-14).[3] As a result of this alliance the North lost its possessions in Transjordan (i. e., Abel Beth-maacah, Ijon, Dan, and Chinneroth), and the Arameans penetrated deep into Israel's territory, drastically reducing the North. Also, Asa advanced northwards and recaptured Ramah, using abandoned material he found there to fortify Mizpah and Geba of Benjamin. This marked the beginning of Israel's wars with its neighbors in the northeast, which lasted for decades, and the virtual fixing of the boundary between Israel and Judah.[4]

Second, during the dynasty of Omri (i. e., Omri, Ahab, Ahaziah, Joram [also named Jehoram - 2 Kgs. 3:1; 8:16] - 1 Kgs. 16:21-22:54; 2 Kgs. 3:1-27; 8:16-24[5]) a new phase in the relations between Israel and Judah began. At this time, the territory of Israel had been greatly reduced and the kingdom of Damascus was the most powerful in Syria-Palestine. In light of the growing power and threat of the Assyrians, Damascus made alliances with Tyre and other Syrian states, its main preoccupation being Assyria. Cognizant of these negotiations Omri forged peaceful relations that precipitated prosperity, including an alliance with Judah, that was concluded with the marriage of his daughter/niece (or Ahab's sister/daughter) Athaliah and Joram of Judah (also named Jehoram - 2 Kgs. 8:26). By means of diplomacy Omri and

Ahab managed to maintain friendly relations with the Arameans, particularly during the time of Shalmaneser III (ca. 858-824 B.C.E.), who made several campaigns toward Palestine. It was during Ahab's reign that Israel experienced its most prosperous period. This prosperity is reflected in the traditio-historical clashes between the Syrian culture of Jezebel indicated by Baalism and the Yahwistic culture represented by Eliyahu and Elisha (1 Kgs. 17-21; 2 Kgs. 1:2-17; 2:1-25; 3:4-8, 15; 13:14-21), which betray the actual, syncretistic culture of the times. The latter two were representatives of strong, independent tribal groups that challenged and countered the Yahwistic monarchies, thereby causing unrest. Most outstanding during Ahab's reign is the relocation of his capital to Shomeron (Samaria - 1 Kgs. 16:24), which was more centralized in his kingdom.[6]

Omri's dynasty was concluded with the revolution or coup d'état of Jehu (2 Kgs. 9:1-10:27), which terminated Israel's relations with Damascus and thereby made possible the ascension of Hazael. It appears that Jehu seized an opportunity to take charge, when Joram was wounded in battle at Ramoth-Gilead, and sought to oppose Joram's anti-Assyrian policies. His pro-Assyrian posture not only spurred his revolt, but agitated Hazael of Damascus (2 Kgs. 11-13; Amos 1:3-5), who probably sought to regain the Israelite territories in northern Transjordan (2 Kgs. 10:32-33)[7] and was anti-Assyrian.[8] Eventually, Israel became isolated and was taken as a vassal of Aram-Damascus, as Shalmaneser was preoccupied with internal affairs and neglected to support his ally.[9] Given the predominance of the North (cf. 2 Kgs. 10:28-31), it is understandable that Judah was inevitably involved in the military enterprises of Israel, that is, the Aramean wars (1 Kgs. 22:2-4; 2 Kgs. 8:28; 9:14) and the war against rebellious Moab (2 Kgs. 3:4).[10] Such political relations were no doubt reflected cultically, for example, Eliyahu and Elisha sought to raise Israelite consciousness regarding the difference between Yahwism and Baalism, though the two ideologies had fundamental similarities.[11]

Third, during the reign of Joash (ca. 798-782 B.C.E.) the North subjugated the South (2 Kgs. 14:1-22). The confrontation was prompted by a challenge by Amaziah of Judah to Joash of Israel, who was freed to wage war due to tribute he had paid to Assyria. He dominated and captured Amaziah at the battle of Beth-Shemesh and demolished Jerusalem, including the palace and the temple.[12] This subjection of Judah probably provided the context for the R[JE] calendar reforms, in which the Northern calendar was superimposed upon the Judean calendar.[13] Also, this provides the backdrop for the reign of Jeroboam II (ca. 786-746 B.C.E.), who probably began as a coregent with his father. Most outstanding about his reign (2 Kgs. 14:23-29) is the regaining of some of the territory that was lost to Damascus and military strength, as he, and probably Uzziah in the South, controlled the key commercial routes between Egypt, Syria, and Mesopotamia.[14] This was possible, because Assyria was suffering a period of political decline. Thus, Jeroboam II's reign marked a period of peace and economic prosperity in Israel and at the same time in Judah under the reign of Uzziah (ca. 783-742 B.C.E.), which was marked by territorial expansion (2 Kgs. 15:1-7 || 2 Chron. 26:1-23).[15] Such prosperity furthered social stratification and exploitation, which prompted the criticism of Amos, a prophet from the South, and Hosea, a prophet from the North.[16] Their indictments and imminent predictions were felt to be verified by history, as the Assyrians recovered from decline and began to expand southwestward.

In 743 B.C.E. many Syrian states had become independent and possibly joined in a coalition, including Tyre, Philistines, and Arabs, to fight with Jeroboam of Israel against Damascus. Also, a coalition of north-Syrian states (Arpad, Gurgum, Melid and Kummu) under the leadership of Sarduri II, king of Urartu, was defeated by Tiglath-pileser III (ca. 745-727 B.C.E.), reducing their territories. As suspected, Tiglath-pileser reformed his administration and then conducted military campaigns to secure the borderlands. This entailed marches into Palestine, which were facilitated by the internal struggles in Palestine. This, in turn, prompted Damascus to work toward formation of a coalition to defend against Assyria.[17] About 738 B.C.E., Tiglath-pileser conducted a campaign on the Syro-Phoenician coast, incorporating the land of Unqi (on the coast of northern Syria) as a province, and then, in 737-735 B.C.E., campaigned in the north and the east against Urartu and the Medes. His latter move was interpreted as weakness in his administration and prompted restrengthening of the Syro-Palestinian coalition. However, in 734 B.C.E., Tiglath-pileser resumed pursuit of his goal of controlling the commerce of the Mediterranean ports.[18] This scenario constitutes the background of the Syro-Ephraimite War of 733 B.C.E. (2 Kgs. 16).

In response to the impending, Assyrian threat, Rezin of Damascus and Pekah of Israel (2 Kgs. 15:8-26)[19] headed a coalition that included Tyre, Ashkelon, Gaza, Edom, Moab, and Ammon. It is very probable that this coalition was supported by Egypt, which also sought to gain control over the Palestinian area as a counter against Assyria.[20] The two leaders tried a coup d'état in Judah, in order, first, to remove Ahaz of Judah, who refused to join the coalition upon their request, following the counsel of Isaiah (Isa. 7), and, second, to install a puppet king that was compliant with their wishes. Their main reason for seeking the collaboration of Judah was neutralization of the garrisons left along the frontier with Egypt. However, against Isaiah's advice,[21] Ahaz surrendered to Tiglath-pileser and paid tribute, along with Qaush-Malaku of Edom, Salamanu of Moab, and Sinipu of Bit-Ammon. Considering that Edom may have sided with and may have been supported by Israel and Damascus, since Edom recaptured Elath (2 Kgs. 16:6), it is very probable that Ahaz was surrounded and had no choice but to resort to the Assyrians for assistance.[22] Nevertheless, in 733-732 B.C.E. the territory of

Israel was reduced and the North was vassalized, as Galilee and Gilead were made Assyrian provinces. Also, the kingdom of Damascus was destroyed. Tiglath-pileser, then, gained commercial control of Palestine and established vassal buffer states to Egypt in the central hills of Palestine.[23] Initially, Assyrian domination was moderate, entailing disposing of Pekah of Israel, who was murdered (2 Kgs. 15:30), and installing of Hoshea as a puppet king.[24] After political stability for almost a decade after 732 B.C.E., Tiglath-pileser III died in 727 B.C.E. and was followed by Shalmaneser V. The change in Assyrian administration prompted rebellions by vassals, including Hoshea, who probably was sponsored by Egyptian support.[25] Now, Assyrian vassalization became most severe, as a three-year siege of Samaria took place, involving reshuffling of peoples through deportation of masses native to Israel and importation of different ethnic groups from foreign lands (2 Kgs. 17).[26] This marked the severest stage of Assyrian vassalization, being directed toward annihilation of the culture and the national unity of the subject peoples.[27] The final result of this episode was the cessation of the Northern Kingdom or Israel.[28]

Hezekiah's Revolution[29]

As a result of Judah's submission to Assyria, the South survived, considering itself the sole legitimate heir of the Israelite traditions. However, all of Palestine was under Assyrian control and thus reflected the cultural mixture caused by this situation: Judah shared a common border with Assyria; Aramaic continued to spread as the international language; and the already syncretistic forms of Yahwism were further blended with new cultic traditions, precipitating a situation in which the god of the land was not worshiped, according to DH (2 Kgs. 17:24-26, 32-34).[30] All in all, a period of relative peace, even cultural and religious revival, ensued throughout the ancient Near East.

Hezekiah came on the throne as a coregent to Ahaz, his father, probably around 728/727 B.C.E. (2 Kgs. 18:1; Isa. 14:28), and reigned with his father 14 years, before the latter died. He continued the pro-Assyrian policy of his father, until he acquired enough political and military stamina to attempt a revolt. He began a religious reform (2 Kgs. 18:3-8), which must be seen as political preparation for solidifying his kingdom.[31] This marked the public debut of P, which was a redaction of JE, that was intended to justify and relocate justice in the Jerusalem temple-cult of the Davidic state as the prime focus of law and order.[32] P, then, revised the calendar and introduced new administrative laws.[33] Also, he defeated the Philistines at Gaza, incorporating territory that had been lost during his father's reign (2 Kgs. 18:8).[34] By 720 B.C.E. a first anti-Assyrian coalition, which was defeated by Sargon, was formed by some city-states in the region, supported by Egypt and including the remnant of Hamath and Gaza and the subject peoples of Samaria.[35] In

712 B.C.E. a second anti-Assyrian coalition, composed of Egypt, Gaza, Ekron, Judah, Moab, Ammon, and Edom and led by Aziru, the king of Ashdod, revolted, prompting the return of Sargon. Once again, he gained control of the situation and reorganized the administration of the cities, installing a new governor over them.[36] In 705 B.C.E. Sargon died in battle against the Cimmerians, who had moved from the Sea of Azov through Caucasus in southern Russia, when they were threatened by the Scythians and later became a threat to Urartu and Assyria and its Anatolian dependencies. Sargon was, then, succeeded by his son, Sennacherib. This change of administration provided opportunity for rebellions, one of which was by a south-Palestinian coalition that was probably led by Hezekiah, which included Egypt and Babylon.[37] Because of delays in countering this threat, Sidqa of Ashkelon and Hezekiah of Judah had time to strengthen their defenses.[38] About 701 B.C.E. Sennacherib suppressed the rebellions in Mesopotamia or Babylon and turned west, first, quelling the rebellion of the Phoenicians, weakening the Palestinian coalition, and second, securing the loyalty of the Transjordanian kingdoms and taking the cities of Beth-Dagon, Joppa, Bene-berak, and Azor. He defeated an Egyptian-Cushite force at Eltekeh and proceeded on to take Ekron and Azekah.[39] Finally, he laid siege to Judah, taking Lachish and Libnah and confining Hezekiah to Jerusalem. However, Jerusalem was not razed, but was spared by tribute Hezekiah paid. Sennacherib's sparing of Jerusalem, though unexplained in Assyrian annals, may well have been due to overworking of his army, resulting in spreading them too thin, and a possible bubonic plague, which could have arisen in such circumstances of war (cf. Ps. 91). This unexplained turn in fortunes was perceived as the work of YHWH and was turned into a propaganda victory (2 Kgs. 18-19; especially 19:20-37;cf. Isa. 36:2-37:37; 38; 39:1-8).[40] Nevertheless, once again, Judah was an Assyrian vassal and this situation continued until 626 B.C.E., when new international changes triggered more rebellions.

Josiah's Revolution[41]

Manasseh inherited the drastically decreased state of Hezekiah and due to circumstance continued the pro-Assyrian policy. His lengthy and peaceful reign (696-641 B.C.E.) was due to his adherence to Assyrian policy. Being a buffer to Egypt, Judah's territory was increased, military fortifications were repaired, and the traditional religion of Judah was restored.[42] Manasseh was followed by his son, Amon (641-639 B.C.E.), who was murdered by court officials who probably sought to join with Egypt to stage a revolt against Assyria.[43] Amon's eight-year-old son, Josiah, was protected from the assassins by the people of the land (עם־הארץ 'am-ha-arez; 2 Kgs. 21:23f).

After 701 B.C.E. Assyria's kings sought to expand their kingdom and extend their control. In 679 B.C.E. Esarhaddon (680-669 B.C.E.) reached the border of Egypt and devastated Arza, a Philistine city. His goal was to subjugate Egypt. In 675 B.C.E. he started his campaign against Egypt, invading them in his tenth year. He reorganized Egypt, making it a province and installing the Assyrian cult of Ashur. Soon after he left, he had to return to stabilize Egypt, but fell sick and died on the way in Haran in 669 B.C.E. His son, Ashurbanipal (668-627 B.C.E.) succeeded him and conquered Egypt, having the support of the Arabs. Now, the empire reached its largest territorial expansion. However, it soon began to crumble. Though Egypt was reunited under Psammetichus I and posed no direct threat, Psammetichus I probably encouraged the creation of a coalition against Assyria, which was supported by parts of Palestine and Phoenicia. Ashurbanipal's main concern to control upper Egypt and maintain the peace of the Delta against the threat of Cush, his real enemy, was continually thwarted by disturbances in his Assyrian empire. It appears that in conquering Egypt, Assyria overextended itself and was not able to maintain control at the distant borders of its empire. The decisive defeat came when Nabopolassar, the Chaldean viceroy of Babylon, declared Babylonia independence and concluded an alliance with the Medes in 614 B.C.E., eventually capturing and destroying Nineveh, the capital of Assyria, in 612 B.C.E.[44]

During this period of Assyrian decline, Josiah (640-609 B.C.E.) assumed his throne in Judah and amassed the largest nation in western Palestine in the latter part of the seventh century. He probably aligned with Egypt and sought to maintain friendly relations with them, while keeping an apparent alliance with Assyria until he could strengthen his position for secession (cf. Jer. 2:18, 36).[45] His religious reforms in 622 B.C.E. marked his declaration of independence from Assyria, thereby endorsing and giving justification to his revolution, which probably had begun earlier.[46] In conjunction with his revolution, he inflicted punitive damages in the territory of north Palestine. Being located away from the main commercial and trade routes, he was able to accumulate great power, which was initially unnoticed by Egypt, who remained an ally of Assyria and thereby sought to control Palestine against the threats of Babylonia and Media. However, his aims evidently became conspicuous in his attempts to gain Meggido, through which a main road went. This, no doubt, was perceived as an apparent severance of ties with Egypt, which caught their attention, and led to his death in battle at Meggido in 609 B.C.E. at the hands of Pharaoh Necho.[47]

The Fall of the Southern Kingdom[48]

After Josiah's death Egypt controlled Palestine and parts of Syria for only a short time (2 Kgs. 24:7) and was eventually supplanted by Nebuchadnezzar in 605 B.C.E., who unimpededly moved through Syria-Palestine to Egypt and destroyed the Egyptian army (Hab. 1:5-10). His concern was to secure the Babylonian frontier from Egyptian threats. However, in 601/600 B.C.E.

Nebuchadnezzar suffered a defeat by Pharaoh Necho of Egypt, who then invaded the southern coast and took Gaza (Jer. 47:1). With the withdrawal of the Babylonians, Jehoiakim, son of Josiah,[49] obviously sided with Egypt against Jeremiah's faction, which, being pro-Babylonian, interpreted the imminent catastrophe at the hands of the Babylonians as the punishment of YHWH (Jer. 24f, 27-29, 37-38)[50] and thereby endorsed surrender to or compliance with the Babylonians. Nevertheless, Nebuchadnezzar resurged in 599 B.C.E., marched through Hatti in 598 B.C.E., and laid siege to Jerusalem in 597 B.C.E. Jehoiakim died before the city was surrendered and his son Jehoiakin who succeeded him and reigned only three months, surrendered, preventing the pillaging of Jerusalem (2 Kgs. 24:11).[51] Jehoiakin was deported and replaced by another son of Josiah, Mattaniah, renamed Zedekiah. A significant number of persons, including the aristocracy[52] and the skilled workers, were deported (2 Kgs. 24:14, 16; Jer. 52:28). Though the total population of Judah was not exiled, its territory was somewhat decimated.[53] This marked the first siege and conquest of Jerusalem.

In 595 B.C.E. Elam challenged Babylonia and was defeated, prompting another occurrence of uprisings in the west. This probably was sponsored again by Egypt and included Judah. However, it was squelched by Nebuchadnezzar in 594 B.C.E., when he came to Hatti. Zedekiah, then, went to Babylon to assure the king of his vassal status (cf. Jer. 51:59-64). At this time, Ezekiel made his debut as a prophet (chs. 1-3), interpreting the domination of Judah by Babylonia as the punishment of YHWH for repeated idolatry (cf. chs. 8-11, especially 8:3, 7, 14, 16; 9:3, 9-10; 10:3-5, 18-19; 11:23; cf. 48:35),[54] thereby unknowingly endorsing the views of Jeremiah (Jer. 24f, 27-29, 37-38) and somewhat engendering acceptance of Babylonian domination. After a brief period, Zedekiah rebelled, joining with Egypt, which marched to Phoenicia in 591 B.C.E. No coalition materialized, and thus Judah felt the full force of the Babylonians, as the latter invaded Palestine in 589 B.C.E. and besieged Jerusalem in 588 B.C.E., meeting its first opposition. Earthen ramps were put up around the city, preventing escape (2 Kgs. 25:1), as the Babylonians attacked from the west, while the Edomites attacked from the south.[55] The siege lasted about a year and a half, as the Babylonians isolated Jerusalem, cutting off communications and supplies (cf. Jer. 32:6-15; 39:3). Once a breach was made and the Babylonians started to enter, Zedekiah and his entourage fled, only to be caught, then blinded after his sons were killed before his eyes, and taken captive to Babylon (2 Kgs. 25:6; Jer. 39:5).[56] Jerusalem was thoroughly destroyed and all items of value were confiscated as booty (2 Kgs. 25:4-7; Jer. 39:8; 52:14, 17-19). This marked, not only the second siege and conquest of Jerusalem, but the destruction of the Davidic kingdom of Judah.

As a result of the Babylonian destruction of Judah, the small territory of Judah was devastated, several members of the leading classes were killed, and a small number including craftsmen was deported (2 Kgs. 24:18 - 25:36; Jer. 40:1-6; 52:4-34). The lower classes were allowed to remain and to continue their existence within the guidelines of the new regime, particularly in light of the probability that the smaller towns and villages were untouched by the war. Gedaliah was appointed governor over Judah, having his residence at Mizpah (2 Kgs. 25:22; Jer. 40:5-7). He was murdered by a faction that possibly had affiliations with Ishmael (Jer. 40-41), prompting the Babylonians to campaign again in Palestine and Transjordan in 582 B.C.E., and probably Ishmael's group to escape to Egypt. It is this group that forced Jeremiah and Baruch to go with them (Jer. 43:3-7). At this time Moab and Ammon were besieged and destroyed, while Edom, a Babylonian ally from 587 B.C.E., was circumvented. Though Nebuchadnezzar may have threatened Egypt in 569 B.C.E., it is probable that an agreement was reached that gave Pharaoh Ahmose a free hand.[57] Most importantly, the remnant of Judah, both deported and remaining in the land, lived in colonies.

Jewish colonialism, then, consisted of several features that continued throughout and beyond the biblical period, with the exception of the Hasmonean Period. First, all of the Jews were not exiled, but only the upper class. So, from 586 to 63 B.C.E. there were a Jewish community in Palestine and parallel communities of Jews widely dispersed. In other words, the situation of the Jews reflected two components: extensive settlement or colonization in foreign lands; and subservience to the political dominion of the larger empires.[58] This twofold situation produced a complex of double loyalties and jurisdictions that tended to run at cross-purposes. Tension developed from the concern to maintain their identity as Jews and to satisfy the demands of the particular overlords, under whose supervision they lived. Because of the deportation of the Aaronite priests, whose absence probably was not mourned by the remaining Jews, and probably the variety of local traditions, including those of the Levites, this tension was acutely felt. This resulted in the birth of Judaism, which emerged in a religiocultural identity that cross-sected location, as the Yahwistic traditions of the Northern Kingdom and the Southern Kingdom were collected, compiled, and reinterpreted in light of the exile. Also, the early traditions were transformed in order to address the prevalent circumstances of the Jews, specifically the catastrophe of the exile. Here, the exile was interpreted as the fulfillment of the prophetic messages, which declared the imminent punishment of YHWH for repeated disloyalty to the Israelite standards[59] (cf. Ezek. 8-11, especially 8:3, 7, 14, 16; 9:3, 9-10; 10:3-5, 18-19; 11:23; cf. 48:35; Jer. 23-24). At this point, the prophetic messages were collected and compiled. This process included sequencing and editing of the messages, whereby they were appropriated for use by later generations.[60] Prophecy gradually began to cease. The contextual particulars in which prophecy occurred had disappeared. That is, the institution of the monarchy was destroyed, and thus the correlating phenomenon of prophecy had no occasion as before to operate. Now, the messages of unconditional judgment were transformed to conditional calls to repentance and later, during the end of the exile, oracles of salvation and of blessings[61] would be announced in the name of YHWH, as new circumstances arose. The Deuteronomistic History (DH) was written during this time, presenting an apologetic theodicy in order to defend the justness/justice of YHWH, and thereby explain the exile as the result of the people's continual refusal to obey Torah, when constantly confronted with it. Its criteria were faithfulness to YHWH evidenced in abandonment of idolatry and maintenance of Jerusalem as the sole, cult center. Its tone was hopeful, that is, according to DH judgment was not the last word of YHWH or history was to be understood as the accomplishment of YHWH's Word as proclaimed by the prophets (cf. Deut. 4:29-31; 18:9-22; 30:1-10; 1 Kgs. 8:46-53).[62] Being Southern and exilic, DH contributed significantly to the creation of Judaism by endorsing Davidic-Zionistic Yahwism minus a monarchy, in order to maintain communal continuity. Third, older customs now grew in prominence and became commemorative vehicles.[63] The custom of Sabbath rest (Gen. 1; Exod. 20:8-11; 23:12; 34:21; 35:2-3; Lev. 23:3; Deut. 5:12-15; et al) became the symbol of sanctification of time and presence with YHWH. Since temple worship was eliminated along with the monarchical administration, local cults and customs were revived. The custom of circumcision (Exod. 4:24-26; Gen. 17:9-14, 23-27) became scrupulously practiced by the paterfamilias and symbolized covenant with YHWH, that is, male members' allegiance or loyalty to the Israelite ideology and lifestyle.[64] Dietary laws ordered daily life, as possible food items were categorized according to a concern for purity and distinction from the prevalent habits of sacrifice and eating within the foreign cultures.[65] Inevitably, a pronounced individualism emerged, as the traditions were democratized and universalized for implementation in the diverse circumstances in which the Jews found themselves. Fourth, and closely related to the previous, a Yahwistic canon continued to emerge. Heretofore, the written, Yahwistic traditions were created at the hands of monarchical personnel and used as political propaganda. Now, these traditions were collected, revised, and used, minus a monarchy and temple, to reconstruct Israelite communities in contradistinction to the extenuating circumstances and the foreign influences that they encountered.[66] This task work necessitated some, regular assemblies, in which the traditions were read, discussed, and interpreted. Thus, the origin of the synagogue is posited in this period, though there is no specific mention of such in the literature from this period.[67] Such institutions marked attempts to counter the foreign influences, particularly cults, that competed for the Jews' allegiance, offering obvious benefits to those who assimilated. Indeed, such assimilation occurred, as evidenced by the temple to YHWH at Elephantine, Egypt and the adoption of Babylonian names.[68] Assimilation must be seen, then, as the mechanism of survival for the Jews, which resulted in the rise to prominence of the Jewish centers in Egypt and Babylonia during the post-biblical periods and their exploitation by the *Jesus* movement during the first century C.E.

Chapter Synopsis:
The Key Dates

9th cent. B.C.E. Rise to Power of the Assyrians
8th cent. B.C.E. Decline of Damascus and Rise of Northern Kingdom under Jeroboam II
745-727 B.C.E. Reign of Tiglath-pileser III of Assyria
733 B.C.E. Syro-Ephraimite War

Causes:
1. threat of the Assyrians
2. threat of the coalition of Damascus and Northern Kingdom to the Southern Kingdom for the latter not supporting war-efforts against Assyria

Developments:
1. destruction of the Northern Kingdom or Israel
2. dispersement or deportation of northern Israelites

Effects:
1. Southern Kingdom or Judah makes alliance with Assyria and becomes an Assyrian vassal [2 Kgs. 16]
2. Isaiah of Jerusalem counsels against foreign alliances and predicts the collapse of the opposing coalition [Isa. 7; cf. also 20:1-6; 30:1-5; 31:1-3]
3. Damascus is conquered in 732 B.C.E.
4. Northern Kingdom or Israel is subjected to Assyria, later ceased paying tribute in 727 B. C.E. under Hoshea, and finally fell to the Assyrians in 721 B.C.E.

Interpretations:
1. fall of the Northern Kingdom as punishment by YHWH for idolatry [2 Kgs. 17]
2. sparing of the Southern Kingdom by YHWH for the sake of His promise to David [2 Sam. 7; 1 Kgs. 11:12, 13, 32, 34, 36; 15:4; 2 Kgs. 8:19; 19:34; 20:6]
3. universalism of YHWH's sovereignty [cf. Amos 1-4; Hos. 11; Jer. 1:11-19] as argued by the Yahwistic prophets

733-705 B.C.E. Southern Kingdom or Judah as Assyrian Vassal
720 B.C.E. Uprisings in Syria-Palestine sponsored by Egypt are suppressed
705 B.C.E. Hezekiah's Reforms or Revolution

Causes:
1. XXV Egyptian Dynasty comes to power and sponsors uprisings in Palestine
2. desire for freedom or self-determination

Developments:
1. decrease of territorial base of Southern Kingdom
2. increased association of YHWH with Jerusalem [proto-deuteronomistic revision of JE, i.e., Gen. 20:18; 21:33; 22:14-19; 28:21b; 30:18aβ; Exod. 9:30; 17:8-16; 22:17-30; 23:1-33; 24:13aβ; 14]

Effects:
1. temporary removal of vassal status under the Assyrians
2. re-kindling of old traditional hopes
3. loss of all territory of Southern Kingdom except Jerusalem and heavy payment of tribute
4. renewed subjection to Assyria (701-626 B.C.E.)

Interpretations:
1. survival of Jerusalem as deliverance of city by YHWH and birth of conception of 'insurmountability' of Jerusalem [2 Kgs. 18-19; especially 19:20-37]
2. positive assessment of Hezekiah by D-Hist. [2 Kgs. 18-20; especially 18:1-8]

625 B.C.E. Babylon asserts independence from Assyria
622 B.C.E. Josiah's Reforms or Revolution

Causes:
1. rise of Babylon as a formidable power
2. pre-occupation of Assyria and extensive spreading of its military forces in (multi-fronted) battle with the neo-Babylonians, the Medes, and the Scythians

Developments:
1. further elevation of Jerusalem as cult center, which began with David and Solomon and Hezekiah
2. beginning of hierarchization of Jerusalem priesthood

3. beginning of canonization of Scripture as Torah was used/enforced as 'written' rules of YHWH

Effects:
1. revocation of vassal relationship with Assyria, i.e., breach of treaty, removal of elements of Assyrian religion, cessation of tribute-payments, assertion of political independence
2. political enforcement of Yahwistic principles, i.e., effort at singularization of cult at Jerusalem, abolition of numerous local sanctuaries, covenant-renewal
3. eventual death of Josiah in battle against Pharaoh Necho of Egypt, an ally of Assyria, [609 B.C.E.]
4. extension of territory in the direction of the Northern Kingdom

Interpretations:
1. positive assessment of Josiah by D-Hist. [2 Kgs. 22-23; especially 23:21-25]
2. failure of revolt due to sins of Manasseh [2 Kgs. 23:26-27]

587 B.C.E. Fall of the Southern Kingdom or Judah to the Babylonians

Causes:
1. fall of Assyria to the Babylonians in 610 B.C.E.
2. need to secure Babylonian frontier from Egyptian threats
3. revolution of Judah under Zedekiah after initial vassalization in 598 B.C.E.

Developments:
1. birth of Judaism
2. beginning of Jewish Colonialism as extensive settlements in foreign lands and Palestine and as subservience of all Jews to the political dominion of the stronger empires

Effects:
1. production of a complex structure of double loyalties and jurisdictions that tended to run at cross-purposes
2. establishment of an identity that cross-sected location
3. mixture of Israelites with foreign peoples is continued
4. establishment of prominent centers in Egypt and Babylon
5. elevated esteem for Jerusalem and Palestine as home
6. destruction of temple of Solomon and palace of southern kings
7. deportation of the aristocracy

8. canonical use of Yahwistic traditions

Interpretations:
1. Shabbat rest as symbol of sanctification of time and presence with YHWH [cf. Gen. 1; Exod. 20:8-11; 23:12; 34:21; 35:2-3; Lev. 23:3, et al; Deut. 5:12-15]
2. circumcision as symbol of covenant with YHWH [cf. Exod. 4:24-26; Gen. 17:9-14, 23-27]
3. exile as punishment of YHWH for unfaithfulness and as fulfillment of the prophetic messages [cf. Ezek. 8:3, 7, 14, 16; 9:3, 9-10; 10:3-5, 18-19; 11:23; 43:1-2; 48:35]
4. Babylon as instrument of YHWH [cf. Jer. 24f, 27-29, 37-38]

The Selected Interpretations
#1: The Fall of the Northern Kingdom as Punishment by YHWH for Idolatry [2 Kgs. 17]

#2: The Sparing of the Southern Kingdom by YHWH for the sake of His Promise to David [2 Sam. 7; 1 Kgs. 11:12, 13, 32, 34, 36; 15:4; 2 Kgs. 8:19; 19:34; 20:6]

A. Perspectives:
    1. Speaker: the Southern, or Zionistic, Yahwists
    2. Writer: Deuteronomistic Historian [DH]

B. Addressees:
    1. of the Speaker: the sympathizers with the Northern (Mosaic-Sinaitic) Yahwists that were in, or the proponents, of the Southern Yahwistic regime
    2. of the Writer:
        a. the exilic Judeans including the Judean sympathizers with the early (Mosaic-Sinaitic) Yahwists
        b. the Northern Yahwists or the Samaritans

C. Contexts:
    1. of the Speaker:
        a. the aftermath of the destruction of the Northern Kingdom or Israel by the Assyrians
        b. the continuance of the Southern Kingdom or Judah as an Assyrian vassal
    2. of the Writer: the exile and the demise of the Judean (and last Yahwistic) monarchy

D. Issues:
   1. of the Speaker:
      a. national security, i.e., "public relations"
      b. ideological contamination, i.e., violation of the constitution and handling of Yahwistic diversity
   2. of the Writer:
      a. sanity, i.e., comprehension of the national crisis/catastrophe
      b. management of cultural diversity

E. Purposes:
   1. of the Speaker:
      a. solicitation of the remnants of the Northern Yahwists to join the South
      b. discouragement of rebellions against the Southern Kingdom's policy, which would signify revolt against Assyrian domination
      c. explanation of the Southern Kingdom's survival, i.e., "public relations"
      d. denigration of the Northern Kingdom's ideology (i.e., Mosaic-Sinaitic Yahwism) and anti-Assyrian policy
      e. explanation of the Yahwistic diversity within the territory of the former Northern Kingdom
   2. of the Writer:
      a. explanation of the national crisis as punishment for departure from the early Yahwistic orthodoxy, and the subsequent future possibilities
      b. engendering of hope through endorsement of Davidic-Zionistic Yahwism
      c. explanation and endorsement of the continuation of the Davidic lineage and right to administrative privilege through qualified criticism
      d. explanation and attempt at reconciliation of Yahwistic diversity

F. Presuppositions:
   1. of the Speaker:
      a. YHWH as being with David [1 Sam. 16:1, 12f, 18; 17:37, 45-48; 18:12, 14, 28-29; 23:14; 30:6; 2 Sam. 3:1; 5:10; 8:6, 14]
      b. YHWH as King/Sovereign of Israel and Judah
      c. King as Adopted Son of YHWH and the Eternality of the Davidic Dynasty [2 Sam. 7]
      d. the oneness of YHWH, i.e., the political solidarity of Yahwistic monarchalism
      e. the historicity of YHWH's activity
   2. of the Writer:

    a. YHWH as being with David [1 Sam. 16:1, 12f, 18; 17:37, 45-48; 18:12, 14, 28-29; 23:14; 30:6; 2 Sam. 3:1; 5:10; 8:6, 14]

    b. YHWH as Universal Sovereign

    c. King as Adopted Son of YHWH and the Eternality of the Davidic Dynasty [2 Sam. 7]

    d. the oneness of YHWH, i.e., exclusive Yahwistic monotheism and the political solidarity of Yahwistic colonialism

    e. Zionistic Yahwism as the Legitimate (Sole) Heir of early Yahwism

    f. the historicity of YHWH's activity

    g. Jerusalem (or Mount Zion) as the City of YHWH and the Sole Yahwistic Cult Center

#3: The Universalism of YHWH's Sovereignty as argued by the Yahwistic Prophets [cf. Isa. 7; 18; Jer. 1:11-19; 7:1-15; 18:1-12; Amos 1-4; 7; Hos. 4; 11; Hab. 1-3]

A. Perspectives:
    1. the proponents of early (Mosaic-Sinaitic) Yahwism
    2. the proponents of a Southern (Davidic-Zionistic) Yahwism that emphasized the early traditions

B. Addressees:
    1. the Yahwistic kings and their courts
    2. the supporters of the Yahwistic monarchies
    3. the masses/populace that was exploited and soured by the policies of the Yahwistic monarchies

C. Contexts:
    1. the debut of national crises/catastrophes
    2. the domestic affects (usually, negative or oppressive) of foreign policy within the Yahwistic kingdoms

D. Issues:
    1. national security, i.e., "public relations"
    2. ideological contamination, i.e., violation of the constitution and handling of Yahwistic diversity
    3. determination of the most appropriate courses in foreign (and domestic) policy
    4. sanity, i.e., comprehension of the national crises/catastrophes
    5. management of cultural diversity

E. Purposes:
   1. advocacy of the earlier (usually, anti-monarchical), and partisan, strands of Yahwism in contradistinction to, and/or as criticism of, the extant monarchical strands of Yahwism, sometimes anti-government activities (e.g., conspiracy, censure, etc.)
   2. representation of those who are dominated/exploited by the monarchical policies, i.e., the Yahwistic tribal cultures, the defenseless, the vulnerable
   3. counsel of the Yahwistic kings regarding foreign and domestic (usually, military) policy
   4. explanation of the national circumstances (i.e., prevalent Yahwistic diversity or cultural diversity) and crises/catastrophes as punishment for departure from the early Yahwistic orthodoxy, and the subsequent future possibilities
   5. explanation, and attempt at reconciliation, of Yahwistic diversity

F. Presuppositions:
   1. YHWH as Warrior, Deliverer, and Judge
   2. YHWH as King/Sovereign of Israel and Judah
   3. the oneness of YHWH, i.e., the political solidarity of Yahwistic monarchalism
   4. Exclusive Yahwistic Monotheism
   5. the historicity of YHWH's activity

#4: The Survival of Jerusalem as Deliverance by YHWH and the Birth of the Conception of the 'Insurmountability' of Jerusalem [2 Kgs. 18-19, especially 19:20-37]

#5: The Positive Assessment of Hezekiah by DH [2 Kgs. 18-20, especially 18:1-8]

A. Perspectives:
   1. Speaker: the Southern, or Zionistic, Yahwists
   2. Writer: Deuteronomistic Historian [DH]

B. Addressees:
   1. of the Speaker: the sympathizers with the Northern (Mosaic-Sinaitic) Yahwists that were in, or the proponents, of the Southern Yahwistic regime
   2. of the Writer:
      a. the exilic Judeans including the Judean sympathizers with the early (Mosaic-Sinaitic) Yahwists

    b.   the Northern Yahwists or the Samaritans

C. Contexts:
    1. of the Speaker:
        a.   the decrease of the territorial base of the Southern Kingdom or Judah by the Assyrians
        b.   the continuance of the Southern Kingdom or Judah as an Assyrian vassal, specifically Jerusalem as a City-State
    2. of the Writer: the exile and the demise of the Judean (and last Yahwistic) monarchy

D. Issues:
    1. of the Speaker:
        a.   national unity, i.e., "public relations"
        b.   morale
    2. of the Writer:
        a.   sanity, i.e., comprehension of the national crisis/catastrophe
        b.   management of cultural diversity

E. Purposes:
    1. of the Speaker:
        a.   consolidation of the remnants of the Southern Kingdom
        b.   discouragement of rebellions against the Southern Kingdom's policy, which would signify revolt against Assyrian domination, while fostering a "propaganda victory"
        c.   explanation of the Southern Kingdom's territorial decrease and survival
        d.   positive enhancement of the image of Hezekiah as a counter to the prevalent public perceptions
    2. of the Writer:
        a.   explanation of the national crisis as punishment for departure from the early Yahwistic orthodoxy, and the subsequent future possibilities
        b.   engendering of hope through endorsement of Davidic-Zionistic Yahwism
        c.   explanation and endorsement of the continuation of the Davidic lineage and right to administrative privilege through qualified criticism
        d.   explanation and attempt at reconciliation of Yahwistic diversity
        e.   approval of Hezekiah's efforts toward achieving freedom/self-determination

F. Presuppositions:
1. of the Speaker:
    a. YHWH as being with David [1 Sam. 16:1, 12f, 18; 17:37, 45-48; 18:12, 14, 28-29; 23:14; 30:6; 2 Sam. 3:1; 5:10; 8:6, 14]
    b. YHWH as King/Sovereign of Judah
    c. King as Adopted Son of YHWH and the Eternality of the Davidic Dynasty [2 Sam. 7]
    d. the oneness of YHWH, i.e., the political solidarity of Yahwistic monarchalism
    e. the historicity of YHWH's activity
    f. Zionistic Yahwism as the Legitimate (Sole) Heir of early Yahwism
    g. Jerusalem (or Mount Zion) as the City of YHWH and the Sole Yahwistic Cult Center
2. of the Writer:
    a. YHWH as being with David [1 Sam. 16:1, 12f, 18; 17:37, 45-48; 18:12, 14, 28-29; 23:14; 30:6; 2 Sam. 3:1; 5:10; 8:6, 14]
    b. YHWH as Universal Sovereign
    c. King as Adopted Son of YHWH and the Eternality of the Davidic Dynasty [2 Sam. 7]
    d. the oneness of YHWH, i.e., exclusive Yahwistic monotheism and the political solidarity of Yahwistic colonialism
    e. Zionistic Yahwism as the Legitimate (Sole) Heir of early Yahwism
    f. the historicity of YHWH's activity
    g. Jerusalem (or Mount Zion) as the City of YHWH and the Sole Yahwistic Cult Center

#6: The Positive Assessment of Josiah by DH [2 Kgs. 22-23, especially 23:21-25]

#7: The Failure of the Revolt as Due to the Sins of Manasseh [2 Kgs. 23:26-27]

A. Perspectives:
1. Speaker: the Southern, or Zionistic, Yahwists
2. Writer: Deuteronomistic Historian [DH]

B. Addressees:
1. of the Speaker: the sympathizers with the Northern (Mosaic-Sinaitic) Yahwists that were in, or the proponents, of the Southern Yahwistic regime
2. of the Writer:
    a. the exilic Judeans including the Judean sympathizers with the

early (Mosaic-Sinaitic) Yahwists

    b. the Northern Yahwists or the Samaritans

C. Contexts:
1. of the Speaker:
    a. the decrease of the territorial base of the Southern Kingdom or Judah by the Assyrians
    b. the continuance of the Southern Kingdom or Judah as an Assyrian vassal, specifically Jerusalem as a City-State
    c. the defeat, and murder, of Josiah in battle against Pharaoh Necho
2. of the Writer: the exile and the demise of the Judean (and last Yahwistic) monarchy

D. Issues:
1. of the Speaker:
    a. national unity, i.e., "public relations"
    b. morale
    c. management of Yahwistic diversity
2. of the Writer:
    a. sanity, i.e., comprehension of the national crisis/catastrophe
    b. management of cultural diversity

E. Purposes:
1. of the Speaker:
    a. consolidation of the remnants, and the diverse (Yahwistic) factions, of the Southern Kingdom
    b. discouragement of rebellions against the Southern Kingdom's policy, which would signify revolt against Assyrian domination
    c. explanation of the defeat, and the murder, of Josiah
    d. positive enhancement of the image of Josiah as a counter to the prevalent public perceptions
2. of the Writer:
    a. explanation of the national crisis as punishment for departure from the early Yahwistic orthodoxy, and the subsequent future possibilities
    b. engendering of hope through endorsement of Davidic-Zionistic Yahwism
    c. explanation and endorsement of the continuation of the Davidic lineage and right to administrative privilege through qualified criticism
    d. explanation and attempt at reconciliation of Yahwistic diversity
    e. approval of Josiah's efforts toward achieving freedom/self-determination

F. Presuppositions:
    1. of the Speaker:
        a. YHWH as being with David [1 Sam. 16:1, 12f, 18; 17:37, 45-48; 18:12, 14, 28-29; 23:14; 30:6; 2 Sam. 3:1; 5:10; 8:6, 14]
        b. YHWH as Universal Sovereign
        c. King as Adopted Son of YHWH and the Eternality of the Davidic Dynasty [2 Sam. 7]
        d. the oneness of YHWH, i.e., the political solidarity of Yahwistic monarchalism
        e. the historicity of YHWH's activity
        f. Zionistic Yahwism as the Legitimate (Sole) Heir of early Yahwism
        g. Jerusalem (or Mount Zion) as the City of YHWH and the Sole Yahwistic Cult Center
    2. of the Writer:
        a. YHWH as being with David [1 Sam. 16:1, 12f, 18; 17:37, 45-48; 18:12, 14, 28-29; 23:14; 30:6; 2 Sam. 3:1; 5:10; 8:6, 14]
        b. YHWH as Universal Sovereign
        c. King as Adopted Son of YHWH and the Eternality of the Davidic Dynasty [2 Sam. 7]
        d. the oneness of YHWH, i.e., exclusive Yahwistic monotheism and the political solidarity of Yahwistic colonialism
        e. Zionistic Yahwism as the Legitimate (Sole) Heir of early Yahwism
        f. the historicity of YHWH's activity
        g. Jerusalem (or Mount Zion) as the City of YHWH and the Sole Yahwistic Cult Center

#8: Shabbat Rest as Symbol of Sanctification of Time and Presence with YHWH [cf. Gen. 1; Exod. 20:8-11, 23:12, 34:21, 35:2-3; Lev. 23:3, et al; Deut. 5:12-15]

#9: Circumcision as Symbol of Covenant with YHWH [cf. Exod. 4:24-26; Gen. 17:9-14, 23-27]

A. Perspectives:
    1. Speaker: the Southern, or Zionistic, Yahwists
    2. Writer: the Holiness School [HS]

B. Addressees:
    1. of the Speaker: the proponents of the Southern Yahwistic regime
    2. of the Writer:
        a. the post-exilic Judeans or Southern Yahwists

    b.   the Northern Yahwists or the Samaritans

C. Contexts:
1. of the Speaker:
    a.   the re-organization of the Southern Kingdom or Judah during Hezekiah's revolution
    b.   the alliance with Babylon and others against Assyria
2. of the Writer: the aftermath of the Babylonian exile and the post-exilic restoration of Judah

D. Issues:
1. of the Speaker: synchronization with the Babylonian regime
    a.   national unity and security
    b.   management of Yahwistic diversity
2. of the Writer:
    a.   management of cultural diversity
    b.   reconstruction of Judah (particularly, Jerusalem) as a Persian borderpost on the front against Egypt

E. Purposes:
1. of the Speaker:
    a.   consolidation of the remnants and the diverse (Yahwistic) factions of the Northern Kingdom
    b.   organization of the revolution against Assyria
    c.   re-definition, and re-identification, of community according to Southern Yahwism
2. of the Writer:
    a.   establishment of a transcultural identity according to Southern-Zionistic strands of Yahwism, i.e., re-definition, and re identification, of community
    b.   establishment of relevant symbols from traditional Yahwistic customs, that can transcend location
    c.   explanation and endorsement of the continuation of the Davidic lineage and right to administrative privilege through a theocracy
    d.   explanation and attempt at reconciliation of Yahwistic diversity

F. Presuppositions:
1. of the Speaker:
    a.   YHWH as being with David [1 Sam. 16:1, 12f, 18; 17:37, 45-48; 18:12, 14, 28-29; 23:14; 30:6; 2 Sam. 3:1; 5:10; 8:6, 14]
    b.   YHWH as Universal Sovereign

    c.   King as Adopted Son of YHWH and the Eternality of the Davidic Dynasty [2 Sam. 7]

    d.   the oneness of YHWH, i.e., the political solidarity of Yahwistic monarchalism

    e.   the historicity of YHWH's activity

    f.   Zionistic Yahwism as the Legitimate (Sole) Heir of early Yahwism

    g.   Jerusalem (or Mount Zion) as the City of YHWH and the Sole Yahwistic Cult Center

    h.   YHWH as Creator-Savior

2. of the Writer:

    a.   YHWH as Universal Sovereign

    b.   the oneness of YHWH, i.e., exclusive Yahwistic monotheism and the political solidarity of Yahwistic colonialism

    c.   Zionistic Yahwism minus the monarchy as the Legitimate (Sole) Heir of early Yahwism

    d.   the historicity of YHWH's activity

    e.   Jerusalem (or Mount Zion) as the City of YHWH and the Sole Yahwistic Cult Center

    f.   YHWH as Creator-Savior

#10: Babylon as Instrument of YHWH [cf. Jer. 24f, 27-29, 37-38]

#11: Exile as Punishment of YHWH for Unfaithfulness and as Fulfillment of the Prophetic Messages [cf. Ezek. 8:3, 7, 14, 16; 9:3, 9-10; 10:3-5, 18-19; 11:23; 43:1-2; 48:35]

A. Perspectives:
1. Jeremiah: the moderate Southern, or Zionistic, Yahwist, i.e., DH
2. Ezekiel: the progressive/reformed Southern, or Zionistic, Yahwist, i.e., P

B. Addressees:
1. of Jeremiah: the proponents of the Southern Yahwistic regime
2. of Ezekiel: the exilic Judean aristocracy

C. Contexts:
1. of Jeremiah: the impending attack of Babylon
2. of Ezekiel: the Babylonian exile

D. Issues:
1. of Jeremiah:
    a.   national unity and security

      b.   determination of foreign policy, i.e., alliance with Egypt against Babylon or surrender to Babylon

  2. of Ezekiel:

      a.   maintenance of communal identity

      b.   sanity, i.e., comprehension of the national crisis/catastrophe

E. Purposes:

  1. of Jeremiah: endorsement of surrender to and alliance with Babylon

  2. of Ezekiel:

      a.   explanation of the destruction of Judah by Babylon as the result of ideological contamination (i.e., violation of the constitution)

      b.   engendering of hope through endorsement of Davidic-Zionistic Yahwism

      c.   explanation and endorsement of the continuation of the Davidic lineage and right to administrative privilege through a theocracy

F. Presuppositions:

  1. of Jeremiah:

      a.   YHWH as being with David [1 Sam. 16:1, 12f, 18; 17:37, 45-48; 18:12, 14, 28-29; 23:14; 30:6; 2 Sam. 3:1; 5:10; 8:6, 14]

      b.   YHWH as Universal Sovereign

      c.   King as Adopted Son of YHWH and the Eternality of the Davidic Dynasty [2 Sam. 7]

      d.   the oneness of YHWH, i.e., the political solidarity of Yahwistic monarchalism

      e.   the historicity of YHWH's activity

      f.   Zionistic Yahwism as the Legitimate (Sole) Heir of early Yahwism

  2. of Ezekiel:

      a.   YHWH as Universal Sovereign

      b.   the oneness of YHWH, i.e., exclusive Yahwistic monotheism and the political solidarity of Yahwistic colonialism

      c.   Zionistic Yahwism minus the monarchy as the Legitimate (Sole) Heir of early Yahwism, i.e., Yahwistic theocracy

      d.   the historicity of YHWH's activity

      e.   Jerusalem (or Mount Zion) as the City of YHWH and the Sole Yahwistic Cult Center

      f.   YHWH as Creator-Savior

Endnotes

1. J. Alberto Soggin, *An Introduction to the History of Israel and Judah* (trans. John Bowden; Valley Forge, PA: Trinity International, 1993), 209; Gösta Ahlström, *The History of Ancient Palestine from the Palaeolithic Period to Alexander's Conquest* (ed. Diana Edelman; JSOT Sup. 146; England: Sheffield, 1993), 562-568. Only the dates of Soggin are cited here.

2. Burke O. Long, *1 Kings* (FOTL; Grand Rapids, MI: Eerdmans, 1984), 160f. The *introductory regnal resumé* for the Southern kings has an accession date given by a synchronistic accession formula; the king's age; a statement on the length and place of his reign; the name of the queen mother; and a theological appraisal. The *introductory regnal resumé* for the Northern kings has a notice which provides an accession date given by a synchronistic formula, together with the length and place of his reign, sometimes having these separate; and a theological appraisal. The *concluding regnal resumé* for the Southern kings has a citation formula; notices of the death and burial (usually a death and burial formula); and a notice of the successor given with a succession formula.

3. Soggin, *History*, 209f; Ahlström, *History*, 564-567. Ahlström sees the Egyptian involvement as a reflection of post-exilic problems, and not historical. However, the support of Egypt could well give weight to Asa's request for severance of the treaty between Damascus and Israel and formation of a new alliance with Judah.

4. Soggin, *History*, 210; Ahlström, *History*, 565-568.

5. Included in these texts are the legends of Eliyahu (1 Kgs. 17-19; 2 Kgs. 1:2-17), the legends of Elisha (1 Kgs. 19; 2 Kgs. 2:1-25; 3:4-8, 15; 4; 13:14-21), the account of Ahab's Aramean wars (1 Kgs. 20, 22), the war against Moab (2 Kgs. 3), and another Aramean war (2 Kgs. 6:8-23). For reading the Eliyahu legends, see Robert L. Cohn, "The Literary Logic of 1 Kings 17-19," *Journal of Biblical Literature* 101 (1982): 333-350.

6. Soggin, *History*, 212-214, 216-220; Ahlström, *History*, 568-579; Siegfried H. Horn, "The Divided Monarchy," in *Ancient Israel: A Short History from Abraham to the Roman Destruction of the Temple* (ed. Hershel Shanks; Washington, D. C.: Biblical Archaeology Society/Englewood Cliffs, NJ: Prentice-Hall, 1988), 120-123. One of the most outstanding campaigns of Shalmaneser III of Assyria is the battle of Qarqar in 853 B.C.E., in which the allied armies of Syria and Palestine were able to arrest his invasion. See "Ashurnasirpal II (883-859): Expedition to the Lebanon," translated by A. Leo Oppenheim (*ANET*, 188); "Shalmaneser III (858-824): The Fight Against the Aramean Coalition," translated by A. Leo Oppenheim (*ANET*, 188-192).

7. This reduction of Israel that was due to Hazael is attributed to YHWH (2 Kgs. 10:32).

8. Soggin, *History*, 222-224; Ahlström, *History*, 590-596, 604-606; Hannelis Schulte, "The End of the Omride Dynasty: Social-Ethical Observations on the Subject of Power and Violence," *Semeia* 66 (1994): 133-148.

9. Ahlström, *History*, 595f, 607-610.

10. Soggin, *History*, 225-228; Ahlström, *History*, 596-601. The alliance between the two Israelite kingdoms was symbolized by the marriage of Athaliah to Jehoram and the paralleling of the social situations in the two kingdoms, e.g., the influx of the cult of the Phoenician Baal.

11. Soggin, *History*, 217f; Ahlström, *History*, 585-588. E. Theodore Mullen, Jr. ["The Royal Dynastic Grant to Jehu and the Structure of the Book of Kings," *Journal of Biblical Literature* 107 [1988]: 193-206] argues that Dtr explains the dynasty of Jehu as the result of a limited "royal grant" [2 Kgs. 10:28-31] of the same unconditional type given to David, because of Jehu's compliance with the *tôrah* of YHWH, thereby accounting for its length yet maintaining condemnation of the northern kings [194, 195, 196 n. 12, 198, 206].

12. Soggin, *History*, 226f; Horn, "The Divided Monarchy," 126f; Ahlström, *History*, 612-614.

13. Bernard Goldstein and Alan Cooper, "The Festivals of Israel and Judah and the Literary History of the Pentateuch," *Journal of the American Oriental Society* 110 (1990): 20-22; idem, "Exodus and Massot in History and Tradition," *MAARAV* 8 (1992): 25. Goldstein and Cooper ("The Festivals") regard Exod. 23:10-19 as the Northern calendar and Exod. 34:18-26 as the Judean calendar that derives exegetically from the former. When the North subjugated the South, they reformed the calendar, introducing the Northern lunar determination of the festivals, de-emphasizing and replacing the fall enthronement festival with the harvest festival, displacing Months 2 and 8 with Months 1 and 7, and combining the *Mazzot* (מצות) of the North with the *Pesach* (פסח) in Judah, interweaving the etiologies of both (24). Here, the regulation of daily life, particularly the offerings, is at stake. Their basic point is that the history of the festivals, in the light of the political and religious interaction between the Northern kingdom and Judah during the eighth century B.C.E., is the crucial period of development (20). Also, they argue that *Mazzot* (מצות) has to be disengaged both conceptually and historically from the other two haggim, the "Canaanite" agricultural festivals of *Qazîr* (קציר) and *Asîph* (אסיף), since its association with the Exodus is primary and its significance lies in being a foundational festival of national identity, serving as cultic commemoration or re-enactment of the myth of national origin, the Exodus from Egypt. (22)

14. Horn, "The Divided Monarchy," 126f; Soggin, *History*, 228f; Ahlström, *History*, 617-620, 628f. Ahlström assumed that the Transjordan down to the Plains of Moab, Galilee, and the coastal area north of Philistia to

Carmel were regained, restoring control over the trade routes from Philistia up through Galilee and through Transjordan north of Moab to the borders of Damascus. For a overview of the eighth century B.C.E., see Philip J. King, "The Eighth, the Greatest of Centuries?" *Journal of Biblical Literature* 108 (1989): 3-15, especially 3-5, 7, 9, 10, 11, 13, 14.

15. Horn, "The Divided Monarchy," 126f; Soggin, *History*, 229-232; Ahlström, *History*, 620-628; King, "The Eighth, the Greatest of Centuries?" 7, 10, 11, 13. Uzziah extended the southern frontier as far as the Red Sea, fought against the Philistines and in the Transjordan, and strengthened the fortifications of Jerusalem, possibly sustaining successes against the Arabs, the Meunites, and the Ammonites.

16. Cf. Amos 2:6-7; 3:10, 15; 4:1; 5:7-13; 6:4-6; 7:10-17; 8:4-6; Hosea 2:8, 13, 17; 4:1-2, 8; 6:10; 9:1, 9. The beginning of the classical prophets is marked by the debut of Amos and Hosea and is characterized by the assertion of the universalism of YHWH's sovereignty, which counters the claims of foreign cults that YHWH is being defeated, when Israel and Judah suffer political or national demise. Here, they argue that the sovereignty of YHWH includes control of foreign nations and powers as His instruments of punishment of Israel and Judah, when they violate the covenant stipulations. Existentially and somewhat psychologically, these interpretations serve the purpose of preservation of sanity, and of promotion of ideological adherence in light of undergoing crises.

17. Ahlström, *History*, 628f.

18. Ahlström, *History*, 630f; "Tiglath-pileser III (744-727): Campaigns Against Syria and Palestine," translated by A. Leo Oppenheim (*ANET*, 193f).

19. Jeroboam II was succeeded by his son Zechariah (ca. 746-745 B.C.E.), who was killed by Shallum (ca. 745 B.C.E.), who in turn was killed by Menahem (ca. 745-738 B.C.E.). Menahem secured Israel by paying tribute to Tiglath-pileser, along with Rezin of Damascus. He was succeeded by his son Pekahiah (ca. 738-737 B.C.E.), who was deposed by Pekah, son of Remaliah (ca. 737-732 B.C.E.). Pekah reversed the policy of his predecessors and became anti-Assyrian. See Soggin, *History*, 238f; Ahlström, *History*, 631-632. Also, note that this impending disaster is perceived to be incited by YHWH (2 Kgs. 15:37).

20. Soggin, *History*, 238f; Ahlström, *History*, 631-633. Cf. 2 Kgs. 16; Isa. 7:1-7; 8:1-15; 10:27; 17:1-11; Hos. 5:1-7; 5:8-6:6; 8:7-10.

21. It is to be noted that Isaiah 1-39, including most of the prophetic collections, reflect domestic or foreign policy advice that was disregarded or not taken.

22. Ahlström, *History*, 631, 633f; Soggin, *History*, 239-243; Horn, "The Divided Monarchy," 129. In rebut of Ahaz, Isaiah (22:8-11; 28:1-14, 16-18; 30:15) contrasted the solid foundation of YHWH with the flimsy foundation that the administration sought to establish, that was based

upon political alliances [see J. J. M. Roberts, "Yahweh's Foundation in Zion (Isa. 28:16)," *Journal of Biblical Literature* 106 (1987): 27-45, especially 39-45].

23. Ahlström, *History*, 630f, 636, 640-644, 658, 662, 665f; Soggin, *History*, 240f.

24. Ahlström, *History*, 636-638; Soggin, *History*, 235f. Soggin notes that Assyrian vassalization occurred in three phases. First, it entailed limited sovereignty, a foreign policy of complete dependence upon Assyria, and exaction of heavy tribute. Rebellions were directly countered through military intervention, resulting in nomination of a pro-Assyrian ruler, drastic changes of the frontiers, incorporation of new territory, and redistribution of this land to loyal vassals. Third, if any opposition arose, it was put down, the remaining territory was incorporated into the Assyrian empire, an Assyrian governor was assigned to the area in replacement of its ruler, and the leading class was deported, while new ethnic groups that are loyal were imported. See Mordechai Cogan ("Judah under Assyrian Hegemony: A Re-examination of Imperialism and Religion," *Journal of Biblical Literature* 112 [1993]: 403-414), who argues that there is no clear evidence that imposition of the Assyrian cult was a regular feature of their domination, particularly in regard to vassal states, thus revealing a distinction in Assyrian policy toward provinces and vassal states (403-405).

25. Ahlström, *History*, 669f; cf. 640-644, 665f; Soggin, *History*, 242f.

26. Cf. K. Lawson Younger, Jr., "The Deportations of the Israelites," *Journal of Biblical Literature* 117 (1998): 201-227. Younger states: "There appears to have been a difference in the deportation policies of Tiglath-Pileser III and Sargon II in their dealings with the northern kingdom of Israel. Sargon II clearly conducted a more common Assyrian bidirectional deportation, deporting Israelites from Samaria and settling others there. However, Tiglath-Pileser III seems to have utilized a unidirectional deportation policy in his deportations of Israelites from Galilee, and possibly from Gilead and Dor. The reason for the difference between the two appears to be linked to the overarching Assyrian economic and military concerns regarding the Philistine coast and Egypt over against the separate economic and security concerns of Samaria. Both kings incorporated Israelite troops into the Assyrian army. The plight of the deportees apparently varied between minimal existence and treatment within the elite of Assyrian societal structure. One thing is certain: the impact of these two kings' policies was felt for many generations to come as evinced by the archaeological survey evidence and historical, textual data" (227; cf. 206, 215, 219, 221, 222f, 225f).

27. Ahlström, *History*, 636-638; cf. 676-680; Soggin, *History*, 235f; "Sargon II (721-705): The Fall of Samaria," translated by A. Leo Oppenheim (*ANET*, 195-198).

28. The fall of the Northern Kingdom was interpreted by DH as punishment by YHWH for idolatry (1 Kgs. 13:1-10; 2 Kgs. 17, especially vv. 7-18, 20-23, 34-40; 18:9-12; 23:17-20), while the survival of the Southern Kingdom was understood as the consequence of a promise that YHWH made to David, i.e., as being spared "on account of David" (lema'an dawid 'avdî למען דוד עבדי): 2 Sam. 7; 1 Kgs. 11:12, 13, 32, 34, 36; 15:4; 2 Kgs. 8:19; 19:34; 20:6). See Mordechai Cogan, "Israel in Exile—The View of a Josianic Historian," *Journal of Biblical Literature* 97 (1978): 40-44, especially 41, 43.

29. 2 Kgs. 15-23; Isa. 7; 20:1-6; 30:1-5; 31:1-3.

30. Ahlström, *History*, 675-684; Soggin, *History*, 244-246. Frank Crüsemann (*The Torah: Theology and Social History of Old Testament Law*, trans. Allan W. Mahnke. (Minneapolis: Fortress Press, 1996]) locates BC (Exod. 20:22-23:33 = Exod. 34:11-26 + Exod. 21f, the Jerusalem Code: ham-mishpatîm המשפטים) during this time, considering its authors to be the priests of the Jerusalem court (142, 166), who addressed the free individual landowners who headed clans (142, 189), regarding the conflicts between the two population groups and their religions that had ensued since the beginning of Assyrian domination and the competition among the Yahwistic shrines that ensued after the fall of the Northern Kingdom (120, 124, 126, 173-174). Specifically, they were concerned with the possible annihilation by the Assyrians (130), the absence of formalized responsibility and power, and the potential inclusion of any free males and aliens from the North (124, 184, 189), which evidently had resulted in lack of sympathy due to animosity, denial of justice to the poor (e.g., slavery) (154-159), exertion of pressure by the majority, and domination of justice by money and power (146, 154, 191). BC serves as meta-norms and a critical authority, that is intended to hinder the activities of the guilty, with a twofold message: (1) justice for the poor should not be perverted by the powerful and (2) partiality toward the weak in a lawsuit should not occur in court (190-191). This was achieved through radicalization and intensification of the understanding of older texts (128-129), parallel historicization of these texts (i.e., former instructions became/functioned as God's Word to the Israelites in the present situation [129-130]), and marginalization (i.e., separation from the non-Yahwistic Canaanites) (130-131).

31. Ahlström, *History*, 689-691, 701-704; Soggin, *History*, 248f; Horn, "The Divided Monarchy," 131-134. During this time Hezekiah had built a 1,749-foot tunnel in Jerusalem, from the Gihon Spring in the Kidron Valley to a lower pool inside the city, in order to secure his water supply in case of siege, and he promoted trade and agriculture (2 Kgs. 18:3-8).

32. This dating of P differs with those who follow the post-exilic dating of P [see, for example, Robert B. Coote [*In the Beginning: Creation and the*

Priestly History (Minneapolis: Fortress, 1991), 32, 36, 38, 41, 47, 49, 56, 85, 89, 95, 104, 108, 117-118, 132].

33. Goldstein and Cooper, "The Festivals," 25-30. Hezekiah postponed *Pesach* (מלך) until Month 2 (cf. 2 Chron. 30) as part of a Judean revival in reaction to R[JE], and in the fall, the old festival of Month 8, Day 10 was incorporated into the Davidide royal festival (25, 26). Originally, Month 2, Day 10 was the conventional Judean date for the heliacal rising of the Pleiades, which marked the New Year and the beginning of summer. The Judean festivals were conjoined to a mythic pattern of creation, flood, temple-building, and enthronement (cf. Gen. 2-9) (25). Month 2, Day 17 (Gen. 7:11-P)—"the cleaving of the well-springs of the Great Deep"— was associated with God's enthronement over the flood (Ps. 29:10), with the founding of the Temple "upon the seas" (Ps. 24:2), and with the Exodus event (Exod. 15) (13). There is the possibility that the existence of a festival complex in Month 2 corresponded to the fall festivals in Month 8, making the two halves of the year exactly symmetrical. (25) Solomon had subsumed the pastoral rites of Months 2 and 8 to his Temple ideology. The construction of his Temple began in Month 2 and ended in Month 8 (1 Kgs. 6:1, 37-38) (26). The principal commemoration of the Davidide enthronement was, then, reserved for the fall complex in Month 8 of *Teru'ah* (תרועה, *Kippurim* (כפרים), and *Sukkoth* (סכות) (26). So, *Sukkoth* (סכות) commemorated the establishment of the Davidide dynasty and its royal sanctuary on Month 8, Day 15 (Ps. 132), similar to Jeroboam, who sought to transfer it to the North (1 Kgs. 12:32-33) (26f). In sum, Hezekiah's attempt was to restore the authentic Judean traditions via commissioning P, a Jerusalemite priest, to revise R[JE] in the light of Hezekiah's reform program. The intent of P was to reestablish the authenticity and centrality of the Davidide cult in Jerusalem. Thus, the fundamental innovation of P was reinterpretation of the old Judean enthronement myth, i.e., establishment of a weekly cycle predicated on God's seven-day creation of the world instead of the annual cycle of flood and enthronement, thus asserting that the real basis for the scheme is authentic Judean cosmology (cf. bases in R[JE] for the 7-day scheme: Exod. 23:10-12, 15; 34:21) and interpretation of Exod. 23:12 and 34:21 as references to his weekly *Shabbat* (שבת) (30).

34. Ahlström, *History*, 690; Soggin, *History*, 249.

35. Soggin, *History*, 249; Ahlström, *History*, 692. According to Ahlström in 719 B.C.E. Sargon fought the Manneans and Urartu, and in 717 B.C.E. he marched against Carchemish and annexed it. In 715 B.C.E. Egypt was subjected, and forced to pay tribute, while Sargon settled Arabian tribes in Samaria. In 714 B.C.E. Sargon annexed Cilicia and made it a province. At this time, the demographic complexure of the Near East became more complex, and the Greek influences slowly increased.

36. Ahlström, *History*, 692f.
37. Ahlström, *History*, 694-696; Horn, "The Divided Monarchy," 134f; Soggin, *History*, 250f. Egypt began resurging under the XXV Ethiopian Dynasty, led by Pharaoh Shabako (713-698? B.C.E.) around 716 B.C.E., while Merodach-baladan had come back into power in Babylon around 703 B.C.E.
38. Ahlström, *History*, 689-691, 696-706; Soggin, *History*, 248f; Horn, "The Divided Monarchy," 131-134.
39. William H. Shea ["Sennacherib's Second Palestinian Campaign," *Journal of Biblical Literature* 104 (1985): 401-418] argues for a two-campaign theory, in which 2 Kgs. 18:13-16 refers to the first campaign and 2 Kgs. 18:17-19:36 refers to the second. He is followed by Christopher Begg ('Sennacherib's Second Palestinian Campaign": An Additional Indication," *Journal of Biblical Literature* 106 [1987]: 685-686), who suggests that Hezekiah's statement (2 Kgs. 19:18a) should be read as a hyperbolic, rhetorical generalization that was inspired by Sennacherib's annihilatory measures against the Babylonian cult in 689 B.C.E. However, Shea is challenged by Frank J. Yurco ("The Shabaka-Shebitku Coregency and the Supposed Second Campaign of Sennacherib against Judah: A Critical Assessment," *Journal of Biblical Literature* 110 [1991]: 35-45), who argues that the Yamani affair of 713-712 B.C.E. marks a synchronism between Egypt and Assyria, at which time Shabaka took control of Lower Egypt and with the falling of Shebitku's accession in 702-701 B.C.E., necessitated a coregency between the two (37, 38, 39, 45).
40. Ahlström, *History*, 707-716; Soggin, *History*, 251f; Horn, "The Divided Monarchy," 135f; Niels Peter Lemche, *Ancient Israel: A New History of Israelite Society* (England: Sheffield, 1995), 172; "Sennacherib (704-681): The Siege of Jerusalem," translated by A. Leo Oppenheim (*ANET*, 199-201). In spite of Hezekiah's concessions to Assyria (2 Kgs. 18:13-16), the lost of most of his territory (2 Kgs. 18:17-37), and his ambivalence toward Yahwism (2 Kgs. 19:3-4), he is applauded by DH probably for his freedom-quest and attempts at homogenization of his kingdom (2 Kgs. 18:1-9).
41. 2 Kgs. 22-23; Lemche, *Ancient Israel*, 168-171.
42. Ahlström, *History*, 730-737; Soggin, *History*, 253f; Horn, "The Divided Monarchy," 136f. In contrast to the North and in disfavor of DH, the traditional religion of Judah included many anthropomorphic or tauromorphic figures (2 Kgs. 21:5-7).
43. Ahlström, *History*, 739f. Pharaoh Psammetichus I (664-610 B.C.E.) had reunited Egypt, and probably inspired hope for a new attempt at rebellion against Assyria. Also, during this time the Qedarites and the Nebaioth of Syria and Palestine revolted against Ashurbanipal, and were subdued along with Acre and Ushu in Phoenicia. Frank Crüsemann (*The*

Torah) argues that after 701 B.C.E., when Sennacherib's reduction of Jerusalem and the centralization of all cults that led to the increased significance of Jerusalem and its temple, and the appointment of a king by the people after the murder of Amon (2 Kgs. 21:24; 23:30; cf. Deut. 17:14-20) had occurred, a resistence/farmers' liberation movement that was led by "the people of the land" (עַם־הָאָרֶץ 'am-ha-arez) seized power from the aristocratic Jerusalem families and drafted D (Deut. 12-26), addressing the free landowners or the Judean 'am-ha-arez, legitimating their acts (Deut. 16:18; 17:8-13; 2 Kgs. 11:14, 18; 22:1; 23:31, 36) (212-215, 219, 223, 235, 238, 240, 247, 249, 266, 268-269). They addressed the following concerns: (1) provision of a counter to polyYHWHism (Deut. 6:4); (2) security for social problems, for example, provision for the weak (Deut. 14:22-29, 15:19-22); (3) regulation of behavior in time of war (Deut. 20); and (4) handling of intra-familial conflicts, that is, curtailment of the rights of the *pater familias* (Deut. 21:18-21; 22:13-21, 22, 25-29; 25:5-10) (222, 225, 244-245, 252-257). This was done through employment of several themes: (1) the tithes are the inner design of D (207); (2) abolition of the tithe, that is, payment of it every third year to the socially underprivileged groups (i.e., those without land) (Deut. 12:6f, 11f, 17f; 16:10f, 14; 26:12-15) (217-218); (3) the freedom that is represented by the exodus and the land is made to include freedom from the requirements of payment of tributary or compulsory labor to the state (Deut. 14:22f; 23:16; 24:6, 14) (234); and (4) the central court holds the same dignity as Moses or the Mosaic lawbook (Deut. 16:18-20;17:8-13; 19:1-13) (238-240).

44. Ahlström, *History*, 741-757; Horn, "The Divided Monarchy," 141f; Soggin, *History*, 256f.

45. Ahlström, *History*, 763-766.

46. Ahlström, *History*, 770-779; Horn, "The Divided Monarchy," 137-141; Soggin, *History*, 257f. For a discussion of the redaction of Isaiah 1-39 as a critique of Josiah's time, see Gerald T. Sheppard, "The Anti-Assyrian Redaction and the Canonical Context of Isaiah 1-39," *Journal of Biblical Literature* 104 (1985): 193-216.

47. Ahlström, *History*, 764-766.

48. 2 Kgs. 24-25; cf. also 2 Kgs. 20:14-19; 21:1-18; 25:1-21, especially vv. 8-21.

49. Ahlström, *History*, 767. The people of the land put up Shallum, renamed Jehoahaz, as king in succession to Josiah. This situation was corrected by Necho, who put up Eliakim, the rightful oldest son of Josiah, who was renamed Jehoiakim. See Soggin, *History*, 261f; Horn, "The Divided Monarchy," 144f. See Alberto R. Green, "The Chronology of the Last Days of Judah: Two Apparent Discrepancies," *Journal of Biblical Literature* 101 (1982): 57-73. Green argues that Nebuchadrezzar's accession period

began on 8 Ab, 605 B.C.E., such that the Judahite writers employed a Tishri system, having Nebuchadrezzar's first regnal year begin 1 Tishri 605 B.C.E. and his eighth year begin 1 Tishri 598 B.C.E., and so establishing Jehoiakim's eleventh year in parallel with this year, if his accession took place after Tishri 609 B.C.E. (62, 63, 71f).

50. Ahlström, *History*, 788-791; Soggin, *History*, 263f; Jer. 25:9-13; 26:24; 2 Kgs. 22:11. Examining six texts concerning Babylon (Jer. 42:9-17; 50:41-43; Isa. 47:5-7; 1 Kgs. 8:46-53; 2 Chr. 36:15-21; Dan. 4:19-27), Brueggemann ["At the Mercy of Babylon: A Subversive Rereading of the Empire," *Journal of Biblical Literature* 110 (1991): 3-22] argues that "when Israel's speech about Babylon is drawn into Israel's speech concerning God, the power of the empire is envisioned and reconstructed around the issue of mercy (רחם rachêm). The intrusion of the rhetoric of mercy into the *Realpolitik* of Babylon derives from the uncompromising character of God. It also arises from the deepest yearning of the exilic community which must have mercy to live, which expects mercy from God, and which by venturesome rhetoric dares to insist that the promised, yearned-for mercy cannot be ignored by the empire" (5).

51. Ahlström, *History*, 781-786.

52. It is most probable that Ezekiel was deported with this group (1:2-3). Such aristocracy included the royal officials, i.e., scribes, advisors, prophets, priests, and administrators. Specifically, the Aaronite priests were deported. These were the primary Jerusalemite priests.

53. Ahlström, *History*, 785-788; Soggin, *History*, 261f; Horn, "The Divided Monarchy," 144f.

54. Ezekiel explains the exile as the result of YHWH's departure and relocation from Jerusalem (cf. 8:3, 7, 14, 16; 9:3, 9-10; 10:3-5, 18-19; 11:23; cf. 48:35) to Babylon (cf. chs. 1-3).

55. Ahlström, *History*, 791-798; Soggin, *History*, 263-265; Horn, "The Divided Monarchy," 146-148.

56. See Niels Peter Lemche, "Kings and Clients: On Loyalty between the Ruler and the Ruled in Ancient "Israel"", *Semeia* 66 (1994): 119-132, especially 127-129 (n. 5); "The Conquest of Jerusalem," translated by A. Leo Oppenheim (*ANET*, 112f).

57. Ahlström, *History*, 798-803; Soggin, *History*, 264f; Horn, "The Divided Monarchy," 147-149.

58. Norman K. Gottwald, *The Hebrew Bible: A Socio-literary Introduction* (Philadelphia: Fortress, 1985), 421f; Ahlström, *History*, 799f; Soggin, *History*, 265-270; James D. Purvis, "Exile and Return," in *Ancient Israel: A Short History from Abraham to the Roman Destruction of the Temple* (ed. Hershel Shanks; Washington, D. C.: Biblical Archaeology Society/Englewood Cliffs, NJ: Prentice-Hall, 1988), 156-165.

59. Martin Noth, *The History of Israel* (3d ed.; trans. Peter R. Ackroyd; New York: Harper and Row, 1958), 296f; Gottwald, *The Hebrew Bible*, 482-492; Soggin, *History*, 266f.

60. Claus Westermann, *Basic Forms of Prophetic Speech* (trans. Hugh Clayton White; Philadelphia: Westminster, 1967), 205-210; Klaus Koch, *The Prophets: Volume One. The Assyrian Period* (trans. Margaret Kohl; Philadelphia: Fortress, 1978), 130-132, 138-140; Gerhard von Rad, *The Message of the Prophets* (New York: Harper and Row,1962, 1965), 229-239; cf. Michael De Roche, "Yahweh's *rîb* Against Israel: A Reassessment of the So-Called "Prophetic Lawsuit" in the Preexilic Prophets," *Journal of Biblical Literature* 102 (1983): 563-574.

61. Westermann, *Basic Forms*, 205-210; idem, *Prophetic Oracles of Salvation in the Old Testament* (trans. Keith Crim; Louisville, KY: Westminster/John Knox , 1991), 42, 195, 229, 244, 246f.

62. DH argues that the impact of cultural diversity that was evidenced in allegiances to the arrangements of the dominant or foreign nations (cf. "other/foreign gods" אלהים אחרים:—1Kgs. 9:6, 9; 1Kgs. 11:4, 10; 1 4:9; 2Kgs. 5:17; 17:7, 35, 37, 38; 22:17; and "high places/shrines... ashteroth" במות...אשרות—1Kgs. 3:2, 3; 12:31, 32; 13:2, 32, 33; 14:23; 15:13, 14; 16:33; 18:19; 22:44; 2Kgs. 12:4; 13:6; 14:4; 15:4, 35; 16:4; 17:9, 11, 29, 32; 18:4; 21:3, 7; 23:4, 5, 6, 7, 8, 9, 13, 15, 19, 20) led to violation of Yahwistic standards (cf. "statutes...ordinances...law...commandments" — חקות...משפטים...תורה...מצות 1Kgs. 3:3; 18:18; 2Kgs. 17:8, 13, 16, 19, 34, 37; 18:36; 21:8; 22:8, 11; 23:9, 24), which resulted in national catastrophes. These disasters were especially caused by repeated disobedience of "the word of YHWH" (דבר־יהוה :1Kgs. 2:27; 5:19; 6:11; 8:20; 12:15, 24; 13:1, 2, 3, 5, 9, 17, 18, 20, 26, 32; 14:18; 15:29; 16:1, 7, 12, 34; 17:2, 5, 8, 16, 24; 18:1, 31; 19:9; 20:35; 21:17, 23, 28; 22:5, 19, 28, 38; 2Kgs. 1:17; 3:12; 4:44; 7:1, 16; 9:26, 36; 10:10, 17; 14:25, 27; 15:12; 19:21; 20:4, 16, 19; 23:16; 24:2, 13; also consider the preponderance of messenger formulae - "thus said YHWH" כה אמר יהוה 1Kgs. 11:31; 12:24; 13:2, 21; 14:7; 17:14; 20:13, 14, 28, 42; 21:19; 22:11; 2Kgs. 1:4, 6, 16; 2:21; 3:16, 17; 4:43; 7:1; 9:3, 6, 12; 19:6, 20, 32; 20:1, 5; 21:12; 22:15, 16, 18).

63. Noth, *History*, 297-299; Soggin, *History*, 268; Purvis, "Exile and Return," 159f.

64. Robert B. Coote and David Robert Ord, *In the Beginning: Creation and the Priestly History* (Minneapolis: Fortress Press, 1991), 67-70. Their thesis is that P is the supplement to the Davidic cult history of the founding of the nation of "Israel," which located justice in the Jerusalem temple-cult as being the center of the world, the prime focus of law and order in the state, and the pinnacle of creation, that was written by the Aaronite priesthood as a function of the Persian policy to resurrect the temple priesthood in Palestine (32, 36, 38, 95, 104, 118). The perspective of P is

southern, i.e., Aaronite priestly (36, 38, 41, 47, 49, 56, 85, 89, 108, 117f, 132) dating to middle to late sixth century B.C.E. (37, 38, 39, *et al*). However, Goldstein and Cooper (*The Festivals*) date P earlier than the Babylonian exile, during the time of Hezekiah, while Israel Knohl (*The Sanctuary of Silence: The Priestly Torah and the Holiness School* [Minneapolis: Fortress Press, 1995]) dates P earlier than Hezekiah, locating the beginning of the activity of HS during the time of Hezekiah (200 [n. 4], 207f [n. 25], 223 [n. 84], 224). See Jerome C. Ross, *The Composition of the Holiness Code (Lev. 17-26)* (Dissertation: University of Pittsburgh, 1997), 106-126.

65. Coote and Ord, *In the Beginning*, 62-66; Mary Douglas, *Purity and Danger: An Analysis of Concepts of Pollution and Taboo* (London: Routledge and Kegan Paul, 1966); idem, "Deciphering a Meal," in *Implicit Meanings* (London: Routledge and Kegan Paul, 1975), 249-275. Douglas (*Purity and Danger*) argued that morality may be motivated by fear of pollution, and that pollution occurs as a result of violation of expected standards (133). Also, she ("Deciphering a Meal") noted four common elements in meal situations: (1) the greater the social import and intimacy, the greater in concentration the elements appear; (2) meals can be arranged on a scale from less to more important and complex; (3) the smallest, meanest meal metanymically figures the structure of the grandest, and vice-versa; and (4) the more complex the meal, the more intimate the participants. See also John G. Gammie, *Holiness in Israel* (OBT series; Minneapolis: Fortress, 1989), 9-12. He proposes that "in response to the divine holiness the priests perceived that God required an ethical and ritual purity as well as the ingestion only of foods that the priestly logic of separation and appropriateness would allow them to declare clean" (12). Also, see Douglas ("The Forbidden Animals in Leviticus." *Journal for the Study of the Old Testament* 59 (1993): 3-23), especially 9-12. The "ring composition" consists of: a prologue, which explains the program to be developed, and introduces the theme; the mid-point, or turning-point, that is flanked by parallel chapters on each side which lay out the steps inside each section; the ring, grand peroration, or conclusion, which summarizes the program that has been developed, and returns to the initial theme by means of a latch (i.e., the final concluding device that ties into the prologue) (9). According to this rubric Leviticus is structured as follows: 1. the prologue: chs. 1-9—things and persons consecrated to the Lord; 2. steps: (a) ch. 10— the holy place defiled; (b) chs. 11-15—blemish and leprosy; (c) ch. 16— atonement for the tabernacle; (d) ch. 17—the bridge or summary; 3 the mid-turn: (a) preceding flank: ch. 18— regulation of sex; Molech; (b) the mid-point: ch. 19—equity between the people; (c) the succeeding flank: ch. 20—regulation of sex; Molech; 4 steps: (a) chs. 21-22—blemish and leprosy; (b) ch. 23—holy

times, including the Day of Atonement; (c) ch. 24—the Name defiled; (d) ch. 25—things and persons belonging to the Lord; 5 the conclusion: ch. 26—equity between God and people, having ch. 27 (i.e., redemption of things and persons consecrated, or belonging, to the Lord) as the latch (10f). The connections in Leviticus are chapters that parallel one another: (1) chs. 1-9 parallel ch. 25; (2) ch. 10 parallels ch. 24; (3) chs. 11-15 parallel chs. 21-22, and ch. 16 parallels ch. 23, both of these parallels being chiastically connected; (4) ch. 18 parallels ch. 20; and (5) ch. 19 parallels ch. 26 (10f). The key to reading Leviticus is recognition that the meaning is delayed, or retarded, until the completion of the rounds (12). See Harold C. Washington, "The Strange Women זרה/נכריה of Proverbs 1-9 and Post-Exilic Judean Society," in *Second Temple Studies 2: Temple and Community in the Persian Period* (eds. Tamara C. Eskenazi and Kent H. Richards; JSOT Sup. 175; Sheffield: JSOT Press, 1994), 217-242; R. A. Oden, "Religious Identity and the Sacred Prostitution Accusation," in *The Bible without Theology: The Theological Tradition and Alternatives to it* (San Francisco: Harper and Row, 1987), 131-53; F. Barth, ed., *Ethnic Groups and Boundaries: The Social Organization of Culture Difference* (Boston: Little, Brown, 1969), 9-38. Washington, drawing upon Oden, who in turn references Barth, an anthropologist, regards prohibitions against prostitutes and dietary rules as instances of *ethnic boundary marking*, a process by which an ethnic group develops sensational accounts, often erroneous, of the customs of other groups as a way of delineating its own self-understanding (224).

66. Cf. Philip R. Davies, *In Search of "Ancient Israel"* (JSOT Sup. 148; Sheffield: JSOT Press, 1992). Davies argues that an idealized Israel was created in Yehud—that is, the creation of a new society, historical Israel or Judaean society, was accompanied by the creation and development of an ideological superstructure which denied its more recent origins, its imperial basis (and probably bias), and indigenized itself. Here, the literate class created an "Israel" that explained their own post-exilic society and the rights and privileges of the immigrant elite within that society (87, 90, 92f).

67. Ross, *The Holiness Code*, 148f; Lee I. Levine, "The Nature and Origin of the Palestinan Synagogue Reconsidered," *Journal of Biblical Literature* 115 (1996): 425-448.

68. Purvis, "Exile and Return," 160-164; Soggin, *History*, 268; Peter R. Ackroyd, *Exile and Restoration: A Study of Hebrew Thought of the Sixth Century B. C.* (Philadelphia: Westminster, 1968), 40-48. Ackroyd observed four typical responses to the exile: (1) return to the old familiar deities of Canaan (Ezek. 8; Jer. 44); (2) acceptance of the religion of the conquerors (Isa. 44:9-28; 46:1-2; Ezek. 20:32); (3) recognition of divine judgment, or the fulfillment of prophecy (Am. 9:11-15; Mic.

2:12-13; 4:1-14; 5:1-14; 7:8-20); and (4) comprehension of the exile as a moment of judgment, or the day of YHWH historicized (Am. 5:18-24; Ezek. 13:5); cf. "Letters of the Jews in Elephantine," translated by H. L. Ginsberg (*ANET*, 278-282).

CHAPTER FIVE:
THE PERSIAN PERIOD[1]

Due to the poor documentation of Palestine during the period of 582-539 B.C.E. only general sketches can be made. It is probable that Judah continued as a governmental district under the military command of the Babylonians. Its location in the mountainous regions put it away from the main activities, which occurred along the commercial routes near the coast. However, after Nebuchadnezzar rebuilt and enlarged his empire, he died in 562 B.C.E., triggering a period of instability. Awil-Marduk (Evil-Merodach), his successor, was ousted in 560 B.C.E., before Nebuchadnezzar's death by a brother-in-law, Neriglissar (559-556 B.C.E.). The latter's son, Labashi-Marduk, reigned three months before being replaced by a revolt by one of Nebuchadnezzar's high officials, Nabuna'id (Nabonidus), who reigned for seventeen years, though not stabilizing the empire. He campaigned in Cilicia and Syria, having his son, the crown-prince Belshazzar, handle administrative and military duties.[2] However, in 550 B.C.E. Cyrus, who was a vassal king of the Medes, revolted against his overlord and grandfather, King Astyages (585-550 B.C.E.), took Ecbatana, dethroned Astyages, and became king of the Median empire. He was accompanied by Nabuna'id, who broke off relations with him after the revolt and joined with Ahmose of Egypt and Croesus of Lydia in order to fight against Cyrus. Then Cyrus marched north of Mesopotamia into Anatolia, took Cilicia, Armenia, and Cappadocia, and captured Sardis in 546 B.C.E., ending the Lydian kingdom and prompting the submission of the Greek city states in Western Asia Minor. In 540 B.C.E. he attacked Babylonia, which was internally deteriorating due to economic, political, and religious problems. These internal problems generated defectors who included the priesthood of Marduk and were sympathetic to Cyrus. They proclaimed Cyrus as the savior, providing the propaganda that influenced Deutero-Isaiah, who regarded him as the Anointed of YHWH (44:28; 45:1; 47)[3], evidently supported his efforts, and thereby recruited exiled Jews for Cyrus's mission in Judah[4] under the auspices that Cyrus was YHWH's agent of deliverance. Finally, in 539 B.C.E., Cyrus emerged as the king of Anshan and defeated the Babylonian army at Opis, marking the end of Babylonian rule and the official beginning of widespread Persian rule.[5]

Cyrus introduced a new policy for the subject peoples, which furthered his political and military aims. He allowed the subject peoples to return to their homelands, repair their temples, and keep their cultic traditions. The return to the homeland was regarded as a "second exodus" (cf. Isa. 40; 43:15-21) by some of the *gôlah* party or exiled Jews who mixed themes of creation and salvation as they interpreted this new turn of events. For them YHWH's salvation was now being shown in re-creation (Isa. 40-45). However, this change of fortunes for the *gôlah* party must be understood in the context of Cyrus's aims to facilitate peaceful and compliant relations among the subject peoples, diminishing any stimulants to unrest and revolt, and to spawn economic growth and development, solidifying his political and military salients. In his concern to secure his border against Egypt Judah became a target area for reconstruction. It had been severely weakened socioeconomically by the Babylonian conquest, which destroyed as well as depopulated its major sites.[6] Internally, Judah was disorganized, reflecting loss of identity and rights to land due to uncontrolled syncretism caused by marriage to foreign women[7] (Neh. 10:30; 13:23-24; Ezr. 9-10; Mal. 2:10-16) and unregulated market practices such as selling on the Sabbath (Neh. 10:31; 13:15-18), neglect of the seventh-year land-rest (Neh. 10:31), neglect of the Levites and the sanctuary (Hag. 1:1-11; Mal. 2:4-9; Neh. 10:32-39, 13:10), abuse/misuse of the sanctuary and offerings (Mal. 1:1-14, 3:6-12; Neh. 13:4-5), and infidelity among the priests (Mal. 2:13-17). These features were obviously caused by the termination of the Davidic monarchy, which had provided economic and political structure, including its royal officials and the temple, the rivalry among the leaders who remained in the land—particularly the priests—the lack of a politically endorsed ideology for the community, and the increased de-urbanization of the Jewish population. The general problems which persisted in Judah during the Persian Period were the weakened socioeconomic fabric of Judah, which was reflected in indentured servitude of Jews to Jews due to loss of land and debts (Neh. 5:1-15), the conflicts of interest between the Palestinian Jews who remained in the land and the Jews who returned, which were reflected in the interference of the Samaritans (Neh. 3:10, 19; 4:1-3, 7-8; 6:1-2, 6-7), in the interference of "adversaries" of Judah and Benjamin (Ezr. 4:1-5), in the rivalry among the priesthoods (i.e., the Levites and the Aaronites), and the thin population of Judah.[8] In response to the structural deficiencies, Cyrus's policy then involved establishment of local autonomy within the supervision of the Persian government, which was effected through repopulation of devastated areas strategic for political stability and military security, endorsement of the cults and the respective ideologies of the deportees from the targeted areas, and moderate redevelopment of the structures of key sites. These now became the agenda items for the missions of several Persian-authorized, exilic descendants who returned to Judah.

Four major missions to Judah were attempted. These efforts were hindered by the reluctance of the Yahwists who had remained (i.e., Jews as well as Samaritans) to embrace the *gôlah* party—those who returned. The mixed population of the territory had diverse interests, and thus the *gôlah* party was perceived as a threat to the non-exiled Yahwists. The returnees represented both the remnants of the Davidic regime and the new phase of subjugation under the Persians. Essentially the difference between the two groups pertained to property rights and political control.[9] The agendas of the two groups conflicted in light of the autonomy given to and enjoyed by the non-exiled Jews and the desires for resumption of political dominance fostered by the returnees. In this respect, reconstruction of the temple was significantly delayed and the Persian "restoration" policy had to be enforced by the overlords. First, in 538 B.C.E. Sheshbazzar sought to lay the groundwork for reestablishing the community of Judah (Ezr. 1:5-11; 5:13-15; 1 Chron. 3:17-18).[10] His efforts may be seen in light of the prophecies of Trito-Isaiah (Chapters 56-66), which reflect the hope prompted by the victories of Darius and the delay in fulfillment of the prophecies of Deutero-Isaiah (Chapters 40-55; e.g., 59:1, 9). The main concern was subservience, including economic exploitation and dependency, which was to be addressed by reconstruction of the temple and establishment of the temple-cultus. Being a function of the city-state or imperial government, the temple functioned as a landholder, a mechanism of employment through work forces or temple slaves, a bank advancing loans, a representation of the imperial government, and a custodian of legal traditions.[11] Obviously the *gôlah* party sought the re-establishment of Jerusalem, particularly the temple-cultus, regarding it as the prerequisite for the in-dwelling of YHWH's presence and thereby a blessing (cf. Hag. 1; Zech. 8; Mal. 1-3). In their thinking the reconstruction of the temple was directed by YHWH (cf. Ezr. 1; 6:1-12; 7:11-26; Neh. 2:4, 8, 12, 18, 20; 4:8, 14), above and beyond the political aims of the Persian overlords. However, this view did not go unchallenged by the non-exiled Jews.[12] The political aspects of the temple, no doubt, engendered the anti-temple polemics of Trito-Isaiah (56:1; 58:2, 5-9) which countered the prevalent views endorsing the temple (cf. Isa. 57:14-21; 60:1f, 62:8f, 10-12; 65:15, 25).[13]

In 520 B.C.E. Zerubbabel, the son of Shealtiel and grandson of Jehoiakin, and Joshua the priest led a second campaign to reconstruct the temple. It must be assumed that Sheshbazzar encountered opposition to his mission and was forced to delay or cease his efforts.[14] Again the concerns of the Persians are foundational for understanding the particulars. Judah had not been significantly reconstructed as a frontier post against Egypt. Also, the community center—the temple-cultus—had not been repaired and re-established. Third, interference came from some Samaritans, who probably fostered a local, even Yahwistic, cult in contradistinction to the *Zionistic* form of Yahwism perpetuated by the *gôlah* party, that is, the descendants of the Jerusalemite aristocracy and also of the Davidic lineage.[15] Zerubbabel and

Joshua achieved some success, and this may be attributed to support from a Levitical faction in the land. They did construct an altar on the Temple Mount in Jerusalem during the second year of Darius's reign (520 B.C.E.) and completed their work on the temple in 516 B.C.E. Though Haggai and Zechariah endorsed the project, declaring holiness as an essential factor for *shalom* that is acquired through rebuilding of the temple (Hag. 1:8; 2:3-19; Zech. 2:9; 3:8-10; 8:13), it seems after completion of the project hopes diminished, in light of unfulfillment of expectations regarding the kingdom of God.[16]

In 512 B.C.E. a revolt by the Ionian cities in western Anatolia occurred. Darius suffered defeat in battle at Marathon in 490 B.C.E. and made further preparations for war with Greece. At the same time Egypt revolted, and before he could encounter them in battle, he died in 486 B.C.E. and was succeeded by Xerxes, his son (486-465 B.C.E.). Xerxes and his successors sought to conquer Greece, a policy which weakened the strength of their empire.[17] Also, the influence of the Greeks was increasingly felt, as Hellenism began to spread. However, this did not directly impact Palestine, especially Judah. Trade in Palestine was mainly controlled by the Phoenicians. Since they were anti-Greek, the Persians sought to exploit these feelings to their advantage. In 481 B.C.E. Persia managed to forge an alliance with most of the peoples of Greece and Thessaly, splintering their strength, which provided the Persians an edge in battle against the Athenians in 480 B.C.E. On the other front, Xerxes was defeated by the Greeks in a bay at Salamis. Also, in 484 and 482 B.C.E. Babylon revolted but was suppressed by Megabyxos, brother-in-law of Xerxes. A significant result of these wars was the emergence of the Phoenicians, who waged war against the Athenians from 465 to 390 B.C.E. and sided, along with King Achoris of Egypt, with Evagoras of Salamis in his revolt against the Persians in 389-380 B.C.E. This emergence occurred against the backdrop of the rise of the Greeks. So the Phoenicians served as a check and an indicator of the inevitable emergence of the Greeks.[18]

In 445-433 B.C.E. Nehemiah, a strong lay representative of a strict Yahwism based upon D and that was pro-Levitical, conducted his first mission. His work was probably necessitated by the effects from the recent military campaigns, which drained resources and caused reshuffling of peoples. He encountered opposition from Geshem the Arab, located in southern Palestine. Their policies conflicted: Nehemiah was separatistic, utilizing religion as a mechanism for distinction of Yahwists from non-Yahwists, while Geshem endorsed a more conciliatory and syncretistic posture of Yahwism.[19] Pervading these ideological differences were political ones. The control of the region was at stake, or at least Geshem's authority was threatened by that of Nehemiah. That Nehemiah is accused in the biblical presentations of treason indicates the political nature of his tasks and motives. His work included re-fortification of Jerusalem (Neh. 6), re-population of Jerusalem by moving every tenth man there (Neh. 11:1), release of property that had been seized because of debt in order to stop exploitation of the lower classes (Neh. 5:1-5), attempts to end selling of Jews as slaves (Neh. 5:5-13), and release of tax burdens by not overtaxing the people (Neh. 5:14-15).[20] During his second mission (ca. 432 B.C.E.?), which was triggered by relapses among the people, he sought to address social issues. His work then included forbidding of work on the Sabbath, including disallowance of the operation of the Tyrian markets which drained economic resources from the local Jews, giving the outsiders an undue advantage, use of the Levites as a police force to close and guard the gates on the Sabbath (Neh. 10:33-40), reorganization of the temple personnel and the system of tithes in response to abuse/misuse of the temple (Neh. 13:10-14), and attempts to dissolve mixed marriages to Ashdodites, Ammonites, and Moabites which had resulted in children who could not speak the language of Judah (Neh. 13:15-30).[21] Nehemiah's work was mainly *externally* structural, addressing the political, military, and economic issues.

In 398 B.C.E. Ezra, an Aaronite scribe, came to Jerusalem. His main concern was to supervise the administrators of the province and to insure the sacred and civil laws were followed. Prior to his coming, power struggles between priests had occurred, resulting in the murder of Jeshua (Joshua) by his brother, the high priest Johanan, and reflecting anti-Persian sentiments. Also, the loss of Egypt no doubt stimulated Persian efforts at securing its control in the south-Palestinian area.[22] His focus upon the operation of the temple betrays this concern with administration—that is, governance and collection of taxes. This was addressed by the laws he brought. It must be understood these laws constituted the laws of the state—they were Persian-screened and Persian-approved. His work included delivery of donations for the temple cult, supplementation of donations with state funds, appointment of judges to enforce his laws, and introduction of a law collection as the basis for civil and religious jurisprudence in Judah.[23] His enforcement of these laws included addressing mixed marriages[24] and adjusting the cultic calendar.[25] The cultic feasts were stringently denaturalized and historicized. The covenant renewal that occurred no doubt reflected the annual atonement that would finally be canonized in Lev. 16 as *Yom Ha-Kippurim*. Also, *Sukkoth* was taught and celebrated (Neh. 8:13-17; Lev. 23:33-43), commemorating the Wanderings in the Wilderness and the reception of the Sinai Laws. These two traditions corresponded to the prevalent circumstances and solicited exclusivity in worship of YHWH. This was accompanied by an emphasis on purity which was separatistic. Membership in the society was now based upon exclusive allegiance to a *Persian-authorized* version of *Aaronite* Yahwism.[26]

As a result of the missions of Nehemiah and Ezra, several trends were started. Initially, their work led to rigidification of societal norms and parochialization, as they somewhat uncompassionately defined the Yahwistic community according to principles of heredity. These efforts may be regarded as mechanisms for survival.[27] Their postures were different: Nehemiah's was that of the Levites, while Ezra's was Aaronite.[28] The traditions which reflect these postures are DH and P. Attempts at reconciliation of these two postures may be found in CH, whose views reflect re-unification through reconciliation and tolerance of the rival parties, ritualized formality—re-absorption of prophecy into the cult,[29] association of righteousness with observance of the Torah or emphasis upon inspired interpretation of prophecy through institutionalization of exegesis and projection of a future reality (what I call "past prophesying"), and openness toward the possibility of the return of the northern Yahwists.[30] CH is also significant in that it argues the legitimacy of the Jerusalem temple-cultus over the Samaritan cultus in light of the latter's establishment upon Mount Gerizim. This argument is internecine or within the community or among persons of similar postures. In this case, two Yahwistic parties differ, challenging the control of one another, with the deciding factor being political. Subsequently, the major developments were parochialization (Neh. 7; 10:1-27; 11:3-12:26; Ezr. 2; 7:1-6; 8:1-14; 10:18-28), and canonization of Jewish writings as a political tool for structuring the Jewish community. Determination of the laws for the community was based upon the need for order and security as perceived by the political overlords and political endorsement of the Aaronite priestly traditions through Ezra and the friendly relations of Jeshua of the Jerusalem high priestly family and the Persians, making the Zadokite leadership its benefactors and proponents (Ezek. 44:15; 1 Chron. 6:33-48; Zech. 3:8).[31] Once Ezra's group gained precedence over its rivals, the Aaronite traditions (i.e., P + H) became the canon or the ideological standard for the community in contradistinction and deposition to the Levites. In this respect, canonization entailed the establishment and authorization of leadership, the ideological determination or endorsement of the rules for the community, and the establishment of a sociopolitical center for community.[32] Canonization then was accompanied by displacement and factionalization of priestly groups, as the Aaronites were authorized, the Levites were deposed, and other dissatisfied factions (e.g., displaced Aaronites; cf. Hag., Trito-Isa., Lev. 17-26) arose.[33] So the Jewish community leaders were responsible for oversight of temple construction, oversight of wall-building or political and military solidification, economic re-development, re-population or re-occupation of Judah, and re-organization of community. Their roles consisted of being liaisons *of* the Persian government, liaisons *of* the Palestinian Jewish community, and local supervisors or deputies (i.e., "governor," "scribe"). Dual positions of administration ensued. The community was ruled by a governor and a high priest, with the latter often dominating. Here, a theocracy emerged, in which the governor was the liaison of Persian authority and the high priest was the liaison of Jewish community. Nevertheless, the crucial thread is the persistence of the community as they survived the assorted circumstances that challenged and threatened them.[34]

Chapter Synopsis:
The Key Dates

546 B.C.E.   Cyrus of Persia defeats Croesus

538 B.C.E.   Cyrus of Persia defeats Nabonidus of Babylon and permits the return of Jews to Palestine

Causes:

1. conquest of Babylon
2. institution of new administration, e.g., extension of local autonomy and respect for indigenous cultural and religious lives of subject peoples
3. concern for political solidification and re-establishment of Judah as a strategic military and political salient on the frontier with Egypt
4. weakened socio-economic fabric of Judah

Developments:

1. re-establishment of Judah and Jerusalem as the main center of Judaism
2. military solidification and re-establishment of the economic base of Jerusalem by Nehemiah
3. re-organization of the Jewish community by Ezra
4. canonization of Israelite literature as a political tool for structuring the Jewish community
5. enforcement of "separatism" as survival tactic
6. elevation of Zadokite priestly leadership via backing of Persian authorities

Effects:

1. interference of the Samaritans
2. conflict of interests of Palestinian Jews and Jews repatriated from Babylon
3. numerous attempts at or stages of restoration, i.e., Sheshbazzar, Zerubbabel and Joshua, Nehemiah, Ezra
4. innovations made by the Jerusalem religious community:
    a. establishment of a priestly hierarchy with a high priest and closed priesthood from the lineage of Zadok
    b. further historicization of the cultic feasts or calendar [cf. Lev. 23; Ezek. 45:18-25]
    c. addition/institution of *Yom Ha-Kippurim* [Lev. 16] and *Sukkoth* [Lev. 23:33-43; Neh. 8:13-17]
    d. further/extensive canonization of Israelite literature:
        i.   fixation of the Pentateuch
        ii. collection and redaction of the prophetic messages

Interpretations:
1. Cyrus as "Anointed of YHWH" [cf. Isa. 44:28; 45:1; 47]
2. return to homeland as "second exodus" [cf. Isa. 43:15-21; 40]
3. salvation as re-creation by YHWH [cf. Isa. 40-45]
4. re-establishment of Jerusalem and the temple-cultus as (pre)requisite for in-dwelling of YHWH's Presence and thereby blessing [cf. Hag.1; Zech. 8; Mal. 1-3] and thus directed by YHWH [cf. Ezra 1; 6:1-12; 7:11-26; Neh. 2:4, 8, 12, 18, 20; 4:8, 14]
5. marriage of foreign women as breach of faith [cf. Ezra 10; Neh.10]
6. assumption of Zadokites as legitimate priests and their version of Torah as the rule due to Persian authorization according to YHWH [cf. Ezra-Nehemiah]
7. eventual publication of the Chronistic History to argue the legitimacy of the Jerusalem cultus over the Samaritan cultus in light of the establishment of the latter on Mount Gerizim

The Selected Interpretations
#1: Cyrus as Anointed of YHWH [cf. Isa. 44:28, 45:1, 47]
#2 Return to Homeland as Second Exodus [cf. Isa. 43:15-21, 40]
#3 Salvation as Re-creation by YHWH [cf. Isa. 40-45]

A. Perspective/Speaker: the exilic Judeans who favored Cyrus

B. Addressees: the exiled Jews

C. Contexts:
1. the imminent conquest of Babylonia by Cyrus
2. the indecision regarding which group with which to align

D. Issues: determination of the most appropriate course for the survival of the Jews, i.e., which foreign administration to support

E. Purposes:
1. recruitment of exiled Jews for support of Cyrus
2. solicitation of exiled Jews to undertake Cyrus' mission (i.e., re-organization of Judah) to Judah
3. endorsement of defection from Babylonia

F. Presuppositions:
1. YHWH as Universal Sovereign
2. the oneness of YHWH, i.e., exclusive Yahwistic monotheism and the political solidarity of Yahwistic colonialism
3. Zionistic Yahwism as the Legitimate (Sole) Heir of early Yahwism

4. the historicity of YHWH's activity
5. Zionistic Yahwism minus the monarchy as the Legitimate (Sole) Heir of early Yahwism, i.e., Yahwistic theocracy
6. Jerusalem (or Mount Zion) as the City of YHWH and the Sole Yahwistic Cult Center
7. YHWH as Creator-Savior

#3: Re-establishment of Jerusalem and the Temple-Cultus as (Pre)Requisite for the Indwelling of YHWH's Presence and thereby Blessing [cf. Hag. 1; Zech. 8; Mal. 1-3] and thus directed by YHWH [cf. Ezra 1; 6:1-12; 7:11-26; Neh. 2:4, 8, 12, 18, 20; 4:8, 14]

#4: Assumption of the Zadokites as Legitimate Priests and their Version of Torah as the Rule due to Persian Authorization according to YHWH [cf. Ezra-Nehemiah]

#5: Marriage to Foreign Women as Breach of Faith [cf. Ezra 10; Neh. 10]

A. Perspective/Speaker: repatriated Jews who were employed by the Persian administration

B. Addressees:
   1. the diverse, non-Judean Yahwists, e.g., the Samaritans
   2. those Yahwists who remained in the land during the Babylonian exile and were opposed to the re-establishment of a Persian-endorsed Davidic-Zionistic theocracy
   3. the competing priestly factions, e.g., the Levites, the displaced Aaronites

C. Contexts: the Jerusalem/Judean community during the Persian domination

D. Issues:
   1. determination of the most appropriate course for the survival of the Jews, i.e., administrative structure and ideological standardization
   2. provincial control, i.e., loss of land-rights via exogamous marriages
   3. execution of the Persian administration's program for Judah

E. Purposes:
   1. endorsement of the Persian-authorized Judean Yahwists and the Judean theocracy
   2. recruitment of opposing Yahwists and non-Yahwists, i.e., solicitation of popular support for the new regime
   3. legitimation of Zionistic Yahwism, i.e., its arrangement, personnel, and policy

4. acquisition of land-rights and stabilization of the local economy
5. re-construction and re-definition of the Yahwistic community at Judah

F. Presuppositions:
1. YHWH as Universal Sovereign
2. the oneness of YHWH, i.e., exclusive Yahwistic monotheism and the political solidarity of Yahwistic colonialism
3. Zionistic Yahwism as the Legitimate (Sole) Heir of early Yahwism
4. the historicity of YHWH's activity
5. Zionistic Yahwism minus the monarchy as the Legitimate (Sole) Heir of early Yahwism, i.e., Yahwistic theocracy with the Zadokites as the Legitimate Priests and Leaders [Ezek. 44; Ezra-Neh.; Lev. 17-26]
6. Jerusalem (or Mount Zion) as the City of YHWH and the Sole Yahwistic Cult Center [Chronicles]
7. YHWH as Creator-Savior
8. YHWH and Israel as Holy [Lev. 17-26]

Endnotes

1. Cf. Ezra-Nehemiah, Chronicles, Malachi, Haggai, and Zechariah 1-8, Isaiah 56-66, Esther.
2. Gösta Ahlström, *The History of Ancient Palestine from the Palaeolithic Period to Alexander's Conquest* (ed. Diana Edelman; JSOT Sup. 146; England: Sheffield, 1993), 804, 806f, 810; J. Alberto Soggin, *An Introduction to the History of Israel and Judah* (trans. John Bowden; Valley Forge, PA: Trinity International, 1993), 275.
3. Cf. Claus Westermann, *Basic Forms of Prophetic Speech* (trans. Hugh Clayton White; Philadelphia: Westminster, 1967), 205-210; idem, *Prophetic Oracles of Salvation in the Old Testament* (trans. Keith Crim; Louisville, KY: Westminster/John Knox , 1991), 42, 195, 229, 244, 246; Klaus Koch, *The Prophets: Volume One. The Assyrian Period* (trans. Margaret Kohl; Philadelphia: Fortress, 1978), 130-132, 138-140; Gerhard von Rad, *The Message of the Prophets* (New York: Harper and Row,1962, 1965), 229-239; Ahlström, *History*, 812-817. Presenting Cyrus as YHWH's agent of deliverance and interpreting the circumstances that ensued under Cyrus's lenient policy as the termination of YHWH's imprisonment of the Jews (cf. Isa. 40), Deutero-Isaiah endorses Cyrus by recruiting Jewish exiles for Cyrus's mission to Judah. See "Cyrus (557-529)," translated by A. Leo Oppenheim (*ANET*, 206-208).
4. Many of the exiled Jews had assimilated to Babylonian society, possibly following the advice of Jeremiah (see Jer. 24f; cf. 27-29, 37-38) and were uninterested in returning.
5. Ahlström, *History*, 814-816; Soggin, *History*, 276; James D. Purvis, "Exile and Return," in *Ancient Israel: A Short History from Abraham to the Roman Destruction of the Temple* (ed. Hershel Shanks; Washington, D. C.: Biblical Archaeology Society/Englewood Cliffs, NJ: Prentice-Hall, 1988), 165.
6. Ahlström, *History*, 816f, 834f, 839, 841-843; Soggin, *History*, 277-280; Purvis, "Exile and Return," 165-175; Norman K. Gottwald, *The Hebrew Bible: A Socio-literary Introduction* (Philadelphia: Fortress, 1985), 428f; Charles E. Carter, "The Province of Yehud in the Post-Exilic Period: Soundings in Site Distribution and Demography," in *Second Temple Studies 2: Temple and Community in the Persian Period* (eds. Tamara C. Eskenazi and Kent H. Richards; JSOT Sup. 175; Sheffield: JSOT Press, 1994), 106-145.
7. Harold C. Washington, "The Strange Women (זרה/נכריה) of Proverbs 1-9 and Post-Exilic Judean Society," in *Second Temple Studies 2: Temple and Community in the Persian Period* (eds. Tamara C. Eskenazi and Kent H. Richards; JSOT Sup. 175; Sheffield: JSOT Press, 1994), 219-221, 230-238; Daniel Smith-Christopher, "The Mixed Marriage Crisis in

Ezra 9-10 and Nehemiah 13: A Study of the Sociology of Post-Exilic Judaean Community," in *Second Temple Studies: 2. Temple and Community in the Persian Period* (eds. Tamara C. Eskenazi and Kent H. Richards; JSOT Sup. 175; Sheffield: JSOT Press, 1994), 243-265; Tamara C. Eskenazi and Eleanore P. Judd, "Marriage to a Stranger in Ezra 9-10," in *Second Temple Studies: 2. Temple and Community in the Persian Period* (eds. Tamara C. Eskenazi and Kent H. Richards; JSOT Sup. 175; Sheffield: JSOT Press, 1994), 266-285; Beth Glazier-McDonald, "Intermarriage, Divorce, and the *Bat-'El Nekar*: Insights into Mal. 2:10-16," *Journal of Biblical Literature* 106 (1987): 603-611, especially 605, 607, 611.

8. Gottwald, *The Hebrew Bible*, 429f, 433; Shemaryahu Talmon, "The Emergence of Jewish Sectarianism in the Early Second Temple Period," in *Ancient Israelite Religion* (eds. Patrick D. Miller, Jr., Paul D. Hanson, and S. Dean McBride; Philadelphia: Fortress, 1987), 597; Ahlström, *History*, 831f, 839, 841f, 846f.

9. Ahlström, *History*, 824-835, 839, 846f; Washington, "The Strange Women," 230-242. Washington observes that these struggles over property rights included women, thus necessitating prohibition of exogamous marriages and genealogical reckoning as 'ideologies of descent' (234-238).

10. Gottwald, *The Hebrew Bible*, 430; Soggin, *History*, 281; Ahlström, *History*, 837-839; Purvis, "Exile and Return," 166f.

11. Joseph Blenkinsopp, "Temple and Society in Achaemenid Judah," in *Second Temple Studies: 1. Persian Period* (ed. Philip R. Davies; JSOTS 117; England: Sheffield, 1991), 22-24, 26, 29, 32, 37, 39, 40, 45, 47, 49; cf. David L. Petersen, "The Temple in Persian Period Prophetic Texts," in *Second Temple Studies: 1. Persian Period* (ed. Philip R. Davies; JSOTS 117; England: Sheffield, 1991), 143f; see also Joel Weinberg, *The Citizen-Temple Community* (trans. Daniel L. Smith-Christopher; JSOT Sup. 151; Sheffield: JSOT Press, 1992).

12. Robert P. Carroll, "So What Do We *Know* about the Temple? The Temple in the Prophets," in *Second Temple Studies 2: Temple and Community in the Persian Period* (eds. Tamara C. Eskenazi and Kent H. Richards; JSOT Sup. 175; Sheffield: JSOT Press, 1994), 34-51; David J. A. Clines, "Haggai's Temple Constructed, Deconstructed and Reconstructed," in *Second Temple Studies 2: Temple and Community in the Persian Period* (eds. Tamara C. Eskenazi and Kent H. Richards; JSOT Sup. 175; Sheffield: JSOT Press, 1994), 60-87; Peter Marinkovic, "What Does Zechariah 1-8 Tell Us about the Second Temple?" in *Second Temple Studies 2: Temple and Community in the Persian Period* (eds. Tamara C. Eskenazi and Kent H. Richards; JSOT Sup. 175; Sheffield: JSOT Press, 1994), 88-103.

13. Klaus Koch, *The Prophets: Volume Two. The Babylonian and Persian Periods* (trans. Margaret Kohl; Philadelphia: Fortress, 1978; English, 1982), 152-156, 158f; cf. John W. Wright, "The Founding Father: The Structure of the Chronicler's David Narrative," *Journal of Biblical Literature* 117 (1998): 45-59. Wright reads 1 Chron. 10-29 as a series of three narrative movements: 1. David's establishment as king (10:1-14:2); 2. the acts of David as king (14:3-22:1); and 3. the Chronicler's succession narrative (22:2-29:30)]. He argues that the Chronicler focused upon David's political impact, perceiving him as a model king and uplifting his control of Temple properties, personnel, and rites as the norm for Judah (45, 47, 50, 51, 59).

14. Ahlström, *History*, 838-840; Soggin, *History*, 281.

15. Ahlström, *History*, 838-841; Soggin, *History*, 280-282; Purvis, "Exile and Return," 166-169; Gottwald, *The Hebrew Bible*, 431f; Clines, "Haggai's Temple," 82-85.

16. Koch, *The Prophets II*, 163; Purvis, "Exile and Return," 167; Soggin, *History*, 282; Clines, "Haggai's Temple," 82-85.

17. Ahlström, *History*, 853; Soggin, *History*, 282.

18. Ahlström, *History*, 853-858.

19. Ahlström, *History*, 859-863; Soggin, *History*, 288f; Purvis, "Exile and Return," 168f, 171-173. Here, the sequencing of Ahlström and Soggin will be followed. They place Nehemiah before Ezra. For arguments see Ahlström (880-882). As suggested later, the reason for sequential priority of Ezra in the biblical text is his endorsement of the Aaronites and his promulgation of their standards, which were authorized by the Persians. See also Lester L. Grabbe, *Judaism from Cyrus to Hadrian: The Persian and Greek Periods*, vol. 1 (Minneapolis: Fortress Press, 1992), 1-145, especially 92f, 136-138.

20. Ahlström, *History*, 864-866; Soggin, *History*, 288-293; cf. Martin Noth, *The History of Israel* (3d ed.; trans. Peter R. Ackroyd; New York: Harper and Row, 1958), 323-328.

21. Ahlström, *History*, 867; Soggin, *History*, 293f.

22. Ahlström, *History*, 873-877, 879-882; Soggin, *History*, 289-293.

23. Ahlström, *History*, 873-875, 876f, 879f; Gottwald, *The Hebrew Bible*, 435-437; Purvis, "Exile and Return," 169f.

24. Washington, "The Strange Women," 219-221, 230-238; Daniel Smith-Christopher, "The Mixed Marriage Crisis in Ezra 9-10 and Nehemiah 13: A Study of the Sociology of Post-Exilic Judaean Community," in *Second Temple Studies 2: Temple and Community in the Persian Period* (eds. Tamara C. Eskenazi and Kent H. Richards; JSOT Sup. 175; Sheffield: JSOT Press, 1994), 243-265; Tamara C. Eskenazi and Eleanore P. Judd, "Marriage to a Stranger in Ezra 9-10," in *Second Temple Studies 2: Temple and Community in the Persian Period* (eds. Tamara C. Eskenazi and Kent H. Richards; JSOT Sup. 175; Sheffield: JSOT Press, 1994), 266-285.

25. Israel Knohl, *The Sanctuary of Silence: The Priestly Torah and the Holiness School* (Minneapolis: Fortress Press, 1995), 222-224. Knohl sees the final redaction of the Pentateuch as the work of HS, which began with Ezra and his circle and continued through the *haburot* of the Pharisees (224). See Jerome C. Ross, *The Composition of the Holiness Code (Lev. 17-26)* (Dissertation: University of Pittsburgh, 1997), 131-146, 147-161.

26. Ahlström, *History*, 884-888; Gottwald, *The Hebrew Bible*, 437.

27. Paul D. Hanson, *The People Called: The Growth of Community in the Bible* (San Francisco: Harper and Row, 1986), 296f, 300.

28. Robert B. Coote and David Robert Ord, *In the Beginning: Creation and the Priestly History* (Minneapolis: Fortress Press, 1991), 32-33, 37-38. Coote and Ord argue that the Levites claimed descent from Levi, Moses, Abiathar. The Zadokites, then, claimed descent from Levi, Aaron, and Zadok. That Solomon ousted Abiathar and established Zadok provides the background for understanding the rivalries among the priests. Coote and Ord regard Nehemiah and Ezra as pro-Levites, though Ezra was a Zadokite, and argue that they were sent to counter the local Zadokites, who were backed by the Greeks and thus were a threat to the Persians. Cf. Num. 16:1; Exod. 6:16, 18, 21; also Aelred Cody, *A History of Old Testament Priesthood* (Rome: Pontifical Biblical Institute,1969), 116-117, 123-124, 129, 131, 133-134, 137, 139, 144, 159-162, 165, 169-170, 171-173; Frank Moore Cross, *Canaanite Myth and Hebrew Epic* (Cambridge: Harvard University Press,1973), 201, 206-207, 211, 215; Saul Olyan, "Zadok's Origins and the Tribal Politics of David," *Journal of Biblical Literature* 101 (1982): 185, 187-191, 193; Rodney K. Duke, "The Portion of the Levite: Another Reading of Deuteronomy 18:6-8," *Journal of Biblical Literature* 106 (1987): 193, 195-199, 201; Stephen L. Cook, "Innerbiblical Interpretation in Ezekiel 44 and the History of Israel's Priesthood," *Journal of Biblical Literature* 114 (1995): 193-208. The general view is that, prior to the exile, the Levites were probably considered priests of equal standing to the Aaronites (cf. Exod. 32), but their status varied due to political preferences (cf. 1 Kgs. 2:26-27; 12:25-33). Also, the references that mention the Levites are crucial. In Exod. 32, which is JE, the Levites are elevated. However, in 1 Kgs. 2:26-27; 12:25-33, which are DH and exilic, the Levites are deposed and Zadok is elevated. Ezekiel 44 confirms this degraded status of the Levites, basing it upon a negative assessment of their role in affairs at Jerusalem prior to the exile. Thus, it is probable that the distinction between the Aaronites (or Zadokites) and the Levites is late, even exilic, and was read back into the traditions (e.g., DH) and continued by H (Num. 8, 16). Furthermore, if the Levites are representative of a popular form of Yahwism, their deposition can possibly be considered an indication of H's redaction of DH and the Pentateuch, in order to justify the elevated

status of the Aaronites, which H endorses. See Gary N. Knoppers ["Hierodules, Priests, or Janitors? The Levites in Chronicles and the History of the Israelite Priesthood," *Journal of Biblical Literature* 118 (1999): 49-72], who reads CH (especially 1 Chr 23:28-32) as empowering the Levites and stressing cooperation and complementarity, not competition and hierarchy, between the Aaronites (Zadokites) and the Levites (59, 62-68, 69, 70-71).

29. During this time, the phenomenon of prophecy does not cease, but is assumed to exist. However, it is incorporated by the cult under the auspices of the priests (e.g., levitical preaching). See Frederick E. Greenspahn, "Why Prophecy Ceased," *Journal of Biblical Literature* 108 (1989): 37-49, especially 37, 39, 40, 41, 47; also Joseph Blenkinsopp, *Sage, Priest, Prophet: Religious and Intellectual Leadership in Ancient Israel* (Louisville: Westminster John Knox ,1995), 82-83, 96.

30. Hanson, *The People Called*, 302-305, 306; Joseph Blenkinsopp, *A History of Prophecy in Israel: From the Settlement in the Land to the Hellenistic Period* (Philadelphia: Westminster, 1983), 252-254, 256; also Roddy Braun, "Solomonic Apologetic in Chronicles," *Journal of Biblical Literature* 92 (1973): 503-516; idem, "Solomon, the Chosen Temple Builder: The Significance of 1 Chronicles 22, 28, and 29 for the Theology of Chronicles," *Journal of Biblical Literature* 95 (1976): 581-590; idem, "A Reconsideration of the Chronicler's Attitude toward the North," *Journal of Biblical Literature* 96 (1977): 59-62. Braun ("Solomonic Apologetic") argues that the Chronicler lays the foundation for the invitation to the northern Yahwists to return to their former allegiance by portraying the reigns of David and Solomon as a single unit centering in the construction of the Jerusalem temple and demonstrating the unique position of the Jerusalem temple and its sponsor-builders as unanimously accepted by all Israel [cf. idem, "The Significance," 581, 590, also 582, 583, 584, 587, 589; idem, "A Reconsideration," 59, 61-62].

31. Gottwald, *The Hebrew Bible*, 437; Hanson, *The People Called*, 292f, 297, 300f; J. Maxwell Miller and John H. Hayes, *A History of Ancient Israel and Judah* (Philadelphia: Westminster, 1986), 475; cf. Thomas B. Dozeman, "The Wilderness and Salvation History in the Hagar Story," *Journal of Biblical Literature* 117 (1998): 23-43. Dozeman reads the Hagar story (Gen. 16, 21) as a P tradition that develops the wilderness theme in conjunction with the theme of family conduct, so as to address the concern of how Israel must live in "the wilderness", thereby emphasizing controlled (i.e., covenant) interrelationship, while maintaining purity through fierce independence from surrounding culture (32, 42-43).

32. In this context, H was composed, that is, ca. 350-300 B.C.E. See Ross, *The Holiness Code*, 106-126, especially 157 n. 40.

33. Ross, *The Holiness Code*. Based upon two findings, that the core of H is not Lev. 18-20 and that the compositional grid of H is multi-tiered, structurally having primary and secondary chapters and substantially consisting of the dialectical pair, holiness-profanation (חלל - קדוש) I have argued that H has a three-tiered, five-part structure, and is best classified as a manual of discipline for some faction of the Aaronite priests. By comparing H with other pentateuchal traditions and Ezra-Nehemiah, especially the passages relating to *Sukkoth*, I have shown that the publication of H as a whole occurred between the time of Ezra, particularly the writing of Ezra-Nehemiah and the translation of the Pentateuch into Greek about 350-300 B.C.E. Furthermore, consideration of the dynamics of the dialectic, "holiness-unholiness," in the historical context of H shows that holiness is generally used as a multi-faceted "boundary-marker" and a mechanism of survival for the post-exilic Jewish community. Thus, I have determined that H addresses the confusion regarding the standards for the community that had ensued due to competing priestly factions within their socially mixed community and argues that anyone, regardless of origin or prior affiliations, who lives in the province of Judah and follows the rulings of the H-faction of the Aaronite priests, is a legitimate Yahwist and thereby holy.

34. From study of Nehemiah the following observations have been noted: (1) religious concerns are always intertwined with social concerns, e.g., politics, economics, customs, etc. (2) faith is the ideology by which a people live that is manifested in customs, symbols, practices, institutions, and concepts, statements, or theories (i.e., doctrines or dogmas, which entail criteria, norms, principles, or standards, e.g., for Israel the *prioritization* of YHWH, the *selective imaging* of YHWH, and the historicity of YHWH's activity) (cf. Neh. 1:1-2:20); (3) Israelite community is never monolithic but eclectic or pluralistic in its expression(s) of its beliefs; (4) sociopolitical differences often reflect differences in ideological interpretations, i.e., political factions result from varied understandings and applications of the basic principles for the Israelite community; (5) legitimacy or validation, usually, is not immediate in the context of an intra-communal controversy; thus, the surviving faction or group often counts itself as justified (cf. Neh. 1-3); (6) the sanctuary or religious institutions should reflect, and often do, the attitudes of those who construct, implement, or utilize them (cf. Neh. 6); (7) community requires people, purpose, and place within some tangible structure (cf. Neh. 7); (8) once a tradition is written: (a) the more obsolete it becomes to each successive or subsequent generation; (b) it must be supplemented in successive or subsequent generations in ways that are consistent with its essential principles in order to maintain relevance for the community that uses it (cf. Neh. 8); (9) salvation is communal (i.e., re-establishment of proper

identity in relationship) and comprehensive (i.e., encompassing all areas of life or having political, economic, cultural, and social ramifications) (cf. Neh. 9); (10) religious rituals or practices (e.g., offerings) have greater social ramifications (i.e., economic, sociopolitical, and cultural dimensions); (11) the sociopolitical structure and the economic base are expressions of the prevailing cultic orientation or posture (cf. Neh. 10); (12) the cult provides the ideal or pattern for communal life via its traditions and history; (13) survival of a people is determined somewhat by the balance they maintain between their ideals and the sociopolitical circumstances that confront and challenge them (cf. Neh. 11); (14) the quality and quantity of a congregation's offerings directly determine the character of its identity or mission (cf. Neh. 12:1-13:14); (15) the requirements for survival of a people are: (a) administrative structure (cf. Neh. 8, 10, 11); (b) economic independence (cf. Neh. 13:15-22; 10); (c) intra-communal organization or ideological standardization (cf. Neh. 13:23-31a); (d) common language (cf. Neh. 13:23-24); (e) balance of extra-communal influences and intra-communal accommodation, i.e., selective appropriation or assimilation of the dominant culture by the minority culture; (f) population or people [cf. lists]; and (g) land or place; (16) faith is necessarily inclusive, i.e., the theology or Israelite ideology is intentionally considerate of the respective, sociopolitical contexts (cf. Neh. 13:15-31). See Ross, The Holiness Code, 131-146, 147-161.

Excursus Two:
Research on Ezra-Nehemiah

"The Composition of Ezra-Nehemiah"

Japhet argues that Ezra-Nehemiah is connected by sources and a unified plan in which there was interweaving according to a chronological reckoning based on the reigns of the Persian kings coupled with historical periodization according to events in Judah.[1] Also, Kraemer presents the thesis that the relationship between the books of Ezra and Nehemiah is analogous to that of 1 and 2 Maccabees—they report an overlapping, but identical, historical period from significantly different ideological perspectives.[2] Third, Eskenazi examines the use of lists in Ezra-Nehemiah and concludes the lists of people in Ezra-Nehemiah shape the book, affirm its integrity, help to differentiate the work from Chronicles, and express one of the major themes of the book—the shift away from individual heroes to the centrality of the people as a whole.[3]

That Nehemiah elevates the Levites while Ezra presents them in a subordinate posture and that Ezra holds sequential priority over Nehemiah are reflections of the superimposition of Ezra upon Nehemiah by the Aaronites, who probably gained prominence under Persian rule. Evidently the fact and the importance of Nehemiah's mission were undeniable, thus warranting the qualification or modification (i.e., toning down) of its significance by the Aaronites, who prioritized Ezra. Regarding this superimposition, Neh. 8 is viewed as belonging to the Ezra narrative, and Neh. 7:5-10:40 is considered to have been inserted into the Nehemiah Memoir—that is, Neh. 7:4 continues in 11:1.[4] However there are dissenting views. Emerton suggests Nehemiah does not presuppose Ezra or the work of Nehemiah preceded that of Ezra, and there are no organic relations between the two,[5] while DeVries sees Ezra-Nehemiah and Chronicles as a collocation reflecting two different authors.[6]

"The Date of Ezra-Nehemiah"

Kellermann dates Ezra earlier than Nehemiah (i.e., ca. 448 B.C.E.) based upon examination and consideration of Ezra 7:12-26 as the only authentic material in a comparison of Ezra 8-10 and Nehemiah 8-12.[7] Second, McFall builds upon the consensus view that Ezra 9-10 and Nehemiah 8-10 belong together and the reference to Ezra's first year in Jerusalem, when Nehemiah was absent.[8] He argues that Ezra was a contemporary of Nehemiah from 458-454 B.C.E. (Ezra 7:7; Neh. 8:9-10; 10:1), after Ezra arrived in the seventh year of Artaxerxes, and that Nehemiah was in Jerusalem in 458 B.C.E.[9] He bases his position on the assumption the Artaxerxes in Ezra-Nehemiah is Artaxerxes I (465-424 B.C.E.). Neh. 8:9, 10:1, and 12:36 are historically accurate and two types of dating were used, dynastic reckoning from the beginning of Xerxes's reign and sole-reign reckoning, in which Nehemiah's first visit was dated according to the first (Neh. 5:14; 13:6) while his second visit was dated according to the second reckoning during Artaxerxes's reign (Neh. 2:1).[10]

However Grabbe questions the authenticity of Ezra 7:12-26, since it purports to be an archival source of a Persian decree, but appears in Hebrew in a Hebrew narrative and not in its appropriate place and reflects considerable Jewish theology.[11]

The Relation of Ezra-Nehemiah and Chronicles

Blenkinsopp[12] follows Meyers[13] regarding Ezra-Nehemiah as part of CH, while the rest read the two separately. Meyers dates the completion of the main work about 400 B.C.E., based upon the following points: (1) the list of the Davidic family in 1 Chron. 3:17-24; (2) the mention of Jehohanan in Ezra 10:6; and Neh. 12:10-11, 22 as being the last functioning high priest; (3) the reference to Darius II (424-405 B.C.E.) in Neh. 12:22 as the last Persian king mentioned; and (4) the reference to Bigvai.[14] However, Japhet offers a reasonable proposal. She argues that Chronicles and Ezra-Nehemiah constitute two different works by two different authors, in light of several features of Chronicles: (1) its heterogeneous composition; (2) the presence of late biblical Hebrew in it, with features common to late biblical and extra-biblical works; (3) the genealogy of Jehoiachin (1 Chron. 3:17-24) that dates about 460-320 B.C.E.; (4) the development of the cultic institutions, the organization of the Temple personnel, and the integration of the non-priestly clergy into the levitical order; and (5) the reflections of DH, the Pentateuch, Zechariah, Lamentations, Ezra (1:1-3a), and Nehemiah (11:3-19).[15] She dates Chronicles at the end of the fourth century or at the end of the Persian period and the beginning of the Hellenistic period,[16] based upon two principles: that early dating must entail a specific view of the literary work, with extensive parts of it regarded as secondary or later editions; and that late dating is often determined by a scholar's general view of the chronology of biblical literature, in this instance, by the literary appreciation of Chronicles as a sample of post-biblical genres.[17] Similarly, following Japhet and Williamson, Throntveit denies common authorship of Chronicles and Ezra-Nehemiah, citing: (1) the presence of Ezra 1:1-3a at the end of Chronicles (2 Chron. 36:22-23); (2) the evidence of 1 Esdras, which begins with 2 Chron. 35-36 and continues through Ezra; (3) the linguistic similarities between Chronicles and Ezra-Nehemiah; and (4) the similarity of theological conceptions in both works. However he refutes the latter two features of Chronicles that Japhet distinguished, noting that Chronicles reflects an emphasis on David, or the Davidic covenant, that is not in Ezra-Nehemiah; ignores the exodus tradition in Ezra-Nehemiah; is tolerant of exogamy with Solomon, while Ezra-Nehemiah abhors such and projects immediate retribution, while such is absent in Ezra-Nehemiah.[18]

Moreover, Chronicles and Ezra-Nehemiah share several common features:[19] (1) description of preparations for building the First and the Second Temple (Ezr. 3:7; 1 Chron. 22:2, 4, 15; 2 Chron. 2:9, 15-16); (2) altar is set up before temple to wardoff danger (Ezr. 3:2; 1 Chron. 21:18-22:1); (3) temples are endowed by the heads of ancestral houses (Ezr. 2:68; 1 Chron. 26:26; royal - 2 Kgs. 12:18); (4) interest in sacred vessels (Ezr. 1:7; 7:19; 8:25-30, 33-34; 1 Chron. 28:13-19; 2 Chron. 5:1 [- 2 Kgs. 24:13]); (5) identical order of sacrifices and enumeration of sacrificial materials (Ezr. 6:9, 17; 7:17-18, 22; 8:35-36; 1 Chron. 29:21; 2 Chron. 29:21, 32); (6) close correspondence between descriptions of liturgical music and of musical instruments and players (Ezr. 3:10; Neh. 12:35; 1 Chron. 15:19; 16:5-6; 25:1, 6; 2 Chron. 5:12-13); (7) close correspondence of liturgical prayer, the blessing form, and confessional psalm (Ezr. 3:11; 7:27-28; Neh. 9:5-6; 1 Chron. 29:10-19; 2 Chron. 2:11; 6:4-11; 9:9; 20:5-12).

Endnotes

1. Sara Japhet, "Composition and Chronology in the Book of Ezra-Nehemiah," in *Second Temple Studies 2: Temple and Community in the Persian Period* (eds. Tamara C. Eskenazi and Kent H. Richards; JSOT Sup. 175; Sheffield: JSOT Press, 1994), 209, 212f, 215.

2. David Kraemer, "On the Relationship of the Books of Ezra and Nehemiah," *Journal for the Study of the Old Testament* 59 (1993): 77.

3. Tamara C. Eskenazi, "The Structure of Ezra-Nehemiah and the Integrity of the Book, *Journal of Biblical Literature* 107 (1988): 642, 654, 656.

4. Kraemer, "On the Relationship," 77, 80-83; Niels Peter Lemche, *Ancient Israel: A New History of Israelite Society* (England: Sheffield, 1995), 45; Simon De Vries, *1 and 2 Chronicles* (Vol. XI: FOTL; Grand Rapids, MI: Eerdmans, 1989), 8, 10f; Joseph Blenkinsopp, *Ezra-Nehemiah* (OTL; Philadelphia: Westminster, 1988), 44, 46, 284, 286f, 288; H. G. M. Williamson, *Ezra-Nehemiah* (WBC; Waco: Word Books, 1985), xxviii, 283, 285, 286; John A. Emerton, "Did Ezra Go to Jerusalem in 428 BC?" *Journal of Theological Studies* 17 (1966): 1, 3, 7, 16.

5. Emerton, "Did Ezra Go to Jerusalem in 428 BC?" 1, 3, 7, 16.

6. De Vries, *1 and 2 Chronicles*, 8, 10f.

7. Ulrich Kellermann, "Erwägungen zum Problem der Esradatierung," *Zeitschrift für die alttestamentliche Wissenschaft* 80 (1968): 56, 84, 86f.

8. Leslie McFall, "Was Nehemiah Contemporary with Ezra in 458 BC?" *The Westminster Theological Journal* 53 (1991): 267f, 270.

9. McFall, "Was Nehemiah Contemporary with Ezra in 458 BC?" 270, 272.

10. McFall, "Was Nehemiah Contemporary with Ezra in 458 BC?" 270, 273-274.

11. Lester L. Grabbe, "Reconstructing History from the Book of Ezra," in *Second Temple Studies 1: Persian Period* (ed. Philip R. Davies; JSOT Sup. 117; Sheffield: JSOT Press, 1991), 99, 101-102.

12. Blenkinsopp, *Ezra-Nehemiah*, 48-54. Cf. Eskenazi, "The Structure of Ezra-Nehemiah," 656; Williamson, *Ezra-Nehemiah*, xxii; Roddy Braun, *1 Chronicles* (WBC; Waco: Word Books, 1986), xxix; Raymond B. Dillard, *2 Chronicles* (WBC; Waco: Word Books, 1987), xix.

13. Jacob M. Meyers, *Ezra-Nehemiah* (AB; New York: Doubleday, 1965), lxviii-lxix.

14. Meyers, *Ezra-Nehemiah*, lxxxix, lxix.

15. Sara Japhet, *I & II Chronicles* (OTL; Philadephia: Westminster, 1993), 4-5, 25-27.

16. Japhet, *I & II Chronicles*, 27f.

17. Japhet, *I & II Chronicles*, 24.

18. Mark A. Throntveit, *Ezra-Nehemiah* (Int.; Louisville: John Knox, 1992), 9.
19. Blenkinsopp, *Ezra-Nehemiah*, 53.

Categorization of the Jewish Sectors
in the Hellenistic & the Roman Period

Liberals	Moderates	Conservatives
The Hellenizing Jews	The Assimilationist Jews	The Orthodox Jews
Politically-Conservative	Politically-Moderate	Politically-Radical
Religiously-Liberal	Religiously-Progressive	Religiously-Traditional
Written Torah	Written & Oral Torah	Written Torah w/Pesherim
Double Standards	Equally-Applicable Laws	Strict Legalism
Temple-Controlling	Synagogue-Developing	Withdrawn from Society
The Hasmoneans & Levites	The Hasidim	The Zadokites/Aaronites
The Sadducees	The Pharisees	The Essenes
The Nobility or Aristocracy	The 'Populace Elite'	The Sectarian Rebels

(The Jewish Underground: The Zealots)

CHAPTER SIX:
THE RISE OF HELLENISM[1]

Under Artaxerxes II the Persian empire declined. In 401 B.C.E. Egypt regained its freedom under Pharaoh Nepherites, who also took Gezer and maintained it until 342 B.C.E. He was succeeded by Achoris (393-380 B.C.E.), who made an alliance with Evagoras of Salamis in Cyprus, resulting in invasion of the northern coast of Palestine and of Phoenicia. Following a failed Persian campaign to Egypt in 385-383 B.C.E., Evagoras captured parts of Tyre and Sidon and managed to secure support from Cilicia against the Persians. Then he was defeated by Artaxerxes II of Persia in 381 B.C.E., who unsuccessfully sought to take Egypt. Egypt stood and maintained influence in Palestine.

After an unsuccessful rebellion by Cyrus, who died in battle, Artaxerxes restored power in Anatolia partly by buying out the Greeks and so pitting the Greek cities against themselves. The satraps of the western part of the empire, under the lead of Aroandes, invaded the area of the Euphrates River and advanced into Mesopotamia in 362 B.C.E., having the support of Abd-ashtart of Sidon and Tachos of Egypt, the son of Nectanebos I. Tachos invaded Phoenicia in 360 B.C.E., being supported by Agesilaos of Sparta, but was deposed while in battle and then defected, becoming a general of Artaxerxes. Shortly thereafter in 358 B.C.E. Artaxerxes died, leaving the Persian empire in further decline. Artaxerxes III Ochos (358-337 B.C.E.) then attained the throne by killing all of his brothers and other competitors.

This precipitated a dangerous climate for Persia in light of the advance of the Phoenicians, who revolted during 351-345 B.C.E. (called the Tennes revolt, because Tennes, Abd-ashtart's son and the king of Sidon, was its leader). Also, Philip II of Macedonia rose to power in 359 B.C.E., bringing all of the Greek states under his rule in 338 B.C.E. Not regarding Macedonia as a threat, Artaxerxes III campaigned in Egypt in 353-352 B.C.E., failing and probably triggering the rebellion by the Phoenicians, who thought the Persian empire was on the verge of destruction. Tennes of Sidon, being aided by Egypt, managed to drive out the army of the satraps.

Upon the arrival of Artaxerxes III in 345 B.C.E., Tennes secretly promised to surrender Sidon to him and to help him reconquer Egypt. However, Tennes marched into the other Phoenician kings, who intercepted his army and put him to death. The horror of Sidon scared the other Phoenician cities into submitting to Artaxerxes III, ending the rebellion, and paving the way for the conquest of Egypt in 343 B.C.E. Artaxerxes III then advanced on Egypt, having the Greeks (Argos, Thebes, and the Ionian cities) as aides from the Phoenician battles though they arrived late in countering Sidon. This ended Egyptian independence, as Bagoas, a general of Artaxerxes III, first murdered the old king in 337 B.C.E., permitting Arses to ascend the throne, and second, murdered Arses in 336 B.C.E., permitting Kodomannos to assume the throne under the name Darius III. Eventually, Bagoas was poisoned to death.

The same year Darius III became king, Alexander succeeded Philip II, his father. Having united all of Greece under his reign, Alexander crossed the Hellespont in 334 B.C.E. and invaded Asia Minor. Upon encountering Alexander, the Cypriot and Phoenician commanders deserted the Persians and joined Alexander, contributing to the fall of Persia. The battle at Issos in 333 B.C.E. marked the end of Persian rule and the beginning of Greek rule in the Near East.

Immediately after taking the throne, Alexander marched south, receiving the submission of all of the Phoenician cities except Tyre, which was taken through a seven-month siege. Then he proceeded south toward the coast of Egypt, meeting opposition in Palestine only at Gaza. Since the Persians were hated in Egypt, Alexander was welcomed there as a liberator. In 331 B.C.E. he founded Alexandria as the new capital of Egypt and headed to Babylonia in order to secure the eastern part of his empire.[2] Darius was murdered in 330 B.C.E. by some of his own men, when the war effort seemed hopeless. Thus the Hellenistic empire was finally secured.

During the time of the takeover by Alexander, the situation of Palestine gradually changed.[3] Judah remain relatively untouched, while Samaria became a Macedonian city, welcoming Alexander. Also, Tyre grew in importance after the destruction of Sidon. During the fourth century B.C.E. there was an increase in coins minted in Palestine, which was necessitated by the need to pay the Greek mercenaries in hard currency. Though the territory of Samaria (Samerina) was settled by people of different national and religious backgrounds, the majority of the population was Israelite and the Yahwistic traditions still thrived.

Within the Israelite areas, tensions between the Jews and the Samaritans incited by Ezra and Nehemiah still existed.[4] These peaked when Andromachos, Alexander's governor, was murdered, probably behind sour sentiments pertaining to the building of a temple on Mount Gerizim. This prompted punishment by Alexander, causing some inhabitants to move to Shechem and to rebuild the city and possibly to build a temple there.[5] The temple at Mount Gerizim became the central sanctuary for Yahwistic worshippers of Samaria (Samerina), preserving a conservative form of religion which broke with and became a competitor to Jerusalem. The definitive break between the two traditions and temples came, when John Hyrcanus, motivated by political concerns, destroyed the Samaritan temple. At that time, he attempted to force the Gerizim-Shechem community to assimilate to that of the Jerusalem community. However after the initiation of Roman rule in 64 B.C.E. the Samaritan community resumed its own traditions independently.

Also during the Hellenistic period, the presence of Arabs increased in Transjordan and southern Palestine, particularly along the trade routes and the border areas with Egypt. When the Persian empire collapsed, they lost the trade with Arabia and the Nabateans of Transjordan and other Arab tribes expanded their territory, replacing the Edomites. This trend of increase of Nabatean settlements in Transjordan and the Negev continued through the Roman period.

The Impact of Hellenism upon the Jews[6]

The domination by the Macedonians was effected differently than the previous empires. There was an overt intent to Hellenize the subject peoples. Being a recipient of the traditions and teachings of Aristotle, Alexander's goal was to establish a multi-ethnic culture undergirded by the achievements and perspectives of Greek civilization.[7] This was sought through several means. First, Hellenism was propagated through founding of Greek cities or reconstituting of existing cities, so that the Greek customs were perpetuated. The Greek cities then provided the fixtures of Greek society (i.e., open markets, assembly places, baths, gymnasia, stadiums, theaters, libraries, temples). Through these institutions Greek culture was fostered, as many of the subject peoples benefited from the amenities and thereby were indoctrinated. Second, the newly established Greek cities were usually governed by a local council loyal to the monarch.[8] The governors within the administration, having backgrounds in agriculture, utilized their diverse expertise in ruling their areas and fostering increased production.[9] Nonetheless, Hellenism posed a great challenge to Judaism, not because of its diversity, but because of its enforcement, which in many instances was intolerant. During such moments of intolerant enforcement of Hellenism, the Jews had to assimilate culturally, even to the point of religious syncretism or be eclipsed by the dominant culture.[10] Also the Hellenistic form of local administration was effected through the dual positions of a high priest and a governor. As the high priest grew in importance and overshadowed the governor, internal conflicts ensued regarding control of the local community. This was further fostered by the Hellenistic overlords selling the office to the highest bidder.[11] Such cultural pressures significantly hindered unity among the Jews and conversely led to the splintering of the community.

When Alexander died unexpectedly in 323 B.C.E., his generals (i.e., Lysimachus, Cassander, Ptolemy, Seleucus) assumed responsibility for his empire, becoming a Diadochi. His empire was divided into four regions (i.e., the European territories, Macedonia, Greece, and Thrace; Egypt; Asia Minor; and Babylonia, Syria, and Canaan) and each general was assigned a region. The generals who held jurisdiction over Egypt and Babylonia continued the pattern of contesting one another for control over Syria and Canaan.[12]

The first Hellenistic regime to govern Palestine was the Ptolemies-Lagids of Egypt, who controlled the region from 301 to 198 B.C.E. Ptolemy occupied Canaan and Phoenicia in 312 B.C.E. and deported many inhabitants of Jerusalem to Alexandria, his governmental seat. Such immigrations persisted and resulted in a sizable population of Jews in Alexandria. A policy of royal absolutism rigorously enforced systems of taxes and leases, but considerable local autonomy was granted, provided the taxes and leases were maintained. At this point the Aaronite priesthood was given the responsibility of local rule as the major landholders and the exclusive legal authorities in the land. Under Ptolemaic Hellenism the region prospered, though offset by heavy taxes. Also, improved soil cultivation in Judah increased productivity, which in turn prompted population growth. The cultural development of this period is tangibly evidenced by the translation of the Pentateuch into Greek, called the Septuagint (LXX), which occurred during the reign of Ptolemy II Philadelphus (285-246 B.C.E.).[13] However Ptolemaic Hellenism eventually came under Roman control, as Carthage fell to Rome in the Punic wars of the second century. The kingdom survived until 30 B.C.E., ending with the death of Cleopatra.[14]

The second Hellenistic regime to govern Palestine was the Seleucids, who reigned from 198 to 164 B.C.E. The Seleucid dynasty that was founded by Seleucus I Monophthalmos (called Nicanor) in 312 B.C.E. managed to gain control over Syria and Canaan through Antiochus III's defeat of Ptolemy V Epiphanes in 198 B.C.E. His conquest was facilitated by support from the magnates, in which he exploited family rivalries between the high priestly Oniads and the Tobiads. As a result of these conquests the Seleucid kingdom extended from Egypt to Asia Minor and the Ionian cities. During these initial stages, the policy toward Judah was gratuitous and conciliatory, including a general waiver of taxes for three years and the permanent exemption of the priests and the temple from taxation. Shortly thereafter, as the Seleucid kingdom sought further expansion in the west, a conflict with Rome ensued (190-188 B.C.E.), in which Antiochus III suffered a defeat at the battle of Magnesia. He lost Asia Minor and some eastern holdings and was forced to pay heavy tribute. As Rome continued its conquests toward Egypt, Antiochus III's territory was severely decreased by the Parthians by the mid-third century B.C.E. and reduced to parts of Syria and Cilicia by the mid-second century. The heavy annual indemnity imposed upon Antiochus III by Rome forced him to consolidate his holdings and to exploit the temple treasuries within his domain. This eventually led to sour relations with Judah.[15]

Soon a rivalry within the royal family occurred. This was fostered by Rome, in order to weaken the Seleucid administration. Following the death of Antiochus III in 187 B.C.E. and later of his son, Antiochus IV Epiphanes assumed the throne. He sought to secure money by selling the office of high priest to the highest bidder. His first appointee was Jason, an Oniad, who obviously was very cooperative with Antiochus IV's plans. In 173 B.C.E. Antiochus visited Jerusalem and received favorable response, as the Jews later participated in the athletic games at Tyre, donating their money to the host city's fleet rather than the local deity. The second appointee was Menelaus, a non-Aaronite who made a higher offer than Jason and thereby bought the office of high priest. Under his tenure exploitation became acute. In 172 B.C.E. he was forced to steal in order to satisfy the demands for finances, creating tension between him and Jason. Antiochus IV severely enforced Hellenism, robbing and massacring in Jerusalem, and triggered incidences of violence in 169-168 B.C.E. Following a defeat by Rome in 168 B.C.E., in which he was humiliated, Antiochus IV abrogated the temple law and desecrated the temple altar in the month of Kislev (November/December), 167 B.C.E. He was intentionally punitive, destroying the community and the people. He issued a series of decrees aimed at compulsory Hellenization of Judah. The Jewish community then split: some Jews complied, while the Jews under Matthias, a priest from Modein, and his sons (Judas Maccabee, Simeon, Johanan, Eleazar, and Jonathan) led a revolt (1 Macc. 1-2; Dan. 11:31; 12:11; cf. 3:8-18) named the Maccabean revolution.[16]

The Maccabean revolt succeeded due to several factors. First, the Seleucids underestimated the Jewish rebels and devoted much of their attention to Rome. Because of this preoccupation and the splintering of the Seleucid forces, the Jews were able to mount a significant challenge. Also, there were numerous regions suitable for partisan war, the territories on the eastern side of the hill country dropping down towards the Jordan valley and the Dead Sea, and the valley of the Jordan River and the Dead Sea. Engagement in battle in these areas probably had to be on foot, canceling any chariotry or ramps. Third, the geographical location of the rebels was most suitable for guerrilla warfare. This was proficiently exploited by the Maccabean warriors, who were knowledgeable of the terrain and held the advantage of being on the offense. A fourth and implicit factor is motivation. During this time of acute persecution apocalyptic eschatology emerged in the form of numerous writings circulated among the persecuted underground. These works encouraged faithfulness to the war efforts, placing the historical particulars on a celestial plane. Through cryptic codes and esoteric symbolism (e.g., numerology, demonology, angelology, figurative language) the final judgment of the rebels as well as the oppressors was predicted, in which just or appropriate rewards would be accordingly meted out (cf. Daniel).[17]

The initial goal of the Maccabean rebels was religious freedom. This was expediently sought, as the rebels countered the charges of the Seleucids. Hindered by the major threat of Rome, the Seleucids were not able to overtake the rebels and had to settle for a temporary armistice in the spring of 164 B.C.E. Shortly thereafter, Judas and his army surprised the Syrian garrison in Jerusalem, capturing the city. At this time, on the twenty-fifth of Kislev (November/December) B.C.E. the temple was rededicated and protected by the installation of a small garrison. The occasion of this reclamation of independence marked the first Hanukkah (1 Macc. 4:36-59).[18]

The subsequent goal of the Maccabean rebels was political freedom. During the period of 164-160 B.C.E. the rebels sought to avenge the Jews who had been killed. Jews were returned to Jerusalem from Transjordan, Galilee, and the Mediterranean coast. However in 162 B.C.E. Antiochus V, who succeeded Antiochus IV, after the latter's death in the East, sustained a victory over the rebels near Beth Zechariah, near Jerusalem. A treaty was hastily made, in which the decrees banning Judaism were revoked, and Alcimus, a moderate Jewish Hellenist, was accepted as high priest. At this point the Jewish community again split. A pietistic group called the Hasidim, who had joined the rebels at the inception, now assented to the arrangement, accepting the religious freedom that was offered and declined from further battle. This left the remaining Maccabeans to subsequent war. Also, in 160 B.C.E. Alcimus demolished the wall in the inner court of the temple, causing a faction of the Aaronite priests to desert Jerusalem, relocate on the northwestern bank of the Dead Sea, and found the Qumran/Essene community. In spite of two factions being removed from the war effort, in 161 B.C.E. Judas achieved another victory at Adasa, defeating the Greek general Nicanor. He then made negotiations with Rome, but to no immediate benefit. In 160 B.C.E. Judas was killed in a return battle as his forces were defeated by Bacchides.[19] The remaining partisans dispersed to Tekoa and Michmash, where they lived in semi-isolation from 160-152 B.C.E.

In 153 B.C.E. war ensued between Demetrius and Alexander Balas (150-145 B.C.E.), both pretenders to the Seleucid throne. Bacchides was summoned home, providing the rebels some relief. Both Demetrius and Alexander Balas courted Jonathan, a brother of Judas, seeking to solicit his support for their positions. However, Alexander was successful. In 152 B.C.E. he gave Jonathan the office of high priest, though the latter was not a Aaronite, and later made him governor. Through these maneuvers Jonathan gained control over the civil and the religious offices, combining the two. In 147 B.C.E. Demetrius, son of Demetrius I, rebelled and sought to seize the throne. This distraction among the Seleucids enabled Jonathan to seize the Acra and occupy part of Samaria. Demetrius succeeded in ousting Alexander and was crowned Demetrius II Nicator (145-138, 129-125 B.C.E.). Through diplomacy Jonathan managed to maintain his position, gaining the privileges of Jewish worship, the concession of tax exemptions for the Jewish community, and three districts of Samaria. Nevertheless, later in 143 B.C.E., Jonathan sided with Antiochus, a son of Alexander Balas, against Demetrius, having renewed negotiations with Rome and begun such with Sparta. He refused to withdraw from the Acra and Bethzur and was then killed by Demetrius.[20]

Following Jonathan's death, Simon assumed the position of high priest and of political leadership. He renewed relations with Demetrius II, who then needed help against his rival Trypho, and thus granted the country *de facto* independence. In 141 B.C.E. Simon was able to seize the Acra and extend the frontiers of Judea through several campaigns, continuing contacts with Rome and Sparta. He conquered Gezer, expelled its gentile inhabitants, and resettled it with compliant Jews. Then he took Joppa, which served as the major seaport for the Hasmonean state. During his reign, the titles of *ethnarch* (i.e., head of the people, which was replaced by the title "king" in 104 B.C.E.) and *strategos* (i.e., commander of the army) were assumed, further bolstering his political clout. Thus, he declared independence from Seleucid rule. He ruled until 134 B.C.E., when he was assassinated at Jericho by his son-in-law along with two of his sons, possibly at the instigation of Antiochus VII, the regent of Demetrius II, who was a prisoner (1 Macc. 16:11-24).[21]

Shortly after Simon's death, the Hasmonean dynasty began. Its first ruler was John Hyrcanus (134-104 B.C.E.). He was the third son of Simon, who had escaped the massacre of his father and brothers because he had not gone to Jericho with them. He resumed contacts with Rome, but to no immediate advantage. He soon faced Antiochus VII at Jerusalem and was forced to surrender, because of shortage of food due to the previous year being *Yôbel* (Deut. 15: 1-18; Lev. 25:8-55), in which no work on the land was done. He was offered reasonable terms, though under Seleucid control. However, Antiochus VII died in 129 B.C.E. fighting the Parthians, while Demetrius II, who had been released from prison and had returned to the throne, was assassinated in 125 B.C.E. This freed Hyrcanus to develop and expand his own country.

After his release from Seleucid domination, Hyrcanus sought to expand his control, particularly over the important trade routes and major ports. Samaria was conquered and the temple on Mount Gerizim was destroyed. In 108 B.C.E. the capital of Samaria was captured and later the Idumeans were forced to convert to Judaism and be circumcised. His concern was consolidation and security of his kingdom, which he sought by forced compliance with his ideology and institutions. Positively regarded, his and his successors' policy was intended to motivate allegiance to the Jewish state. The negative side-effect of this forced conversion was the creation of animosity among the non-Jews. Though he was originally a disciple of the Pharisees, by this time Hyrcanus sided with the Sadducees, probably because of the criticism of his holding of civil and religious power and his cruelty in administration. In this respect the Pharisees became staunch, even militant, opponents of the Hasmonean state. The Sadducees, on the other hand, benefited from the acquisition of power and position through affiliation with the Hasmonean administration. Essentially, Hyrcanus organized and operated a monarchy that resembled the Hellenistic models.[22]

Following Hyrcanus' reign, several successors served short terms. Aristobulus I (104-103 B.C.E.) succeeded John, being the first Hasmonean to adopt the title "king" and securing his position by means of execution of his mother and assassination of Antigonus, one of his brothers. The other brothers, among whom was Alexander Jannaeus, were imprisoned. Aristobulus continued the pro-Hellenistic policy of Hyrcanus and annexed Iturean territory in southern Lebanon or northern Galilee, forcing them to convert to Judaism.[23]

Next was Alexander Jannaeus (103-76 B.C.E.), who came out of prison and also resumed the expansionist policy of Hyrcanus. He gained control of Straton's Tower (later Caesurea) and Dor in the southwest, the coastal district, including Gaza, and large areas of Moab, overrunning much of the Golan and Gilead. He suffered a defeat at Shechem by the Seleucids, who were summoned by the Pharisees, his opponents. The Pharisees abandoned the alliance, perceiving Demetrius III Eucarius's aim to re-establish Seleucid dominion, and saved the country. However they suffered severe backlash from Alexander, who crucified many of them and killed their family members before their faces. Alexander became ill and died, ending his treacherous reign.[24]

Alexander was succeeded by his widow, Alexandra Salome (76-67 B.C.E.). Peace ensued after his death, probably due to his reconciliation with the Pharisees before his death. The Pharisees gained control of the country's internal affairs and collided in administrative battles with the Sadducees. By this means his wife enjoyed some significant measure of support. One of the consequences of these differences was the withdrawal of a Saducean faction called the Essenes. Also, Alexander's older son, Hyrcanus II, became the high priest, and the younger son, Aristobulus, became the commander of the army. After the death of Alexandra, Hyrcanus II inherited the throne, only to abdicate, after three months, in favor of his brother.[25]

Aristobulus' reign (67-63 B.C.E.) was marked by serious conflict. Antipater, the governor of Idumea, who was aided by the Nabateans of southern Transjordan, rebelled. He pledged the Nabateans to restore their lost territory and sought to enlist Hyrcanus II's support. He played the Pharisees against the Sadducees, observing that Aristobulus had the support of the Pharisees and Hyrcanus had that of the Sadducees. A stalemate occurred, prompting both sides to appeal to Rome. So, in 64 or 63 B.C.E. Rome annexed Syria and decided in favor of Aristobulus, ordering the withdrawal of the others. However Hyrcanus appealed directly to Pompey, who had arrived in Damascus in 63 B.C.E., simultaneously when a delegation from Jerusalem requested termination of the Hasmonean rule. The delegation proposed a *hierocratic solution*, that is, that Jerusalem would be locally governed by the temple priesthood, while adhering to Roman administration and sovereignty. Though Pompey decided in favor of Aristobulus, the latter deserted him, only later to acquiesce on harsh terms. Aristobulus was requested to surrender his fortresses and the capital to Rome, but refused, prompting a three-month siege, after which Jerusalem fell. Upon penetration of Jerusalem Pompey entered the Holy of Holies in the temple, probably to tear down any religio-political images, but found nothing. Aristobulus was taken by foot to Rome as verification of Pompey's triumph. Thus, the Hasmonean dynasty came to an end and Roman sovereignty was instituted with Hyrcanus, being nominated to high priest and ethnarch and having to renounce the title of "king." Also, Antipater gained momentum and clout through his affiliations with Rome, which secured his position politically, while souring his relations with the local populace.[26]

To conclude this overview of the Jews under the Hellenistic rule, the following features of Jewish life emerged: (1) increased individualism; (2) dissolution of traditional ties; (3) distinction and withdrawal of the synagogue as a counter-action to the assimilation of Hellenism; (4) encompassing of prevalent philosophies in some circles; (5) adoption of Hellenizing tendencies, especially by the Sadducees; (6) furtherance of the separatistic tendency that was started by Ezra and Nehemiah on the part of the Pharisees; and (7) the rise of apocalyptic literature and the preoccupation with early Hebrew narratives.[27] The Jews were unified by their sense of purpose, the belief that they were called by YHWH to embody a certain quality of life that was specified by the Torah. However the most prominent indicators of this unity were Sabbath observance, dietary regulations, and sacred texts now regarded as revelatory due to the presumed inspiration of their speakers and writers.[28] Still, factionalization of the Jewish community due to the volatile political situation[29] was most prevalent. Thus these groups and this delicate situation provide the backdrop for understanding the Greek Testament with its main feature, the *Jesus* movement.

Chapter Synopsis:
The Key Dates

333 B.C.E. Alexander the Great conquers the Mediterranean World
301-198 B.C.E. Rule of Egyptian Hellenism in Palestine
198-164 B.C.E. Rule of Syrian Hellenism in Palestine
167-164 B.C.E. The Maccabean Revolution

Causes:
1. challenge of cultural assimilation and religious syncretism or eclipse precipitated by Hellenism
2. internal conflict that determined control of intra-communal leadership
3. severe or oppressive policy of the Seleucids due to fiscal crisis caused by the defeat of Antiochus III at Magnesia by the Romans (190 B.C.E.) and lost of Asia Minor and some eastern holdings or enforcement of Hellenism by the Seleucids and Hellenizing Jews in effort to consolidate their political domain

Developments:
1. attempted reconciliation of normative political constructs with Yahwism evidenced in the formation of the Hasmonean State
2. exclusion of Hellenistic religious syncretism by an overwhelming Jewish consensus
3. Jewish consensus for maintenance of Torah as ideological basis for community
4. prominence of the synagogue as counter-action to Hellenism and Jewish temple-cultus

Effects:
1. split of the country and Jewish community
2. treaty connections with the Romans in order to keep in check the Seleucids
3. forced conversions of conquered peoples by the Hasmoneans
4. destruction of the Samaritan temple on Mount Gerizim and suppression of Jewish heterodoxy
5. reactive emergence of an independent Jewish state modelled after the Hellenistic structures
6. re-alignment of socio-economic, political, and religious forces of Jews, i.e., origination of various Jewish parties or sects and the particular rivalry of Pharisaism and Sadduceanism and the withdrawal of the Essenes and the Hasidim
7. addition or institution of *Hanukkak* as a Jewish holy day [1 Macc. 4:36-59]

8. rise of apocalyptic literature [Dan., Joel 3-4; Isa. 24-27; Zech. 9-14; Ezek. 38-39]
9. translation of the Pentateuch into Greek

Interpretations:
1. YHWH as Sovereign Judge and Deliverer via apocalyptic concepts, e.g., final judgment, resurrection, etc.
2. imminent conquest of human history and worldly rule by the kingdom of God [cf. Dan.]

The Selected Interpretations
#1: YHWH as Sovereign Judge and Deliverer via Apocalyptic Concepts, e.g., Final Judgment, Resurrection, etc.
#2: Imminent Conquest of Human History and Worldly Rule by the Kingdom of God [cf. Dan.]

A. Perspective: Speaker/Writer
the conservative Jews who were dissatisfied with Hellenism, and were persecuted by their fellow Jews who accommodated Hellenism and represented the interests of the Hellenistic overlords

B. Addressees:
those segments of the Jewish populace that were dominated/oppressed by the Hellenistic overlords by means of the Jewish sympathizers/proponents who were appointed

C. Contexts: the period of Hellenistic domination during the Seleucid reign, specifically Antiochus IV Epiphanes

D. Issues:
1. self-determination and survival of the Jews, i.e., how, and if, to accommodate Hellenism and maintain Torah-compliance
2. determination of the most appropriate administrative structure and ideological standards, i.e., whether and how to organize their community

E. Purposes:
1. motivation of the Jewish masses to join the revolution, i.e., encouragement of the war efforts against the Seleucids
2. solicitation of the undecided or inactive Jews for alignment/alliance with the rebels
3. assurance of the participants in the struggle regarding the righteousness of their compatriots who were killed

F. Presuppositions:
  1. YHWH as Universal Sovereign
  2. the oneness of YHWH, i.e., exclusive Yahwistic monotheism and the political solidarity of Yahwistic colonialism
  3. the historicity of YHWH's activity
  4. Zionistic Yahwism minus the monarchy as the Legitimate (Sole) Heir of early Yahwism, i.e., Yahwistic theocracy with the Zadokites as the Legitimate Priests and Leaders [Ezek. 44; Ezra-Neh.; Lev. 17-26]
  5. Jerusalem (or Mount Zion) as the City of YHWH and the Sole Yahwistic Cult Center [Chronicles]
  6. YHWH as Warrior and Creator-Savior, i.e., the Creation, and the Exodus, traditions
  7. YHWH and Israel as Holy [Lev. 17-26]
  8. YHWH as Just and Merciful

Endnotes

1. For references see Gösta Ahlström, *The History of Ancient Palestine from the Palaeolithic Period to Alexander's Conquest* (ed. Diana Edelman; JSOT Sup. 146; England: Sheffield, 1993), 889-906.

2. J. Alberto Soggin, *An Introduction to the History of Israel and Judah* (trans. John Bowden; Valley Forge, PA: Trinity International, 1993), 300. Soggin notes that Samaria rebelled in 331 B.C.E. and was penalized by the settlement of a Macedonian colony. See also Robert B. Coote and Mary P. Coote, *Power, Politics, and the Making of the Bible: An Introduction* (Minneapolis: Fortress, 1990), 86.

3. For references see Ahlström, *History*, 898-906.

4. Soggin, *History*, 305-309. Soggin notes that there were hostilities toward the Judahites on the part of the Sanballatids, stimulating and perpetuating the mutual animosities.

5. Both Ahlström and Soggin have located the construction of the temple at Gerizim after Alexander's conquest of Palestine.

6. For references see 1 and 2 Maccabees, Judith, Ecclesiasticus, Daniel, and the works of Josephus.

7. Ahlström, *History*, 894; Norman K. Gottwald, *The Hebrew Bible: A Socio-literary Introduction* (Philadelphia: Fortress, 1985), 439.

8. Soggin, *History*, 300-302; Coote and Coote, *Power, Politics and the Making of the Bible*, 86; Lee I. A. Levine, "The Age of Hellenism," in *Ancient Israel: A Short History from Abraham to the Roman Destruction of the Temple* (ed. Hershel Shanks; Washington, D. C.: Biblical Archaeology Society/Englewood Cliffs, NJ: Prentice-Hall, 1988), 177f.

9. Coote and Coote, *Power, Politics and the Making of the Bible*, 86; Gottwald, *The Hebrew Bible*, 443.

10. Soggin, *History*, 313-319; Levine, "The Age of Hellenism," 178-182, 190-194; Gottwald, *The Hebrew Bible*, 439f.

11. Soggin, *History*, 302; Gottwald, *The Hebrew Bible*, 439f, 444.

12. Soggin, *History*, 303; see Levine, "The Age of Hellenism," 178f.

13. Soggin, *History*, 303; Coote and Coote, *Power, Politics and the Making of the Bible*, 87-89; Gottwald, *The Hebrew Bible*, 442f.

14. Coote and Coote, *Power, Politics and the Making of the Bible*, 88.

15. Soggin, *History*, 304f; Coote and Coote, *Power, Politics and the Making of the Bible*, 88f; Gottwald, *The Hebrew Bible*, 444.

16. Soggin, *History*, 304f, 312-324; Coote and Coote, *Power, Politics and the Making of the Bible*, 89-91; Levine, "The Age of Hellenism," 179-183.

17. Soggin, *History*, 323-325; Coote and Coote, *Power, Politics and the Making of the Bible*, 90-91; Levine, "The Age of Hellenism," 183-184; Gottwald, *The Hebrew Bible*, 444-445, 582-594; cf. also Paul D. Hanson,

The Dawn of Apocalyptic: The Historical and Sociological Roots of Jewish Apocalyptic Eschatology (rev. ed.; Philadelphia: Fortress, 1979), 1-31.

18. Soggin, *History*, 325; Levine, "The Age of Hellenism," 183-184.
19. Soggin, *History*, 325-327; Levine, "The Age of Hellenism," 184.
20. Soggin, *History*, 327f; Levine, "The Age of Hellenism," 185f.
21. Soggin, *History*, 328f; Levine, "The Age of Hellenism," 186f.
22. Soggin, *History*, 329-342; Levine, "The Age of Hellenism," 187-189, 197-204; Gottwald, *The Hebrew Bible*, 447-456. Gottwald notes that during the Maccabean-Hasmonean period the Pharisees, the Essenes, and the Sadducees originated, while the Zealots arose as an offshoot of Pharisaic circles in 6 B.C.E. (449). The major causes for these factions and parties were the realignment of socioeconomic, political, and religious forces started by the attempt to Hellenize Judaism radically and the reactive emergence of an independent Jewish state that took on a Hellenistic character in spite of its anti-Hellenistic beginnings (450). The key concern was whether and how Jewish society and state should appropriate the internationally operative Hellenistic socioeconomic and political structures and assumptions (450). The basis for this concern was twofold: the exclusion of Hellenistic religious syncretism by an overwhelming Jewish consensus and the Jewish consensus for maintenance of a Jewish religion based on the Torah (450). Specifically, the Pharisees and the Essenes originated because of the breach of the separation of religious and civil offices by the Hasmonean political rulers. The Sadducees, on the other hand, emerged as a result of being catapulted into positions of power and leadership by the new opportunities for power and wealth that were spawned by the Maccabean war and the Hasmonean expansion (451). Thus a basic rivalry ensued between the Pharisees and the Sadducees, which was intertwined with socioeconomic and political issues, i.e., social class positions and perceived self-interests considerably determined how the Jews aligned themselves on the religio-political issues (453, 456). The Pharisees were members of a sect that voluntarily and strictly took on themselves "the yoke of the Torah", having: a progressive interpretation of Torah via a twofold Law; equal applicability of purity laws; and a negative view of Hellenized politics and culture. The Essenes' posture was the same as the Pharisees but stricter in application of the Torah. They withdrew from society due to its perceived, social and political evil. On the other hand, the Sadducees were persons of privilege in the priesthood or in the lay nobility, who combined pro-Hasmonean sympathies with an elitist religious outlook, having: a narrow, constructionist interpretation of Torah; a double standard of purity for priests and laity; and a dichotomy of religious and sociopolitical life (453f). The Sadducees tended to mandate messianic political action in terms of the prevailing, blunt and cruel forms of

international power politics from a traditional religious view, while the Pharisees tended to mandate messianic loyalty to domestic social equality and justice, eschewing the conceits and excesses of power politics, even to the point of endangering political independence, as long as religious purity and freedom of practice were assured from a traditional religious view (455). Note that Levine and Soggin differ with Gottwald regarding the origin of the Essenes. Both regard them as off-shoots of the Sadducees. However, Soggin sees them as breaking away from the Sadducees and joining the Hasidim, because of the Jewish concessions to Hellenism (338f), while Levine sees two additional factions of Sadducees. One group, the adherents of Onias IV, erected a temple in Leontopolis, Egypt under Ptolemaic auspices to rival the Jerusalem temple under the Hasmoneans in 150 B.C.E. Another group withdrew to the Judean wilderness, and formed the Essene sect (198). Certainly, it is obvious that the tensions between the Pharisees and the Sadducees resulted in the development of distinct social bases of operation. Here, the Pharisees probably worked out of the synagogues [see Lee I. Levine, "The Nature and Origin of the Palestinian Synagogue Reconsidered," *Journal of Biblical Literature* 115 (1996): 425-448; Jerome C. Ross, *The Composition of the Holiness Code (Lev. 17-26)* (Dissertation: University of Pittsburgh, 1997), 148f], while the Sadducees controlled the temple-cults.

23. Soggin, *History*, 330; Levine, "The Age of Hellenism," 187.
24. Soggin, *History*, 330f; Levine, "The Age of Hellenism," 187; Gottwald, *The Hebrew Bible*, 448.
25. Soggin, *History*, 331; Levine, "The Age of Hellenism," 189, 199.
26. Soggin, *History*, 331f; Levine, "The Age of Hellenism," 204; Shaye J. D. Cohen, "Roman Domination," in *Ancient Israel: A Short History from Abraham to the Roman Destruction of the Temple* (ed. Hershel Shanks; Washington, D. C.: Biblical Archaeology Society/Englewood Cliffs, NJ: Prentice-Hall, 1988), 205-207; Gottwald, *The Hebrew Bible*, 449.
27. Martin Noth, *The History of Israel* (3d ed.; trans. Peter R. Ackroyd; New York: Harper and Row, 1958), 393-400.
28. Soggin, *History*, 342-344; cf. Cohen, "Roman Domination," 215-222.
29. See chart, "Categorization of the Jewish Sectors in the Hellenistic and the Roman Period".

CHAPTER SEVEN:
THE JEWS UNDER ROMAN ADMINISTRATION

Though the Hasmonean dynasty came to an end, Herod Antipater succeeded in founding a new but limited dynasty, the Herodians. When Julius Caesar came to Syria in 47 B.C.E., Hyrcanus II was appointed *ethnarch* (literally, ruler of the nation) and was nominated to the office of high priest, and Herod Antipater was appointed *procurator* (literally, caretaker). He made his older son, Phasael, commander of the military region of Jerusalem, and the younger Herod, commander of the northern region. Both were efficient commanders, especially Herod who secured Galilee from robbers. Nevertheless, they were unpopular, because of their foreign origin (i.e., Idumeans were forced to convert to Judaism) and violent style of administration. Upon Caesar's death in 44 B.C.E., Antipater was thrust into a civil war, supporting Cassius, in whose jurisdiction he found himself. A rival assassinated Antipater in 43 B.C.E. and Herod avenged his father's death and took the throne. He managed to appease Cassius and Anthony and to obtain for himself and his brother the ethnarcy of Judea.[1]

In 40 B.C.E. the Parthians invaded Syria, captured Hyrcanus II, and installed Antigonus, the son of Aristobulus, as king and high priest. During this time Herod took refuge in Rome, and when he was given the title of king by Anthony and Octavian, he returned to reclaim his territory. Accompanied by two triumvirs and Roman troops, he took Jerusalem after a short siege, putting Antigonus to flight, and finally killing him in 37 B.C.E. To secure his throne and possibly to legitimate his rule, Herod married Mariamne, the granddaughter of Aristobulus and Hyrcanus, and the sister of Antigonus, the last heir to the Hasmonean throne. Thus he reigned from 37 to 4 B.C.E.[2]

Herod's administration was politically proficient yet ruthless. To secure his reign further he executed surviving members of the Hasmonean aristocracy—his wife's brother, aunt, and father, and other relatives, and eventually his wife. He maintained a posture of non-involvement in conflicts within the Roman administration, always in effort to secure his position by keeping their support. When a conflict broke out between Octavian and Mark Anthony, he first sided with the latter, probably due to his close proximity, but after Octavian defeated Anthony, Herod managed to convince Octavian to keep him in position, even gaining the territories of Samaria and Perea (the region east of Lake Tiberias).

Before pursuing any major endeavors, he consulted the Roman governor of Syria. Given the latitude to govern as he so desired, Herod engaged in no unauthorized activities and vigorously supported the Roman administration. His hunger for power was manifested in many remarkable achievements. He created an aristocracy that was solely dependent upon him, positioning illegitimate persons within the high priesthood. He conducted several building projects to promote the administration, to solicit support from his subjects—both Jews and non-Jews—and to protect his vested interests: the cities of Caesarea, in which he built a harbor, using the latest technology in hydraulic cement and underwater construction, and Sebaste, which was on the ancient site of Samaria; the fortresses of Masada, Herodium, Alexandrium, Hyrcania, Macherus; and the rebuilding of Jerusalem, including the tower of David and the western wall, and the temple. Also, he bestowed gifts and benefactions on cities and enterprises outside of his own kingdom, such as, Athens, Sparta, Rhodes, and the Olympic games.[3]

On the other hand, Herod was not locally popular. His violation of traditional Jewish laws and oppressive taxation soured the feelings of the Jews toward him, though they benefited very much from his endeavors. Certainly, his marginal status as a Jew, being an offspring of the Idumeans who were forced to convert to Judaism under Hyrcanus and Aristobulus, further marred his image in the eyes of the Jews. At his death, numerous riots occurred, as broad sections of the population, particularly the impoverished, sought to assert their freedom from exploitation. From 4 B.C.E. to 6 C.E. chaos persisted, until Judea came directly under Roman procurators, a situation which continued throughout the biblical period, with the exception of Agrippa (41-44 C.E.), the son of Aristobulus IV.[4]

The context for the reign of Herod is the Roman administration. They chose to exercise rule through vassal kings who were native to the respective jurisdictions. These kings were given only local autonomy, provided taxes were promptly paid and no disturbances were incited. In the case of the Jews and Judaism,[5] Rome granted them the status of a *religio licita*, respecting their worship but not always exempting the Jews from erection of statues dedicated to the divinized emperor or the parade of military standards. The Romans did not disguise their contempt for Jewish faith and worship. The concession they granted the Jews was inconsistently enforced, as Roman compliance with this rule varied, based upon the whims of the given rulers. Also, tensions between Jews and non-Jews developed, because of the concession the Romans provided them and the separatistic tendencies of Jewish practices. Third, the Roman administration's failure to create a homogeneity within Judea provided an atmosphere for volatile exchanges between the various social classes. The indiscreet granting of preferences and favors to the aristocracy stimulated hatred among the masses toward them. Thus the administrative corruption, violence, and inconsistency of the Romans regularly led to revolts by the Jewish populace.[6]

After Herod's death, Antipas governed Galilee and Perea, Philip governed the Golan heights and points east, and Archelaus governed Judea. In 6 C.E. Archelaus was deposed by Rome for misrule, and Judea, Idumea, Samaria, and most of the Mediterranean coast were annexed to the province of Syria. It seems that at this time Judah of Galilee incited a revolt against the census ordered by the Romans for fiscal reasons, but was killed and the revolt suppressed. From this brief rebellion, the Zealots, an underground group of Jewish militants, emerged, and later, as an offshoot from the Zealots, the Sicarii originated as a group of Jewish terrorists.[7] So, from 6 to 41 C.E. Judea was governed by Roman *prefects* or (after 44 C.E.) *procurators*, while the rest of the country was governed by Antipas and Philip for about 30 years. These procurators were Coponius (6-8 C.E.), M. Ambivius (9-12 C.E.), Annius Rufus (12-15 C.E.), Valerius Gratus (15-26 C.E.), Pontius Pilate, the most documented one (26-36 C.E.), Marullus (37 C.E.), and Herennius Capito (37-41 C.E.).[8] In 41 C.E. Agrippa I, the grandson of Herod, received kingship over Judea from emperor Claudius, dying in 44 C.E., after which the Roman prefects ruled again. For a few years, Agrippa I's son, Agrippa II, ruled a small portion of Galilee, until the Jewish wars of 66-70 C.E.[9] Due to the brevity of information regarding the tenures of the procurators, the outstanding events during the administrations of the key persons will be sketched.

During the tenure of Pontius Pilate, Jesus, an itinerant preacher in Galilee, made his debut. His messianic-like activities led to him being accused by the Jewish authorities, before the Roman procurator, of being a political and social agitator. He started an egalitarian movement[10] among the masses (עם־הארץ 'am-ha-arez), from a Pharisaic posture, critiquing and condemning the Pharisees and the Sadducees,[11] which apparently ended in confrontation in Jerusalem, around the time of Passover. It is very probable that he incited a riot in the temple at Jerusalem bringing attention to his cause, and thereby forcing the hands of the Jewish leaders and the Roman administration.[12] For his efforts he received Roman capital punishment. However, following his tragic death, his disciples created an apocalyptic sect within Judaism, based on the application of a Pharisaic belief, the resurrection of Jesus. *Apologia* in the form of "gospels," in defense of charges of treason leveled against their leader and them, were written to explain his messiahship. Substantively, they *spiritualized* the messianic traditions and subsumed the traditions of "the Son of God" (בן־אלהים ben-elôhîm; 2 Sam. 7; Pss. 2, 110), "the servant of YHWH" (עבד־יהוה 'ebed YHWH; Isa. 42:1-4; 49:1-6; 50:4-11; 52:13-53: 12), and "the Son of man" (בן־אדם ben 'adam; 1 Enoch) under that of "the Messiah" (משיח mashîach; Isa. 9:2-7; 11). The "servant of YHWH" passages, especially Isa. 52:13-53:12, provided the rubric for integrating the other traditions under that of the Messiah.

Eventually this sect severed its ties with its mother faith, becoming a separate religion by the time of the Jewish wars of 66-70 C.E.[13]

The Jewish wars of 66-70 C.E. were generally precipitated by the tenor of the Roman administration. In 41 C.E. the Romans tried to put an image of the emperor in the temple, sparking backlash from the Jews. On another occasion, Jewish reprisal came when the Torah scrolls of a local synagogue were profaned. In 67 C.E. Gessius Florus took seventeen gold talents from the temple, possibly as a ploy to hide his misconduct. Coupled with the tense situation that persisted within Judea, the procurator was jeered and insulted. In reprisal he allowed his troops to ransack a district and demanded the population give a triumphant welcome to two of his cohorts from Caesarea. The high priest, the Sadducean priests, and the Pharisees urged the people to comply, but the crowd took offense when the cohorts did not respond to their salute. War broke out as the people of Jerusalem occupied the temple, severing ties between it and Antonia, and the Zealots occupied the various fortresses of Herod. Essentially this was a civil war or class struggle among the Jews—revolutionaries from the lower class promoted their apocalyptic aims against the aristocracy, which was backed by the Romans. The apocalyptic traditions, which were fostered by the oppressed Jews of the lower class, regarded the overthrow of the Roman administration, at least locally, as its primary concern. Obviously, the revolutionaries included the Zealots and the Sicarii, while the Sadducees constituted the aristocracy and the Pharisees a pietistic or elitist group. The very make-up of the Jewish community significantly dictated their fortunes in battle, and they were disunited. The initial priestly revolutionaries led by Eleazar, the son of the high priest Ananias, were eventually eclipsed by the Sicarii, led by Menahem, as internecine struggles ensued. Though revolutions outside of Judea arose, the efficiency of the Roman military, particularly its siege-techniques, prevailed in 70 C.E., as a famine ensued, forcing surrender. Vespasian began the assaults upon the Jews, but was replaced by Titus, who completed the siege of Jerusalem in the spring of 70 C.E., when Vespasian assumed the throne after a rapid succession of emperors (Galba, Otho, Vitellius) in 69 C.E. Shortly thereafter, Antonia was captured in July, and the temple-fortress complex was taken in August. Later, Masada, the final fortress, fell in 74 C.E.[14]

This Roman conquest of the Jews resulted in several things. First, a significant portion of the Jewish population was killed in battle. This no doubt included many of the revolutionaries such as the Zealots and the Sicarii. Second, most of the land belonging to the Jews in Judea was confiscated, though they were not expelled. The region became an imperial Roman province and the Romans imposed the *fiscus Judaicus*, "the Jewish tax," which was later abolished under Nerva (96-98 C.E.). Third, the temple was destroyed, terminating the means of subsistence of the Sadducees, who largely disappeared after this time. Institutionwise, the synagogue, which heretofore had complemented the temple, replaced it. Now, only the Pharisees survived as a Jewish sect and the sole inheritors of Judaism, having developed institutions that were acclimated to non-temple worship. Also, in this respect, the Romans permitted Judaism to retain its status as a *religio licita*, probably for the sake of fostering peaceful reconstruction. Fourth, the first Christians were permitted to relocate to Pella in Transjordan, while the Jews under the leadership of Johanan ben Zakkai relocated to Yamnia (Yabne). Both groups began to reorganize, using their respective collections of "sacred traditions." Here, the Jews started the final canonization of the Hebrew texts, which entailed exclusion of practically all apocalyptic-eschatological traditions, particularly those used by the Christians. From this point on, the two groups became separate religions, engaged in evangelistic efforts at the same target audiences and reflecting in varying degrees polemical attacks on one another. Under these circumstances, all of the New Testament Gospels except Mark were written. Fifth and obvious, "sacred texts" called Scripture became the exclusive foundation for both faiths, being interpreted and administered by authoritative personalities in succession with their respective founders (for the Christians, the first disciples and then the early Church fathers; for the Jews, Johanan ben Zakkai and the rabbis).[15] Now, Christianity and Pharisaic Judaism survived as *diaspora* religions.

The Jewish wars of 132-135 C.E. were stimulated once again by the combination of the corrupt and violent administration of the Romans and the volatile, apocalyptic beliefs of the Jews. Expectations of an imminent end of the age and of the Roman dominion over Judea were stimulated by heavy taxation under the penalty of severe punishment. In 115 C.E. a revolt broke out among the Jews of Cyrene, Alexandria, Cyprus, and Mesopotamia, typifying events to come. Though the exact causes for this revolt are unknown, it is reasonable to associate any probabilities with the reign of Hadrian (117-138 C.E.). It appears the disturbance was incited by desecration of the holy places, as Hadrian founded *Aelia Capitolina* on the ruins of Jerusalem and inaugurated a sanctuary there to Jupiter Capitolinus. Also, Hadrian purportedly prohibited circumcision, thereby interfering with Jewish practices. Simon ben Kosiba, acclaimed by his followers as *bar kokba*, led the rebellion, which gained considerable success, in light of Hadrian's initial ignorance of it. Simon and his army recaptured Jerusalem and major portions of Judea and governed from Jerusalem, minting coins and restoring temple worship. No doubt his interference with Roman fiscal affairs, not to mention political escapades, prompted serious Roman intervention. Julius Severus was dispatched, besieging each stronghold and eventually starving the rebels into surrender. The last rebels were trapped in a complex of caves above Wadi Murabba'at, where the majority of them committed suicide rather than surrender. At this time Jerusalem was made a colony and called *Aelia*

Capitolina, and the Jews were prohibited from entering it. Also, traditional Jewish practices, such as circumcision, ceremonies, and production or possession of Torah scrolls were forbidden. Finally, the traditional name Judea was replaced with that of Palestine, from the name of the Philistines.[16] From this point up to the present, the Jews were the targets of persecution and exploitation, while Judaism persisted through the privacy of the family, its most potent center.

Chapter Synopsis:
The Key Dates

65 B.C.E.	Entrance of Romans in Syria-Palestine
64/63 B.C.E.	Pompey appears in Syria and introduces fundamental re-organization in Syria and the Re-starting of the Gerizim cultus
57 B.C.E.	Re-organization of the affairs of the Jerusalem religious community by A. Gabinius, the Syrian Governor
47 B.C.E.	Caesar comes to Syria and confirms Hyrcanus in the office of High Priest
44 B.C.E.	Caesar is murdered
40 B.C.E.	Herod wins over Antony and is appointed king of Judea
37-4 B.C.E.	Reign of Herod as "confederate king" within the Roman administration
66-70 C.E.	Fall of Jerusalem and Destruction of the Temple via Jewish Wars
132-135 C.E.	Bar Kochbar Revolution

Causes:
1. corrupt and violent administration of Roman administration
2. anti-Roman sentiments of Jews in spite of Roman concessions, e.g., qualified exemption of the Jews from emperor worship, recognition of Judaism as a *Religio Licita*
3. apocalyptic or Jewish beliefs, e.g., messianism

Developments:
1. increasing individualization and universalization of religion
2. rejection of apocalypticism and association of the kingdom of God with political constructs or entities
3. spiritualization of the kingdom of God
4. increased focus upon Torah study
5. severance of the Jesus-movement or Christian-movement from Judaism and consequent/ subsequent polemical battles between the two

Effects:
1. after 66-70 C.E.:
   a. Christians moved to Pella and broke with Judaism
   b. Jews moved to Yamnia/Yabne and canonized the Hebrew Bible
   c. Scripture became the exclusive foundation for both faiths
   d. authority was based upon personalities
   e. destruction of the Jerusalem temple
   f. disappearance of Sadducees and Zealots
2. after 132-135 C.E.:

a. Jerusalem became a pagan/Roman province, i.e., *Colonia Aelia Capitolina*
b. Jews were forbidden entrance into Jerusalem
c. name of land was changed from Judea to Palestine (= land of the Philistines)
d. Rabbinic Judaism replaced Yahwistic tribalism and conception of Israel as twelve tribes

Interpretations:
1. Jesus movement and Church as Jewish and/or the New Israel [cf. New Testament]
2. The Church as apostates or heretics [cf. *Birkath Ha-Minim*]
3. Jesus as Messiah [cf. New Testament]

The Selected Interpretations

#1: The Jesus Movement and the Church as Jewish and/or the New Israel [cf. New Testament]
#2: Jesus as the Messiah [cf. New Testament]
#3: The Church as Apostates or Heretics [cf. *Birkath Ha-Minim*]

A. Perspective:
   1. Speakers:
      a. the Christian Jews: those liberal, or Pharisaic, Jews who followed Jesus, and sought to challenge or counter Roman domination
      b. the Orthodox Jews: those Jews who took a more moderate stance, and distanced themselves from or disagreed with Jesus's approach to Roman domination
   2. Writers:
      a. the Church: those inheritors of the traditions of the Jesus movement, which took on a more assimilationistic posture
      b. the Synagogue: those inheritors of the orthodox Jewish traditions, specifically that were transmitted through Pharisaic Judaism

B. Addressees:
   1. of the Speakers:
      a. the Christian Jews:
         i. the Jewish populace
         ii. those gentiles or non-Jews who were sympathetic to the Jews' causes
      b. the Orthodox Jews:
         i. the Jewish populace
         ii. those gentiles or non-Jews who were sympathetic to the

Jews' causes

      iii. those gentiles or non-Jews who were sympathetic to the Christian Jews' causes

  2. of the Writers:

      a. the Church:

          i. those Jews who were sympathetic to the Church's causes

          ii. those gentiles or non-Jews, especially the Roman administrators, who were sympathetic to the Church's causes

          iii. those Roman administrators who suspected the Church of offenses against the State i.e., treason

      b. the Synagogue:

          i. those Jews who were sympathetic to the Church's causes

          ii. those gentiles or non-Jews, especially the Roman administrators, who were sympathetic to the Church's causes

          iii. those Roman administrators who suspected the Jews in general of offenses against the State i.e., treason

C. Contexts: the period of Roman domination

D. Issues:

  1. of the Christian and the Orthodox Jews:

      a. self-determination and survival of the Jews, i.e., how, and if, to accommodate Hellenism as manifested through Roman domination and maintain Torah-compliance

      b. determination of the most appropriate administrative structure and ideological standards, i.e., whether and how to organize their community

  2. of the Church and the Synagogue:

      a. self-determination and survival in light of the recent wars with the Roman administration

      b. determination of the most appropriate administrative structure and ideological standards, i.e., whether and how to organize their community

      c. re-definition or re-identification in light of the recent wars with the Roman administration

E. Purposes:

  1. of the Speakers:

      a. the Christian Jews:

          i. recruitment of Jews to the efforts against Roman domination

          ii. implementation or facilitation of the kingdom of God

      b. the Orthodox Jews:

          i. acquisition and maximization of self-determination

          ii. maintenance of Jewish identity

2. of the Writers:
   a. the Church: "apologetics"
      i. establishment of the Jesus movement and the Church as the legitimate heirs of Yahwism, i.e., the New Israel
      ii. establishment of the compatibility of the Church and the Roman administration, i.e., de-emphasis and disclaiming of the original anti-Roman sentiments through re-interpretation of Jesus's mission
   b. the Synagogue:
      i. acquisition and maximization of self-determination
      ii. maintenance of Jewish identity
      iii. distinction of Pharisaic Judaism from Christianity

F. Presuppositions:
  1. of the Speakers:
   a. the Christian Jews:
      i. YHWH as Universal Sovereign
      ii. the oneness of YHWH, i.e., exclusive Yahwistic monotheism and the political solidarity of Yahwistic colonialism
      iii. the historicity of YHWH's activity
      iv. Jerusalem (or Mount Zion) as the City of YHWH and the Sole Yahwistic Cult Center [Chronicles]
      v. the Hebraic traditions:
        (1) YHWH as Warrior and Creator-Savior, i.e., the Creation, and the Exodus, traditions
        (2) YHWH and Israel as Holy [Lev. 17-26]
        (3) YHWH as Just and Merciful
        (4) the subsumption of "the Son of God" [2 Sam. 7; Pss. 2, 110], "the Son of Man" [1 Enoch], and "the Servant of YHWH" [Isa. 42:1-4; 49:1-6; 50:4-11; 52:13-53:12] under the label "Messiah" [Isa. 9:2-7; 11] with the last "Servant of YHWH" passage providing the rubric
   b. the Orthodox Jews:
      i. YHWH as Universal Sovereign
      ii. the oneness of YHWH, i.e., exclusive Yahwistic monotheism and the political solidarity of Yahwistic colonialism in cooperation with the Roman administration
      iii. the historicity of YHWH's activity
      iv. Jerusalem (or Mount Zion) as the City of YHWH and the Sole Yahwistic Cult Center [Chronicles]
      v. the Hebraic traditions via halakoth:
        (1) YHWH as Warrior and Creator-Savior, i.e., the Creation and the Exodus traditions

   (2) YHWH and Israel as Holy [Lev. 17-26]

   (3) YHWH as Just and Merciful

   (4) the collective interpretation of "Israel" as "the Son of God" [2 Sam. 7; Pss. 2, 110], "the Son of Man" [1 Enoch], and "the Servant of YHWH" [Isa. 42:1-4; 49:1-6; 50:4-11; 52:13-53:12] in conjunction with a future hope for "the Messiah"

2.   of the Writers:

   a.   the Church: toning down or elimination of the emphases upon revolution, and re-capitulation of Jesus as the Son of YHWH who transcends politics and history

   b.   the Synagogue: same as previous minus a sacrifical cult

Endnotes

1. J. Alberto Soggin, *An Introduction to the History of Israel and Judah* (trans. John Bowden; Valley Forge, PA: Trinity International, 1993), 346f; Shaye J. D. Cohen, "Roman Domination," in *Ancient Israel: A Short History from Abraham to the Roman Destruction of the Temple* (ed. Hershel Shanks; Washington, D. C.: Biblical Archaeology Society/Englewood Cliffs, NJ: Prentice-Hall, 1988), 207.
2. Soggin, *History*, 347; Cohen, "Roman Domination," 207.
3. Soggin, *History*, 347f; Cohen, "Roman Domination," 207-209.
4. Soggin, *History*, 348f; Cohen, "Roman Domination," 210f.
5. Cohen, "Roman Domination," 215-222. At this time the main features of Judaism were: 1. belief in the God of Moses; 2. practice of laws and rituals that Moses purportedly commanded; 3. study and practice of "sacred traditions", i.e., the Torah, Nebiim, and Kethubim, within synagogues; 4. regular prayer; 5. individualism; 6. predominance of apocalyptic eschatology, as evidenced in apocalypses; and 7. varied sects, or religious groups, e.g., Pharisees, Sadducees, Essenes, Zealots, 'pietistic extremists'.
6. Soggin, *History*, 349f, 352f; Cohen, "Roman Domination," 209-211, 222-224; Martin Noth, *The History of Israel* (3d ed.; trans. Peter R. Ackroyd; New York: Harper and Row, 1958), 422, 425, 435.
7. Soggin, *History*, 350; Cohen, "Roman Domination," 212.
8. Cf. *The New Oxford Annotated Bible*. The procurators of Palestine from the reign of Herod Agrippa I to the Jewish revolt are: Cuspius Fadus (44-46 C.E.); Tiberius Alexander (46-48 C.E.); Ventidius Cumanus (48-52 C.E.); M. Antonius Felix (52-60 C.E.); Porcius Festus (60-62 C.E.); Clodius Albinus (62-64 C.E.); and Gessius Florus (64-66 C.E.).
9. Cohen, "Roman Domination," 212.
10. Luise Schottroff, "Women as Followers of Jesus in New Testament Times: An Exercise in Social-Historical Exegesis of the Bible," *The Bible and Liberation: Political and Social Hermeneutics* (Revised Edition of A Radical Religion Reader; ed. Norman K. Gottwald; Maryknoll, NY: Orbis Books, 1983), 418-427. Schottroff sees the Jesus movement in Palestine as a self-help community of poor Jews, that fostered equality of the sexes in the context of shared poverty and hope for the impending kingdom of God.
11. See Howard Clark Kee, "Jesus, The King of The Jews," *Explorations* vol. 9, no. 2 (1995): 1-2; David G. Burke, Translating *Hoi Ioudaioi* In The New Testament," *Explorations* vol. 9, no. 2 (1995): 1-3.
12. Jesus was a Yahwist from Nazareth in Galilee. It is possible that he was influenced by Samaritan Yahwism as well as Zionistic Yahwism, thereby embracing a blend of northern and southern traditions. It is safe to say

that his revolutionary fervor attracted followers to him, probably from the north and the south. This caused him to be regarded as messianic in the southern sense, that is, he was interpreted according to the Davidic (or Zionistic) traditions, which believed that a messiah would come from the lineage of David. Also, he is presented in the Gospels of the Greek Testament as Pharisaic. This group was the more progressive of the Jewish sects, operating within society, but not compromisingly working in association with the Roman administration. However, Jesus's quest for freedom at all costs made him appealing to the more radical groups, such as the Zealots and the Sicarii, increasing his circle of followers.

It is reasonable to surmise that Jesus proposed a plan to counter the Roman administration, not to overthrow them, since that was not feasible. His mission was to make a statement about self-determination, that is, that Roman sovereignty could not have full control over his, and orthodox Jewish, life. He evidently practiced and fostered a form of Yahwistic conservatism that included an inherent political radicalism. In other words, his belief in YHWH was strictly monotheistic, such that he refused to recognize any authority but that of YHWH. Thus Jesus's trip to Jerusalem was primarily intended to be confrontational and exemplary. He sought to demonstrate the essence of freedom as presented in the Hebraic traditions! Barring the view that Jesus was religiously fanatic or socially naive, he went to Jerusalem to die—to be a martyr! And in this respect, he accomplished his mission!

At Jerusalem Jesus and his disciples had a physical altercation with the Romans, in which he was captured and sentenced to death for treason or insurrection. Later, many of his original disciples were captured and similarly sentenced. In the aftermath of these tragic happenings, later followers re-interpreted these episodes by spiritualizing the message and the mission of Jesus. They sought to downplay the political dimensions of his message and mission and to emphasize the personal-ideological aspects. Here, Paul was essential, even the primary creator of the Church, for he interpreted the political radicalism (i.e., the anti-Roman stance) of Jesus as the Christ, whose mission was compatible with the Roman administration. Following Paul, the Gospels present a picture of Jesus as sympathetic to Gentiles (including the Romans), being assimilationistic and politically-correct. Except for Mark, the Gospels were written, following the Jewish Wars of 66-70 C.E., in order to show the Roman overlords that Christianity (the product of the Jesus movement, which was originally Jewish, but became heretical and independent of Judaism, its mother faith) was not politically dangerous or offensive to the Roman kingdom. Now, the very instrument of punishment and shame—the cross—became a symbol of honor and commitment unto death. And the freedom and the kingdom of God that Jesus sought were projected onto a metaphysical plane, such that the early believers saw the rule of God within the very harsh every day.

13. Soggin, *History*, 350f; Cohen, "Roman Domination," 212, 218, 222; see Matthew, Mark, Luke, and John; see later "Understanding Jesus: An Old Testament Approach to the New Testament." Also, see Günther Bornkamm, *Jesus of Nazareth* (trans. Irene and Fraser McLuskey with James M. Robinson; New York: Harper and Row, 1960); John Reumann, *Jesus in the Church's Gospels: Modern Scholarship and the Earliest Sources* (Philadelphia: Fortress, 1968); Geza Vermes, *Jesus the Jew: A Historian's Reading of the Gospels* (Philadelphia: Fortress, 1973); Howard Clark Kee, *Jesus in History: An Approach to the Study of the Gospels* (2nd ed.; New York: Harcourt Brace Jovanovich, Inc., 1977).

14. Soggin, *History*, 353-357; Cohen, "Roman Domination," 220-230.

15. Soggin, *History*, 357-358; Cohen, "Roman Domination," 230-235; Noth, *History*, 440-447; see James Parkes, *The Conflict of the Church and the Synagogue* (New York: Atheneum, 1979), 27-150; Jacob Neusner, *First Century Judaism in Crisis* (Nashville: Abingdon Press, 1975); idem, *Judaism in the Beginning of Christianity* (Philadelphia: Fortress, 1984).

16. Soggin, *History*, 359-363; Noth, *History*, 448-454.

CONCLUSION:
UNDERSTANDING JESUS: AN OLD TESTAMENT
APPROACH TO THE NEW TESTAMENT

In order to understand the Greek Testament, particularly Jesus of Nazareth as presented therein, several things must be considered. First and foremost, Jesus of Nazareth was a first century C.E. Jew.[1] This one fact entails his identification and location within history. He was a member of the Hebrew people and by virtue of his residence a descendant of the northern tribes.[2] It is the argument of the Greek Testament that he was a descendant of the Davidic lineage and thus the Jewish Messiah; however, it appears that such association with David was polemical. During his lifetime the Romans controlled Palestine through local rulers, specifically the sons of Herod the Great.[3] The tenor of the Roman administration fluctuated according to the circumstances and the intentions of the respective leaders. The primary aim of the Roman administration was maintenance of peace or security within the area and for that matter its jurisdictions. Second, the Greek Testament was written by Greek-speaking persons, who may not have been very familiar with the Jewish traditions and were mostly Gentiles or non-Jews. Jewish Christianity or the Christian Jews did not last very long. The Gentile-Christian movement, which was facilitated by the missionary journeys of Paul and the like, gained dominance within the Jesus movement and led to an eclipse of the Christian-Jewish movement.[4] In light of the cultural milieu being predominantly Hellenistic, the Greek culture provided the matrix or rubric of thought for the early Church, though its essential content was Hebraic or Jewish. This intertwining of Jewish traditions within a Hellenistic framework obviously distorted the understanding of the former, which was original and primary.[5] Thus, the Jesus of the Greek Testament is a Jewish-Hellenistic hybrid that shows a fluctuating focus of one tradition and then another, based upon the respective, individual documents being read.

To get beneath the Hellenistic crust of the Greek Testament modern biblical criticism is obviously needed.[6] Entailed within the implementation of the methodology is the necessity of thorough and, first, independent study of the Hebrew Testament. Study of the Hebrew Testament offers a valid mechanism for critique of the Greek Testament,[7] which shows reappropriation of the former. Such study offers an in-depth look at the traditions of Jesus of Nazareth—that is, those documents and understandings that were formulative or foundational for his life and ministry. The goal of this preliminary

154

study of the Hebrew Testament is simply comprehension or appreciation of the principles or standards of the individual and cumulative ideologies[8] of the Hebrew people. The basic faith standards of the Hebrew Testament are *prioritization* of YHWH, the *selective imaging* of YHWH, and the historicity of YHWH's activity, which distinctly emerged during the Hellenistic period and in the form of *exclusive Yahwistic monotheism* in the post-exilic period. Numerous other commandments or principles are developed from combinations of the previous three along with adaptations from the respective, cultural contexts within which the Hebrew people existed.[9] These threads must provide the orientation for reading of the Hebrew traditions and the early Church traditions. No doubt they provide a mechanism for critique and assessment of Jesus as presented in the Greek Testament, keeping him within his—a Jewish, context. Also, conceptually, for the Hebrew Bible, function is presented as the primary criterion of existence (i.e., function determines identity) and relationship as the primary basis of existence (i.e., humans are inherently social or the products of personal exchange or interaction).[10] Here, the dynamics of Hebraic thought or conceptualization may provide a means of comparing and distinguishing Jewish from Hellenistic thought.[11] Essentially the statements of the Hebrew and the Greek Testament were written by persons in different cultural contexts, relevant to issues and persons within those respective contexts for the fundamental purpose of survival,[12] particularly in light of the Hebrew people being an oppressed or dominated people for most of its existence during biblical times.[13] This implies that religious concerns are always intertwined with social concerns. Thus assuming that reality is constant and complex, one's experience of reality is most crucial as the looking-glass or interpretive medium for reading and understanding the text.[14]

Most discomforting in taking this approach is the tension produced by the self-criticism that is central to biblical criticism. The exegete-interpreter is forced to re-evaluate, re-formulate, and maybe discard the denominational traditions that have been uncritically and unquestioningly articulated and embraced. Indeed, the present author contends that theological integrity is determined by biblical consistency and existential expediency—a quality faith stance or faith posture requires, demands, and/or reflects affirmation of one's faith-standards (traditionalism)[15] and commitment to the reality in which one lives (realism, relevancy, or realisticness).[16] One must make a genuine effort to read the Hebrew Testament without distorting or biasing its statements, engage the Greek Testament in light of the findings from the prior reading, and dare to correct personal views. Though neutrality is impossible or bias is inevitable, the believing and the non-believing academician should reach conclusions that are mutually consistent! The common denominator is that which is human or one's humanness. Accounting for differences in cultures and their respective literary expressions, one's experience and assessment of reality leads that one in communicating with the biblical writers, getting beyond or piercing through the confines of the cultural-linguistic forms and concepts in order to ascertain that which is historically and thereby existentially, documentable! Here, real humans, real Jews, a real Jesus, at least in sketch or outline, emerge and thereby permit the reader or exegete-interpreter, believing or non-believing, an encounter with the concerns, circumstances, or conditions of persons just like self and their respective solutions or understandings of life! Here, Jesus of Nazareth, the early disciples, Paul, or whoever are located somewhere—within some historical context, some ethnic group, some geographical boundaries, some cultural milieu, etc., and permitted to remain there for the sake of a trans-cultural dialogue about life! For beneath or pervading life itself, or within one's understanding of what is human, one gains a sense of that which is beyond— the Eternal Thou or whoever *there* may be![17]

Endnotes

1. See Geza Vermes, *Jesus the Jew: A Historian's Reading of the Gospels* (Philadelphia: Fortress, 1973); also Marvin R. Wilson, *Our Father Abraham: Jewish Roots of the Christian Faith* (Grand Rapids, MI: Eerdmans/Dayton, Ohio: Center for Judaic-Christian Studies, 1989).

2. Martin Noth, *The History of Israel* (3d ed.; trans. Peter R. Ackroyd; New York: Harper & Row, 1958), 429. If his name and locus are taken seriously, "Jesus of Nazareth," then he must have originated in the old territory of the tribe of Zebulun at the time of him called Galilee.

3. Noth, *History*, 412-428, especially 420; J. Alberto Soggin, *An Introduction to the History of Israel and Judah* (trans. John Bowden; Valley Forge, PA: Trinity International, 1993), 349-351.

4. See Chapter Seven.

5. See Chapter Seven.

6. John H. Hayes and Carl R. Holladay, *Biblical Exegesis: A Beginner's Handbook* (rev. ed.; Atlanta: John Knox , 1987), 1-14. Hayes and Holladay state that there is a degree of difficulty involved in exegeting and interpreting a wide range of texts, as well as in oral communication, due to the distance or proximity of the sender and the receiver in regard to their discourse and experience and the temporality of content and forms of expression. Further factors that introduce complexity are: (1) the "third-party perspective," (2) composition in a language different from that of the interpreter or exegete, (3) the "cultural gap," (4) the "historical gap," (5) the collective and historical growth process under which the text has gone and which has produced it, (6) the existence of multiple and differing texts of the same documents, and (7) classification of some texts as sacred.

7. Wilson, *Our Father Abraham*, 167, 174, 185. He offers three correctives for the Church from its Jewish heritage: (1) humans and the world must be viewed in terms of a dynamic unity and oneness, not dualistically; (2) other-worldliness must be brought back into biblical balance by a return to this-worldly concerns; (3) rugged individualism and private Christianity must be replaced by the greater emphasis on the corporate life of the community of faith.

8. See the discussion of "faith" and "theology" in the Introduction.

9. See Excursus One. Also see Paul D. Hanson, *The People Called: The Growth of Community in the Bible* (San Francisco: Harper & Row, 1986), 3, 5, 7, 22-23, 26-29; also Klaus Koch, *The Prophets: Volume One. The Assyrian Period* (trans. Margaret Kohl; Philadelphia: Fortress, 1978), 5, 13f, 23, 28, 31; idem, *The Prophets: Volume Two. The Babylonian and Persian Periods* (trans. Margaret Kohl; Philadelphia: Fortress, 1978; English, 1982), 78f.

10. See Wilson, *Our Father Abraham*, 146; also Johannes Pedersen, *Israel: Its Life & Culture*, vol. 1 (London: Oxford University Press, 1940), 155; Thorleif Boman, *Hebrew Thought Compared with Greek* (trans. Jules Moreau; New York: W. W. Norton Co., 1960), 31, 39, 100, 205; Martin Buber, *I and Thou* (trans. Walter Kaufmann; New York: Charles Scribner's Sons, 1970), 53, 56f, 69, 78, 80, 85, 112f, 123, 124f.

11. See See Wilson, *Our Father Abraham*, 146; Pedersen, *Israel*, 155; Boman, *Hebrew Thought Compared with Greek* , 31, 39, 100, 205; Buber, *I and Thou*, 53, 56f, 69, 78, 80, 85, 112f, 123, 124f.

12. Survival requires several things: (1) administrative structure; (2) economic independence; (3) intra-communal organization or ideological standardization; (4) common language; (5) balance of extra-communal influences and intra-communal accommodation—that is, selective appropriation or assimilation of the dominant culture by the minority culture; (6) population or people; and (7) land or place.

13. Robert B. Coote & Mary P. Coote, *Power, Politics, and the Making of the Bible: An Introduction* (Minneapolis: Fortress, 1990), ix, x, 8, 11, 18, 28, 34-35, 36-37, 39, 41, 61, 70-73, 75, 78-80, 87, 92-93, 101, 108-109, 112, 123, 128, 135-136, 139, 149-151, 159-161, 162, 164. Both authors contend that the Bible originated as temple scriptures, was the product and the tool of power struggles between the rich or affluent, and was used to legitimate the political or power status/policies promulgated by these rich and powerful. See also Morton Smith, *Palestinian Parties and Politics that Shaped the Old Testament* (London: SCM Press Ltd., 1987); Norman K. Gottwald, *The Hebrew Bible: A Socio-literary Introduction* (Philadelphia: Fortress, 1985), 596-609; Richard Elliott Friedman, *Who Wrote the Bible?* (New York: Harper & Row, 1987).

14. See the Introduction.

15. Traditionalism is the pretexts, doctrines, dogmas, views of reality, etc. bequeathed to one through the believing-community with which one identifies.

16. Realism, relevancy, or realisticness is the pretexts, theories, views of reality, etc. bequeathed to one through the greater, non-believing cultural milieu within which that one lives.

17. See Buber, *I and Thou*, 53, 56-57, 69, 78, 80, 85, 112-113, 123, 124-125. Here, the present author confesses his bias—that is, the contours of the Sacred or the Eternal Thou are drawn based upon genuine inter-personal relations and appreciation of what is human. In other words, these biases are: (1) realism or rationalism; (2) relationalism or dialogical ordering of reality/the world; (3) God as being the Eternal Thou who can never become an It (i.e., who cannot be objectified or fully and adequately explained) and who is Personified Good(ness) who acts in human life; (4) there are no atheists—that is, everyone believes some-

thing; (5) faith is a lifestyle or pilgrimage; (6) life is sacred/valuable, that is, each life, every person, is purposeful within the dialogical ordering of the world; (7) good is essential, fundamental, or primary, that is, the dialogical ordering of the world is good; (8) Jesus of Nazareth is a 'didactic, filtering lense' by which the world may be perceived, comprehended, and engaged. My ultimate goal in biblical studies is to hear the text in context. Thus, my focus in biblical studies is development and employment of sensitivity to the biblical composer-authors' communications as they comprehend their reality/world and to the criteria/mechanism (i.e., Yahwistic beliefs) they employ in comprehending their reality/world.

INDEX OF AUTHORS

Scripture Index